poeticized LANGUAGE

THE

FOUNDATIONS

OF

CONTEMPORARY

FRENCH

POETRY

THE PENNSYLVANIA STATE UNIVERSITY PRESS
UNIVERSITY PARK, PENNSYLVANIA

Library of Congress Cataloging-in-Publication Data

Thomas, Jean-Jacques.
    Poeticized language : the foundations of contemporary French poetry /
Jean-Jacques Thomas, Steven Winspur.
        p.   cm.
    An adaptation and enlargement of J.-J. Thomas' *La langue, la
poésie*, published by Presses universitaires de Lille, c. 1989.
    Includes bibliographical references and index.
    ISBN 0-271-01812-7 (cloth : alk. paper)
    ISBN 0-271-01813-5 (pbk. : alk. paper)
    1. French poetry—20th century—History and criticism.   2. French
language—Versification.   I. Winspur, Steven, 1955–   .
II. Thomas, Jean-Jacques. La langue, la poésie.   III. Title.
PQ441.T465   1999
841'.9109—dc21   98-17597
                                                                      CIP

It is the policy of The Pennsylvania State University Press to use acid-free paper
for the first printing of all clothbound books. Publications on uncoated stock
satisfy the minimum requirements of American National Standard for Informa-
tion Sciences—Permanence of Paper for Printed Library Materials, ANSI
Z39.48–1992.

contents

acknowledgments

This book takes as its starting point a number of essays from various French, English, and Spanish publications. Each chapter of this book also contains additional material not previously found in such publications, as well as updated references to contemporary poets who have appeared during the last ten years. The lengthy introduction, Chapters 7, 10, and 11, and the conclusion and bibliography have been written specifically for the current study and are designed to complete our readers' understanding of the major developments in French poetry from World War I to the present.

First, we wish to thank the Presses Universitaires du Septentrion for allowing us to adapt and translate several chapters of Jean-Jacques Thomas's *La Langue, la poésie: Essais sur la poésie française contemporaine* (1989). Parts of our introduction and of Chapter 9, as well as Chapters 1 through 4, are translated from this work. Chapter 6 is a rewritten version of an essay first published in Spanish ("La Metafora: La imagen y la fórmula," in *Poética Generativa* [Buenos Aires: Hachette, 1990]). An earlier and shorter version of Chapter 5 was published by Steven Winspur under the title "The Poetic Significance of the Thing-in-Itself" (*Sub-Stance* 41 [November 1983]: 41–49).

The authors also wish to acknowledge the permission to reproduce extracts and illustrations given by the following publishers and individuals: Les Editions Flammarion, Les Editions Gallimard, Les Editions du Seuil, Paul Fournel, Hachette, Paol Keineg, Présence Africaine, Slatkine, Ubacs, Keith Waldrop, and Burning Deck.

INTRODUCTION

In the introduction to his *Letter on French Music,* written in 1753, Jean-Jacques Rousseau pinpoints the most widely recognized attribute of the French language. "Although we have had some excellent poets," he concedes, "and even a few musicians who were not lacking in talent, I believe that our language is hardly suited for poetry and certainly not for music." He goes on to note that "the French language seems to me to belong to philosophers and wise people." Such a view of French as being fashioned by Malherbe—a grammarian who even Ferdinand Brunot, his most studious hagiographer, characterized as having no "feeling for poetry"[1]—and by the grammarians who succeeded him is all too common.

---

1. Even if Francis Ponge in his *Pour un Malherbe* (Paris: Gallimard, 1961) writes, "Malherbe is part of my own wood, so to speak. He has been intimately bound to my own substance as I was growing, and has become part of it" (36), one has to remember that Ponge places himself at the top of the tree ("ici-haut") with the most recent leaves of the French language whereas Malherbe is part of the trunk.

It argues that those entrusted with maintaining the language, and who were keen to elaborate a tool perfectly suited to philosophical reflection and scholarly debate, concentrated first of all on turning French into a vehicle for clear and orderly prose that had no room for excessive liberties of style—even if these came under the rubric of "poetic license."

Understood in this way, French did not, however, simply retain its auxiliary role to philosophy. Its forms diversified, its logical structures became less rigid, rhetorical constraints were made less severe and, as a result of these changes, it had an unparalleled success in the nineteenth century through the genre of the novel. Yet at this very moment when all of Europe acknowledged the prowess of French in this domain and tried to emulate its discursive patterns, poetry resisted the shackles imposed by standard linguistic forms with even greater vehemence. Through Rimbaud, Baudelaire, and Mallarmé, poetry tried out new formulations that, at the very least, were an internal resistance to, and a declared attack against, several of the traits French had acquired. For instance, the mimetic representation of reality, which had been carefully cultivated by novelists following Walter Scott's lead, became a pretext for poetic experiments in which unreal descriptions were more and more common. Now considered to be the raw material for different forms of verbal alchemy, the most characteristic structures of the French language were disappearing between the cracks that had opened up in the new semantic fields created by poetic images and by the hypotaxis that characterizes poetry's unexpected formulations.

An example had been set, and the tentative experiments with such hybrid forms as the prose poem or poetic prose were a clear warning that the sharp division between poetry and prose was becoming blurred. More precisely, it became apparent that this division hinged less on an obvious contrast between two basic types of formal structure than on a more subtle contrast between two distinct models of the French language. The formal apparatus of rhymed verse, fixed stanza forms, and so on, which had ostensibly indicated poetry's specificity, was losing its importance and being usurped by a newly liberated prosaic language that had been pushed to its formal limits and constrained by laws other than those of practical communication or referential reporting. New procedures for literary production and new organizing principles were put into place with the result that French acquired a poetic dimension.

We do not want to suggest that the formal apparatus of verse and rhyme that had previously been synonymous with poetry had not initially been a surface reflection of these basic poetic principles. On the contrary, the two were indeed linked. Yet, precisely because this apparatus had become poetry's traditional garb, it no longer had anything but a ritualized function and the underlying causes that had produced it had been more and more forgotten. In French poetry from 1860 onward we are consequently confronted by a return to basics, as it were, since what counts are some fundamental rules of language whose more apparent expression in traditional structures of prosody had only a secondary importance. The remodeling process that poetry underwent at this time certainly made it a lot harder to identify, and harder for the reader to penetrate. This was largely because its commentators and readers had to reflect in a very sustained way on the types of writing produced and gradually identify those linguistic operations indicating the presence of certain verbal exercises that deserved the label of "poetry."

The absence of clearly visible formal criteria also entailed that poetic constructions could not be easily transposed from one author to another. In fact each author created his or her own models for subverting language and the way these models operated varied from one body of work to another, even if the principles underlying the models remained essentially the same. This led to a wide diversity of forms in contemporary poetry that escapes any attempts at explanation in terms of "poetic individualism." For recognizing a text's unique features does not prevent a reader from assigning it to a broader literary movement that is characterized by a single aesthetic precept, even if this means falling back into the dubious practice of classifying works in a literary historical manner. In our days, however, the solitary act of writing is a necessary precondition for a poet's confronting language directly. The forging of individual idiolects is a fundamental fact in the writing of poetry today, and it can thrive only in isolation.

It would be pointless to search for a dominant movement among contemporary French poets, along the lines of the Surrealist group that was so influential before World War II. Individual literary groups can certainly be pinpointed, and have been: *Tel Quel* or the *Change* collectivities, for instance. Yet even in these well-known groups we find that the writing duties are divided up among their members. Jacques Roubaud is *the* poet in the *Change* group, while Denis Roche is, or rather was, the poet of *Tel Quel*. The other group members were novelists, theorists, art critics, or intellectual activists. The groups themselves, then, do not include a large number of poets who share the same ideals or who

use writing strategies that are governed by the same doctrine or under-
lying credo. (An instructive exception to this tendency is the OuLiPo
group, whose meticulous and deliberately collective works will be dis-
cussed in Chapter 9.) In fact the poets who currently receive the most
acclaim are not beholden to any school and, on the contrary, take care to
publicize the individual nature of their writings.

In the first issue of *Hémisphères,* which was one of a series of pri-
vately distributed literary reviews grouping together, from the outset of
World War II, most of the well-known poets of today, there is an editorial
signed by Alain Bosquet that is typical of this new attitude toward poetry.
Its title is "French Poetry Continues" and in it we find the following
declarations:

> Pas d'amitié dans la poésie, surtout pas d'union! Le poète ne doit
> pas s'occuper de ce que fait le poète voisin. Il sait que la poésie est à
> la fois synthétique et exigeante. Il sait que les jeux sont désormais
> interdits et avec eux les grimaces et les chiquenaudes. (...)
>
> Le poète se veut sévère, difficile, sans même avoir ce qu'il
> exige, car ce doute augmente encore sa grandeur.
>
> Il sait surtout que son rôle est d'écrire et non pas de réfléchir.
> (...) Il ne doit pas perdre son temps à devenir trop intelligent, à
> discuter, à prouver, à construire des systèmes.

> (There must be no camaraderie in poetry, and especially no unity! A
> poet should not be worried about what fellow-poets are doing. He
> knows that poetry is an act of both synthesis and internal rigor. He
> knows that playfulness is henceforth forbidden, along with putting
> on airs or ribbing. [...]
>
> Poets want to be strict, difficult, without even possessing the
> strengths they demand, since this lack can only increase their great-
> ness.
>
> Most of all, they know that their job is to write, and not to
> meditate. [...] They must not waste their time becoming too intel-
> ligent, or being involved in discussions, proofs, and the construc-
> tion of intellectual systems.)

This upturned manifesto calls for poets to spread out into their own terri-
tories. It denounces any attempts at writerly brotherhood, as well as the
Surrealists' obsession with explaining poems in minute detail with the

help of a critical paraphrase that is a useless accompaniment to the original act of writing. A great number of poets are consequently cut down to size and brought back to their simplest forms of expression. The phrase "their simplest forms of expression" may lose some of its literal meaning here, since the poems in question were far from being flat declarative statements, but it does stress Bosquet's condemnation of literary pretense, a pretense that has more to do with a poet's status than with the formulations he or she writes.

After World War II writing became more personal, and poetic technique worked solely on what Michel Leiris calls, through the figure of antanaclasis, *le bagage lent* (the slow baggage) that is *le langage* (language). Left in a quandary, poets took with them only what was strictly necessary for their writing and kept poetry in its most basic form, working on the only material that belonged to them: language. By taking refuge in language they were able to map out new paths of phonetic patterning and symbolic composition without worrying about how these would be received by their public or even their fellow poets. Denied its function as a vehicle of intersubjective communication, speech became for these writers the richest source for poetry's revitalization. The phonetic and semantic substance of each word was reworked and the multiple possibilities of each sentence were explored. Such a solitary undertaking, with its refusal to cultivate disciples or future audiences, could only have one outlet once they were left to confront themselves—the forging of a personal poetic dialect that was precisely tailored to the poet's verbal competence. With language now free of the exterior affectations that had made it seem like poetry to the casual reader, it was nevertheless not entirely devoid of social imprints. For the performative experimentation inherent in language allies it closely with an intertextual archaeology that is part of the common linguistic heritage shared by French speakers. The verbal monuments in this archaeology are revisited by the new poetry, but not in any order that has been prescribed by history.

When confronted by the linguistic depth of such poems, some readers complain about their inaccessibility, and then conveniently forget that these texts play the same role in the literary imagination of twentieth-century French writing that the novel played in the nineteenth century. This oversight is probably due to the fact that these same readers fail to realize that the very poems they are characterizing as gratuitous or esoteric are actually a direct consequence of the loosening of formal rules that was enacted by the so-called avant-garde poets at the end of the nineteenth century, whom such readers have no difficulty placing in the French literary canon.

Quite obviously, there is an ascetic dimension inherent in modern poetry's return to its sources, and in its attempt to break free from the sort of exhibitionism with which it was identified for too long. A poetry based on linguistic deciphering and on a sustained labor of well-grounded interpretation is precisely the type of writing that Roger Callois called for in the same issue of *Hémisphères* quoted above:

> Ce langage, qu'on aurait cru arbitraire et assemblage capricieux de syllabes, se laisse donc déchiffrer. De lentes recherches et quelque abandon à ses pouvoirs savent le forcer à livrer ses secrets. La patience et le savoir qu'il faut dépenser pour y réussir privent sans doute un texte si défendu des lecteurs précipités ou peu avertis qui sont le plus grand nombre. Mais il est douteux que l'auteur souhaite les retenir.

> (This language of ours, which one would have thought to be a purely arbitrary and capricious jumble of syllables, finally allows itself to be deciphered. Through lengthy research and by absorbing its powers, its secrets can be forced into the open. The necessary patience for this task and the knowledge that one must devote tremendous effort to it in order to gain anything in return probably deprive such daunting texts of impatient and unsuspecting readers who come in great numbers. But it's doubtful that authors would want to hold on to them.)

In putting forward the critical commentaries that make up this book it was not our intention to set up an honor roll of French poets, for the simple reason that the most well-known among these (Pierre-Jean Jouve, Aragon, Saint-John Perse, Char, Ponge, Du Bouchet, Guillevic, and Dupin, to name but a few) have already come under close critical scrutiny. Being neither a eulogy of already recognized poets, nor a set of predictions for future poetic glory, the following pages are primarily a detailed study of specific poems. By analyzing the literary functions of these texts, we not only gain a better understanding of them but also an overview of the main tendencies in contemporary French poetry as a whole.

It is too often believed that today's poets write only for one another, or for other specialists in poetic technique, and this is in part due to the ease with which poets switch from the role of writer to that of critic—a switch that casts doubt for some readers over the communicative purpose of the poems. Yet this oversimplified portrait of the contemporary poet is at fault, and largely because of the type of poetry criticism that is fostered in universities and elsewhere. When such criticism examines the most stimulating and original works of French literature, it calls on models that are valid only for traditional poetry and limits itself to impressionistic surveys that garner from each work merely its themes, the configuration of symbols that it contains, or else a vague assortment of superficial stylistic features. One can therefore understand why any prospective poetry reader would think that there is nothing particularly new in contemporary works and that the complexity of the latter was specifically designed to ward off the uninitiated. Hence readers' tendency to hold on to well-worn critical concepts and to stick to poems that respect canonical norms and whose meaning has an obvious direction. Unfortunately, this common tendency makes readers forget that the body of poetry they have ignored for the most part is contemporaneous with their own culture, and that the forms and strategies used in such poetry are much more indicative of their times than any putative modern sensibility. To ignore such writings is to turn the act of reading into a nostalgic look backward, rather than an understanding of the present. Who, for instance, remembers that Victor de Laprade was France's foremost poet in the mid-nineteenth century, at the very time when the new prose poem form of Aloysius Bertrand was, and still is, largely unknown? Or that Tristan Derème was held in high esteem in the 1920s when Eluard's *Répétitions* was ignored by the poet's contemporaries?

These last remarks are not intended to question the wisdom that a generation of readers has shown through its choice of texts, but rather to bring into focus the purpose of the present book. Every act of reading implies an apprenticeship in the ways of discovering and identifying those features that make up a text's particular quality and value. So the fame or age of the poets who will be discussed in the following chapters is of little importance alongside the unearthing of some radically new properties that are intrinsic to contemporary poetry.

Some of today's essayists believe that drawing a distinction between prose and poetry is already a step backward since the differences between the two no longer matter, whereas basic definitions of the terms *text* and *writing* do. For these critics the classical genre divisions have been surpassed once and for all. This argument seems to us to be extremely sketchy and hypothetical, despite the fact that certain contemporary writers are lulled into believing that there is an underlying homogeneity to all forms of writing. Yet as we pointed out at the start, the functional properties of the French language have changed over the last two hundred years. A certain number of procedures that have traditionally helped readers identify the language of poetry have been absorbed by authors who, in all good faith, claim to be prose writers. Yet this merely pushes the prose/poetry distinction back to a more basic level, since what we are now faced with is the need to draw a distinction between the most modern literary prose and prosaic texts designed for mass consumption. In fact it was the appeal of poetry, or at the very least the attraction of its governing principles, that gave much contemporary prose its value, and so if it is no longer possible to tell poetry apart from prose it is not because poetry has disappeared but because nineteenth-century novelistic prose has been contaminated and upended by a language whose basic principles are exclusively poetical.

The question therefore becomes: How are we to understand the specificity of contemporary poetry if the bulk of French literature since 1870 has itself taken a poetic turn? The following eleven chapters answer this question by examining the different ways in which poets from Apollinaire onward have "poeticized"[2] even further the language of literature that was handed down to them. More precisely, we examine how the referential capacities of language are poetically transformed (by Eluard and Bonnefoy, Saint-John Perse and Deguy), how language's own intertextuality weaves a poetic persona (for Apollinaire and Césaire) or guides its readers in their search for meaning (in writings by Jacob, Bonnefoy, or Hébert), how syntax and the communicative dimension of a message are replaced by poetic patterning (in Dada, Bernard Noël, and recent visual poetry), and how the formal rules that constitute a poem's significance develop certain mathematical properties of language (in Roubaud's writings and those of the OuLiPo group).

---

2. The concept of poeticizing was already present in Mallarmé's work where he discussed "le besoin de poétiser" (the need to poetize; "Crise de vers," *Oeuvres complètes,* eds. Henri Mondor and G. Jean-Aubry [Paris: Gallimard, Pléiade, 1945], 361). Mallarmé used the term, however, as an intrasitive verb in this passage, in order to give a general definition of poetry's mode of communication. Here we use it transitively (hence the shift from "poetize" to "poeticize") with specific emphasis on the necessary transformations that poetry brings to a language system.

Although each of these transformations or patterns is not sufficient in itself to turn a group of words into a poem (since some of them create jokes in everyday conversation, or mere playfulness in prose), taken as a whole they sketch out many of the necessary conditions that characterize French poetry since World War II. To claim in this way that there are no single properties unique to contemporary French poetry amounts to denying any essential differences between poetic and nonpoetic language. It does not mean, however, that the two are identical; there are differences between these two forms of language, but they are a matter of degree rather than nature. Modern poetry exploits to the full certain linguistic properties that underpin everyday communication but are obscured in normal speech and descriptive prose, where the transmission of a message is paramount.

When considered in this light, the opposition favored by many critics between poetic and nonpoetic language needs to be revised. For instance, when Cleanth Brooks adopts I. A. Richards's dictum that "it is not what a poem says that matters, but what it is,"[3] we are immediately tempted to ask: How can one describe what the poem is without discussing what it says? Moreover, when Brooks argues that "a poem does not *state* ideas but rather *tests* ideas" (256), it is clear that such testing must be conducted at the level of words, and that the meanings within a poem lie at the heart of this evaluation. Any theory that opposes ordinary linguistic meaning to poetic meaning runs up against the same problem: by isolating poetic texts from the normal functioning of language it becomes increasingly difficult to show how a poem produces many of its specific effects that are built on normal linguistic features.[4]

If one turns briefly to some of the earliest analyses done by a twentieth-century French poet on the differences between poetic and everyday language—namely, in essays by Paul Valéry—one discovers that poetry's

---

3. Cleanth Brooks, *The Well Wrought Urn: Studies in the Structure of Poetry* (New York: Harcourt Brace, 1947), 265.

4. Jean Cohen's *Structure du langage poétique* (Paris: Flammarion, 1966) is another victim of this approach since it attempts to prove empirically that poetic language always deviates from common usage. Cohen sums up his argument by claiming that poetry is "anti-prose" (51). However, as Gérard Genette has argued, the "norms" from which poetry is supposed to deviate are extremely hard to define, which makes the notion of deviation rather vague. Yet if poetry is to be defined as a negation, or transformation, of prose, it is essential that prose not have any of the poetic properties that Cohen highlights—and this is, quite simply, not the case. See Genette, "Langage poétique, poétique du langage," *Figures II* (Paris: Seuil, 1969), 123–53.

connection to ordinary speech is not simply oppositional. The links be-
tween the two are more complex. Building on Mallarmé's claim that
poetry draws out a potential, inherent in all language, to create forceful
effects in its listeners,[5] Valéry argues that poetry is to everyday speech
what dance is to walking. Dance and poetry both reveal what a body (or
a language) is capable of, and at the same time clarify the mechanisms
that make daily walking and talking possible.[6] Consequently, poetry
stands not so much in contrast to everyday language as in the form of a
backdrop to all linguistic acts, insofar as it illustrates to the utmost degree
the power of language's effects. Such effects are lessened in prose and
daily communication where words are subordinated to what Valéry calls a
"transitive" use, that of saying something or conveying a message. Mean-
while in poetry one finds "literature reduced to the essential core of its
active principle [where] the quasi-creative or quasi-fictive role of lan-
guage [...] is revealed in the clearest possible way through the fragile and
arbitrary status of a poem's subject."[7]

    Poeticizing language does not, therefore, involve a complete over-
haul of the linguistic properties of French. In some cases it in fact accen-
tuates these properties, with the result that several contemporary poems
appear to be complex developments of phonetic or syntactic patterns oc-
curring within the language itself. One of the poets we examine in Chap-
ter 5, Michel Deguy, has summed up the procedure in this way: "La
poésie prend conscience de, et confiance dans, ce fait qu'elle *est* langage;
ou, renversé, que le langage est poétique" (Poetry draws awareness, and
confidence, from the fact that it *is* language; or, conversely, that language
is poetic).[8] Giving a new impetus to Valéry's meditations on the types of
action that are accomplished by poetic effects, Deguy proceeds in *Actes*
to examine the ways in which "a poem bends back on language and
delves deeper into it" (77), in order to better grasp the poem's own *agir*
(233), or mode of action.

    Three ways of poeticizing language seem to us to be emblematic of

    5. See Mallarmé: "le dire (...) retrouve chez le Poète, par nécessité constitutive
d'un art consacré aux fictions, sa virtualité" (diction [...] rediscovers in the Poet, through
the underlying necessity of any art made up of fictions, its own virtuality; "Crise de vers"
368).
    6. Paul Valéry, "Propos sur la poésie," *Oeuvres,* ed. J. Hytier, vol. 1 (Paris: Galli-
mard, Pléiade, 1957), 1370–72.
    7. Valéry, "Ebauches de pensées," *Oeuvres,* ed. J. Hytier, vol. 2 (Paris: Gallimard,
Pléiade, 1957), 548.
    8. Michel Deguy, *Actes* (Paris: Gallimard, 1966), 46.

French poetry today, and to close this introduction we will characterize them briefly. They are the poetic transformation of historical references, the co-optation of readers' intertextual competence, and the playful exploitation of language's formal rules.

To begin with the first of these, mimesis is the term normally applied to the referential function of writing. Mimesis results from certain linguistic uses based on denotation, and the legibility of mimetic markers is grounded in their quick recognition by readers. Mimesis is not only a trait of the novel (although the term is most commonly used for this genre); it is part of the very structure of language itself—whether this is used in prose or in poetry—since any instance of articulated language serves the function of conveying information. The difference between various types of prose and poetry hinges on the degree to which this function is activated in specific texts. The information can be taken as such and read in connection with a reality that is external to the verbal network, but it can also be analyzed as just another element in this network. Since every reading of a sequence is initially a predicative one, there is a predominance of information in any reading. Indeed, in certain poetic texts the role of information is precisely to give a referential anchor to an extralinguistic context that offers spatial or temporal beacons guiding the reader's interpretation of the text. In such cases information plays the role of an index that is similar to that of deictic markers (*this, that,* and so on) in grammar. There is nothing stopping a reader, however, from taking these signs, which are apparently subservient to an extratextual reality, as elements bound up in a textual sequence and placed there precisely to operate alongside all the other words within the text's framework of semantic and phonetic structures. The informative value of these elements disappears, and it is no longer their indexical value that saturates the verbal chain, but rather the connotative value of the index. For example, Baudelaire's *Croquis parisiens* (Parisian sketches) are hardly "Parisian" at all. They use their topographic reference as a semantic reservoir operating at a metalinguistic level and pointing nonmimetically toward a fictional space in which poems can address poetry directly. Consequently, in this work we are confronted by language grappling with its own resources, and any reference to a material reality beyond the text is pushed aside. Topography simply becomes a metaphorical canvas on which the text's developments are projected. True to the etymology of *topos,* or place (with the proviso that the places in question are consecrated sites of literature, or *commonplaces,* to which successive authors refer in a ritualized manner), topographical markers in poetry are merely inscriptions within a textual system, and their referential value is subordinate to the internal functioning of the poem in question.

From this it should not be inferred that the most stimulating works of modern poetry are candid examples of art for art's sake. The poem's significance, which springs from a roundabout and off-center emphasis on verbal playfulness, erects a secondary meaning that is not necessarily inconclusive or lacking in didactic force. Eluard's poem "La Victoire de Guernica" (The victory of Guernica), discussed in Chapter 3, is a clear example of the ways in which a poeticized topography replaces referential value with didactic authority.

The second way of poeticizing language draws on patterns of intertextuality. Many different definitions of intertextuality abound, from Bakhtin to Kristeva and Barthes, but the one from which we draw below was put forward in 1980 by Michael Riffaterre in his article "La Trace de l'intertexte" (The trace of the intertext).[9] Countering many critics' tendency to expand the notion of intertextuality so that it could designate any allusion a particular reader might infer from a text, Riffaterre distinguishes between "aleatory" allusions in a text and "obligatory" intertextuality. Concerning the latter, he writes that "whatever the size of an intertext is for any given reader, it is made up of certain fixed elements that are totally determined by textual imperatives." He goes on:

> We are dealing here with a type of intertextuality that the reader cannot not perceive, because the intertext leaves an indelible mark in the text which is a formal coefficient that serves as a command for a particular type of reading. This command dictates the deciphering of the text's literary aspects. (5)

From this standpoint, aleatory allusions are simply part of the reader's aesthetic appreciation of a text, whereas obligatory intertextuality corresponds to certain requirements for an understanding of the work in question. It is not just a type of artistic surplus value that is triggered off by a reader's whim; instead it closely matches the way in which the literary text has been encoded.

Consequently, within the infinite expanse of an encyclopedic tex-

---

9. Michael Riffaterre, "La Trace de l'intertexte," *La Pensée, Approches actuelles de la critique*, 215 (October 1980): 4–18.

tual memory it is important that the intertext be a specific and precise reference—for the simple reason that its role is crucial to a text's production. In short, the movement of a text's significance cannot be charted without an explanation of the intertext.

For us, intertextuality imposes even more constraints on the reader, since it does not merely involve calling up the superficial aspects of one text in order to illuminate the apparent obscurity (or what Riffaterre calls the "non-grammaticality") of another. It is not just the need to put two completed works of literature face to face, for a work by Proust does not by itself evoke one by Stendhal (nor is the contrary true, as Barthes would have us believe). This is because the inevitable contamination of one work by another takes place *within language itself* and hence inside those elements that make up literary signs. As we mentioned at the start of this introduction, the substance of each language carries along with it elements of the literary encyclopedia specific to it, for the simple reason that a language is the vehicle through which such knowledge is conveyed. The abundance of intertexts is in fact a plethora of linguistic resources, and these alone chart the course for the workings of literary memory. Each verbal unit, be it long or short, contains elements of this memory that have become identified with the unit itself, so that these elements are not optional supplements to the verbal unit but internal to its functioning. For this reason they cannot be defined as mere "con-notations" or accessory meanings.[10] In Chapters 4 and 7 we show how portions of literary and philosophical discourse (from La Fontaine and Descartes, respectively) are extracted from the encyclopedic memory of French and then reactivated through poetic transformations.

Moreover, within a given poem the intertextual inscriptions are not merely there to guide the reader and give easier access to the text's significance. Such as we have defined it, intertextuality plays an even more basic role since it guarantees that a text will belong to a given linguistic community, by exploiting the mnemonic capacity of language itself. When, through fragmentation, opacity, or a lack of semantic direction, parts of discourse seem to escape the control that comes about through the simple rules of conventionalized communication, it is the anchor of intertextuality that restores the legitimacy of intersubjective verification and that sets up communal conditions for readability and interpretation.

10. For a detailed discussion of this question, see Jean-Jacques Thomas, *La Langue volée* (Bern: Peter Lang, 1990).

In Chapters 7 and 10, for instance, intertextuality is shown to be the glue that binds coherent meanings together in obscure poems by Jacqueline Risset and Denis Roche. The need to recognize such communal *lieux-dits* (signposted sites) is central not only to so-called textual analysis, but also to reader-response interpretations of literature. One could even argue that such intertextual sites are more important in the latter case, where interpretations are often falsely claimed to exist independently of the text's governing system.

The third means of poeticizing language (which will be examined especially in Chapters 2, 8, and 9) is what we call *techno-ludic,* and it is a strain that runs through French poetry from Dada onward. Techno-ludic writing is characterized by a playful development of basic linguistic mechanisms, grounding syntax, semantics, and so on. By using the word "playful" we are not implying that such texts have a gratuitous or throw-away value; instead we use it in the musical sense of a player who develops his or her skill through rigorous exercises that steadily broaden the parameters of artistic value. Such word games (which should be more correctly termed *language games* rather than mere puns or lexical substitutions) certainly have the artificial and arbitrary appearance that comes when anybody attempts to escape the conventions of public communication. However, in order to function at all these ludic exercises must obey specific operating rules, and to do so they must ground themselves in a set of principles that are just as controlled and codified as the ones they left behind.

In order to compensate for its doing away with the basic rules of communication, poetic language develops a supplementary set of rules that, in most cases, manages to bring back the type of elemental formalism that is peculiar to poetry. The characteristic properties of this formalism (systematized derivations, dense patterning, and unity) reappear in many diverse arrangements that are generated from different principles, and yet they all have one thing in common: an underscoring of the rhythmical structure that gives voice to poetry. Contrary to what happened in traditional poetry, this putting into form is not governed by any preestablished canon, but is instead closely linked to the formal logic that is peculiar to each individual text. It therefore plays a more important role than it did in earlier poetry since, instead of merely serving as an external system of constraint, it blends in completely with the particular dynamics that produce the text in question. Typographic arrangements, numerical patterns, or literary structures that are created in an ad hoc way give support to this putting-into-form, and they direct the linguistic expansion that the poem undertakes after it has attacked the communicative rules of speech.

Showing the ways in which poems are already their own metalanguage (or critical commentary on themselves) is one of the goals of Michel Deguy's essays, and also of his poems to which we return in Chapter 5. Developing his enigmatic motto from *Actes* that "le poème recherche le langage du langage" (the poem searches for the language of language; 36), Deguy argues that a poem both states its meaning poetically and also shows (through its formal patterning) how this meaning is created, what its poeticity consists of, and hence what the poetic nature inherent in language really is. "For a poem is a sort of phonic anagram for that 'word of itself' that the poem does not otherwise reveal," he writes (64). In short, each poem hides "the metaphor of itself in its very breaths and arguments" (28).[11]

Although the principle of dissemination and the technique of fragmenting linguistic structures were, historically speaking, begun before the Dada movement, it is largely responsible for the broadcasting and radical development of new poetic forms in which language is cut up and turned into raw material for texts that have no apparent rhyme or reason. In Chapter 2 we examine Dada's antisemiotic project, and in Chapters 8 and 9 we trace the development of typographic and numerical formalisms in various types of visual poetry and the works of the OuLiPo group. The latter are the clearest example of the techno-ludic strain that is to be found, to one degree or another, in all poetry. The self-questioning and uneasiness that give rise to many OuLiPian texts are quite obviously a sign of uncertain times in which literature is undergoing a reexamination. One finds traces of this reexamination in current debates surrounding the term *lyric*. Our book closes with two chapters that discuss the usefulness of this term when discussing today's poetry in France. Chapter 10 argues for a new understanding of lyricism, based on the effects that performative utterances produce in their readers. By shifting the site of lyricism (from the netherworld of a poet's personal experience to the realm of a reader's reactions) we hope to put the discussion of lyrical force on firmer ground—specifically, the pragmatic and linguistic components of the text itself, and the ends to which these components are directed. Our last

11. See also Mallarmé's "Sonnet allégorique de lui-même," in his *Oeuvres complètes: Poésies*, eds. Carl Paul Barbier and Charles Gordon Millan (Paris: Flammarion, 1983), 220.

chapter examines some long poems that seem to have escaped critics'
categorizations, and in it we propose that the study of personal pronouns
in such works reveals their affiliation to both lyric patterns and the ne-
glected genre of epic poetry.

When Mallarmé declared in "Crise de vers" that "Parler n'a trait à
la réalité des choses que commercialement" (Speaking is related to the
reality of things only in a commercial way; 366), he freed literature, in
effect, from its obligations to the real world and cleared a path for the
biggest exploration of language's potential that any society has under-
taken so far. However, he left up to others the task of writing *Le Livre*
(The book) that he did not know how, or perhaps lacked the time, to
finish. Literary monuments of the twentieth century make up its pages
and mark out the contours of our own modernity. Confined as we are by
the networks of meaning into which these monuments direct us, is it not
inevitable that we should want to escape from the book and, like the
OuLiPians, look to some hypothetical workroom for new rules and mate-
rials that would offer a completely different type of poetic language in
which repetition and difference could coexist?

one

ENTOMBED ALIVE

(APOLLINAIRE)

What follows this doubly cryptic heading is an analysis of *L'Enchanteur pourrissant* (The rotting enchanter).[1] It is a little known work and often overlooked—which has led Scott Bates to comment that "in a nutshell, nobody mentions it."[2] With its semantic tension caused by the contrast between things morbid and marvelous, the very title of the work leads one to expect a model text along the lines of so many necrophilic writings where unscrupulous sawbones play out the comedy of death, but under another name. For it is precisely in graves that mortal destiny is inverted into animal parasitism, thus becoming an extended antiphrasis

1. Guillaume Apollinaire, *L'Enchanteur pourrissant.* The first edition of this work was published in Paris in the review *Le Festin d'Esope,* no. 6 (April 1904). The second edition, published in Paris by Henry Kahnweiler, appeared in 1909. All references to the work herein will be made to Jean Burgos's edition (Paris: Minard, 1972).
2. Scott Bates, "Guillaume Apollinaire et 'L'Enchanteur pourrissant,'" *Revue des Sciences Humaines* 84 (October–December 1956): 425–35.

that draws out the ambiguity of the matrix symbol, tomb. Bachelard points out that the French word for a cemetery (*cimetière*) is derived from the Greek *koimétérion,* or bridal chamber.[3] The negative element in the word would seem to trigger off a sprightly optimism—as evidenced by the French expression, "Des fruits tombent, les germes lèvent" (Fruits fall, seeds rise).[4]

When commentators of literature face indecipherable or undecidable extracts they invariably resort to the appealing suggestiveness of this two-way symbol, even if they disguise it with the latest psychoanalytic jargon. Jean Bellemin-Noël offers a case in point when he tackles the two resistant verses from Apollinaire's poem "Les Colchiques" (published in the collection *Alcools*):

> Ils cueillent les colchiques qui sont comme des mères
> filles de leurs filles et sont couleur de tes paupières.
>
> (They pick the autumn crocuses which are like mothers
> daughters of their daughters and are color of your eyelids.)

In the phrase "mothers daughters of their daughters," where Roger Lefèvre spotted "a botanical peculiarity of autumn crocus,"[5] and where Michel Deguy detected "a shore of murmuring and palatal tenderness placed between some harsh and dry syllables,"[6] Bellemin-Noël uncovers "a meaningless statement which consequently points to the site of a libidinal drive: to be born is to already desire death [...] each newborn infant is born-with death (*co-naît sa mort*). For the grown-up [...] to be *mother daughter of her daughter* is one and the same thing for the subject of an utterance."[7] The standard marker for death is, consequently, an invitation to read its own negation. The celebration of things defunct would seem to be merely a prelude to a ritual of endless rebirths.

This metaphorical approach could perhaps give us a reading model for *L'Enchanteur pourrissant*. According to the model, the entombing of

---

3. Gaston Bachelard, *La Terre et les rêveries du repos* (Paris: Corti, 1948), 179.

4. This expression is quoted by Gilbert Durand in *Les Structures anthropologiques de l'imaginaire* (Paris: Presses Universitaires de France, 1963), 318.

5. Apollinaire, "Les Colchiques," *Alcools,* ed. Roger Lefèvre (Paris: Larousse, 1971), 64.

6. Michel Deguy, "Encore une lecture des 'Colchiques,'" *Poétique* 20 (1974): 54.

7. Jean Bellemin-Noël, "Petit supplément aux lectures des 'Colchiques,'" *Poétique* 33 (1978): 69.

the magician in the first chapter would open the way to a deification of the poet-prophet who finally resolves, in the section titled "Onirocritique," the secret of his destiny: namely, the different life patterns for man and woman.

Reading *L'Enchanteur pourrissant* in this way trivializes it, however, by reducing it to a mere phase among others in a long literary tradition. It is the tradition of those "Texts from Beyond the Grave" that occupy a special place in Alain Buisine's category of "tomb prose" and that, in another context, Jean-Pierre Richard has labeled "open-grave" works.[8] Moreover, the type of analysis that Richard proposes clearly shows the limits to this approach. For what he extracts are themes (for instance, those of falling or speed), motifs (those of mirror, grave, or body parts),[9]

8. Alain Buisine, "Prose Tombale," *Revue des Sciences Humaines* 160 (1975). Jean-Pierre Richard, *Microlectures* (Paris: Seuil, 1979), 277–83.
9. Sometimes Richard does not even deal with strictly literary motifs, but with real objects and their presumed extensions within the text. Consider, for instance, the opening remarks in his Apollinaire chapter ("Le Poète étoilée," in *Microlectures*): "Apollinaire's poetic universe contains few objects that are as rich [...] as the star" (150). The actual components of the objects are thus used to determine the generic thematics of the imagery (the Milky Way, constellations, light, and so on), and to limit this thematics. Concerning the poem "Lul de Faltenin," for example, Richard limits his inquiry to the astronomical characteristics of the word *étoile* (star) when he writes: "The thematics of the star already betrays the mark of this modification in such a poem as 'Lul de Faltenin.' In this work, as different commentators have shown, we find the disappearance of the setting sun into the blue body of the sea" (153).
Yet most commentators have actually found autoeroticism running throughout the poem and culminating in "les étolles oblongues" (oblong stars). Jean Burgos confirms this interpretation. "It is clear," he writes, "that in 'Lul de Faltenin' whose erotic inspiration is almost beyond a doubt, we rediscover images of creeping, in various degrees" (*L'Enchanteur pourrissant* 17, note d). The sexual connotations of the word *star* are explicitly mentioned, moreover, in other poems by Apollinaire. See, for instance, "Le Brasier" (*Alcools*): "The sudden gallop of the stars / Not being what will become / Mixes with the male neighing / Of the Centaurs in their stud-farms." There is nothing surprising in this connection since the French sociolect contains a ready-made expression for autoeroticism, based on the interchangeability of *toile* (sheet) and *étoile* (see André Gill, *L'Etoile* [Paris: A. Lemerre, 1873]). The last line from "Lul de Faltenin" is a parody of this switching of terms: "Car c'est moi seul nuit qui t'étoile" (Since it is me alone the night that stars you).
Moreover, J.-P. Richard completely ignores the other meaning of *étoile* that lies at the very heart of *L'Enchanteur pourrissant*—namely, the clearing at the center of a forest to which every path leads and which is dominated by the enchanter's tomb. This omission merely underscores the fact that because a thematic reading stops at the surface of a text, it can only extract from the work in question what it has already added to it, thus failing to clarify the underlying mechanisms that are woven into the networks of meaning already set up in the language used by the text.

and finally myths (narcissism)—in short, all that is needed to prop up the initial symbol. The entire analysis is made up of a catalogue of isolated images that are linked together by thematic bonds whose validity is not necessarily confirmed by the text but derives solely from the analysis itself. These omnipresent symbols seem to congregate on the words' surface and operate purely according to their own rules, as if the text's language were nothing but a pretext for constructing the symbols themselves. Consequently, commentaries of this type bring back the old distinction between written language and its images—a distinction between form and content that tends to be erased by the very mechanisms of a poem. As a result, thematic commentaries give rise to separate mythologies for each author, which wrongly assume that we can isolate, on the one hand, the writing subject with its linguistic rules and, on the other, the subsidiary and ornamental epiphanies offered to the reader. These epiphanies are considered to be privileged myths or symbols for the simple reason that the author deigned to give them a literary form.

We do not analyze *L'Enchanteur pourrissant* in this loose, thematic way. Instead of viewing the text as the mere illustration of a traditional, timeworn, symbolic *system,* we focus on the particular type of symbolic *transformation* that Apollinaire's work accomplishes. This transformation includes the transposing of an experience into poetic writing in such a way that the symbols used by Apollinaire refer back to the scriptural transposition itself. Moreover, the text's central motif of decomposition, along with the ensuing circle of death and birth, will be seen as a metaphor for the motif's own renewed significance.

Consequently, we do not assume that there are two different levels to the text: on the one hand, Apollinaire, the writing subject, and on the other, a set of symbols and attributes that can be cut off from the verbal discourse that produces, or reproduces, them. Basically, we believe it is the verbal and symbolic order that constitutes the writing subject, and not the other way around. Transposed into the aesthetic terms of the nineteenth century, this axiom in effect upturns the proposition whereby art imitates nature, and it maintains instead that what is natural imitates art—or, more precisely, that for humans the life principle is controlled and structured by signs. Apollinaire could not have been the spokesperson for poets of the Modern era if his *Enchanteur pourrissant* (on which he never stopped working throughout his life[10]) had not itself demon-

10. For the importance of *L'Enchanteur pourrissant*'s extended composition during

strated (in the manner of a performative statement) that the self exists only in, and through, writings. This proposition finds its allegory in the inscription placed at the center of the "Onirocritique" section: with the advent of the sacrificer who is his own sacrifice, the three letters *I.O.D.* escape from the victim's excision. According to the esoteric tradition these three letters are the original components of language. In this episode there is paradoxically both an escape from, and entry into, symbolism that is first and foremost a reexamination of poetic language. Consequently, Apollinaire shows that he is surrounded by language, indeed locked up in it to the extent that it inhabits him completely. In his works a poetry of the self takes on body—but it is a poetry of the self that is fashioned out of initially bookish elements. The development of certain fables, symbolic stories, or legendary tales transforms these earlier fragments, and at the same time it gives shape to a writer whose poetry is more *exploratory* than *exploitative*. By dismantling these preliminary symbolic units, Apollinaire gives a cohesion to his entire corpus while also drawing a self-portrait that begins to take on legendary dimensions.

It is generally believed that the text of *L'Enchanteur pourrissant* was expanded when it was first published as a separate volume by Kahnweiler in 1909.[11] It had initially appeared in 1904 in the review *Le Festin d'Esope*, containing textual strata from several different periods, since Apollinaire had been working on it since 1898. The Kahnweiler edition contains two important additions: the introduction, which presents us with the "entombing" of the magician Merlin, and the famous conclusion, "Onirocritique." These two additions are of prime importance for any commentator since they correspond to two explicit, yet different, models for intertextual practice. It would also seem to be significant that the two chapters stand guard over the text, in some way encircling (or entombing) it with borrowed material.

The introduction reveals a direct filiation with the sixteenth-century text of which it is a mere transcription—namely, Philippe Le Noir's 1533 edition of *Lancelot of the Lake*. The importance that critics have made of this filiation can be judged by the fact that three studies of Apollinaire's

Apollinaire's career, see Jean Burgos's detailed analysis in chapters 1 and 2 of his introduction ("Genesis" and "Fragmentation," respectively). See also Michel Décaudin, "Sur la composition du poète assassiné," *Revue des Sciences Humaines* 84 (October–December 1956): 437–45.

11. See Jean Hughes, *50 ans d'édition de D.-H. Kahnweiler* (Paris: Galleries Louise Leiris, 1959), i–vi, 1.

writings offer the Lancelot tale in their appendix.[12] This obvious case of
borrowing-cum-plagiarism has led many critics to apply the label of
hoaxer to Apollinaire. Bonmariage denounced him as a "noble impos-
ter,"[13] and his often used technique of introducing fragments or even
whole passages of earlier texts into his writings leads Roch Grey to write:
"Guillaume Apollinaire, a man devoted to literature and to study, has
subjected himself to every possible influence."[14] A more biting criticism
came from Georges Duhamel who denounced Apollinaire's work in 1913
as "a second-hand bookstore that collects only the odds and ends of
libraries."[15] Despite his defense of Apollinaire's right to incorporate cer-
tain fragments of earlier texts into his own, Jean Burgos also expresses a
certain commentator's disquiet when faced by "these [bookish] influ-
ences which are too obvious and not always properly assimilated" (cxxiii).
This comment about the need to assimilate earlier works raises a problem
since it shifts questions of influence, source, borrowing, parody, and
hence of intertextuality in general, into the area of authoritative decree.
And yet, as Burgos's scholarly and erudite critical edition of *L'Enchant-
eur pourrissant* illustrates, a large part of a commentator's work consists
precisely of locating the originals that anchor all the provocatively scat-
tered borrowings. All commentary must inevitably retrace the paths of
intertextuality.

Whereas literary critics delight first of all in identifying biblical
echoes, borrowings from medieval literature, or extracts from articles on
demonology, and then attempt to locate the proper sources of these
echoes, philologists, on the other hand, have a tendency to treat *L'En-
chanteur pourrissant* as a strange fantasy that has no bearing whatsoever
on the texts they study. In this vein, Mario Roques has pointed out a
large number of errors in the book and has raised serious doubts about
Apollinaire's knowledge of medieval culture.[16] Were we to consult Paul
Zumthor's thesis on the original Merlin legend we would find a similar
view of Apollinaire's hybrid text. "The introduction is a story that copies

12. Marie-Jeanne Durry, ed., *Guillaume Apollinaire—Alcools,* 3 vols. (Paris:
S.E.D.E.S., 1956–64); Scott Bates, "Guillaume Apollinaire et 'L'Enchanteur pourrissant'";
Jean Burgos, ed., *L'Enchanteur pourrissant,* 189–92.

13. S. Bonmariage, "Guillaume Apollinaire ou l'Imposteur Magnanime," *Mercure
de France,* November 1927.

14. Roch Grey, "Apollinaire familier," *La Table ronde,* September 1952.

15. Georges Duhamel, "Alcools d'Apollinaire," *Mercure de France,* 14 June 1913.

16. Mario Roques, *Études de littérature française [de la Chanson de Roland à
Guillaume Apollinaire]* (Lille: Giard, 1949).

virtually word for word the *Lancelot* interpolation," writes Zumthor. "It is a statement of the basic myth, or the primary material. The book then proceeds to lay out a series of infuriatingly obscure symbols that have no obvious link to this material."[17] Consequently, if Apollinaire's book does manage to assimilate disparate elements, such an assimilation is not evident on the level of historiography. This is quite simply because Apollinaire's borrowings come not from works of history but from literary texts. Literature feeds off literature, and, in this particular instance, it feeds off the long hagiographical tradition that was inaugurated by the *Prophetia Merlini* published by Geoffrey of Monmouth in 1134.

Jean Burgos suggests that the only contact Apollinaire had with the "real" Merlin was limited to his reading the entry under that name in the *Grand Dictionnaire Larousse du XIXe siècle*. It is a plausible hypothesis since in *L'Enchanteur pourrissant* the figure of Merlin evolves from that of the sorcerer-magician who can accomplish any magical feat to that of the poet-prophet. Moreover, a brief look at *Myrdhinn ou l'enchanteur Merlin* by Hersart de la Villemarqué, which was published in 1862 and on which the *Larousse* entry was based, reveals that the first part of the tale (titled "The Real Merlin") borrows from Celtic chronicles, especially the Myvyrian one, and describes Myrdhinn as a bard or poet blessed with the gift of prophecy.[18] Consequently, in this particular book that Apol-

---

17. Paul Zumthor, *Merlin le prophète* (Lausanne: Imprimeries Réunies, 1948), 287. One should remember that Apollinaire's "modernism" did not correspond to Zumthor's aesthetic ideas during the war period.

18. Hersart de la Villemarqué, *Myrdhinn ou l'enchanteur Merlin* (Paris: Didier et Cie, 1862). Curiously enough, this work opens with some thoughts on plagiarism, spurred by the author's disquiet with Edgar Quinet's recently published *Merlin l'enchanteur* (Paris: Lévy, 1860). According to Burgos, Quinet's book appears to be a source often used by Apollinaire. De la Villemarqué underscores the distinction between literary and historical works that was drawn above in connection with the intertextual production of *L'Enchanteur pourrissant*. He writes:

> This book, whose arrival has been promised for quite some time and which is the sequel to the author's earlier work (*Les Bardes bretons*), was about to be printed when a work of poetic fantasy with the same name appeared, and in which we were surprised to find the following tirade: "The world is full at the present time of authors who go about stealing heroes whom others have taken the trouble to unearth. I repeat (and in all seriousness) that my hero was stolen from me. . . . To steal a hero who has been entrusted to public faith is clearly a thousand times worse than stealing treasure from someone's old casket. Believe me, the worst evil is to be interrupted in the course of an epic work such as this one, which should have flowed effortlessly and without pause, in the manner of a river enlarged by melting snow." If anyone had the right to complain of being interrupted (let alone robbed), would it

linaire could have consulted there is a study of the Merlin character that is apparently anchored in historical fact and also proposes the poet-prophet figure.

Nevertheless, when situated within the workings of intertextuality, a proper name functions simply as a self-contained repository of cultural knowledge, or "monument-memory," so to speak. Since proper names are also what emerge from historical investigation, we can begin to see why Apollinaire's text could afford to disregard the already established model of the poet-prophet that de la Villemarqué had put forward. By passing over certain historical aspects of Merlin's name, Apollinaire's book instead gives priority to a cultural body of writings in which a community of shared beliefs is more important than scholarly fact.

For Apollinaire, who, in the words of "Les Sirènes" (in *Le Bestiaire*), wished to "manufacture" poetry in the way the modern world was "manufactured," writing entailed making use of texts similar to his own, which would allow for the transpositions that give rise to intertextual effects. This search for sources did not take place within the domain of history proper, tied as ever to the pseudomimesis of contemporary chronicles, but within the publicly charted domain of recognizable history—that is, literary legend.

When Scott Bates juxtaposes the source text and Apollinaire's transcription it is clear that several topical references in the sixteenth-century text were omitted by Apollinaire, thus giving his version a wider relevance and, in effect, preparing us for the processional cycle that begins with the visit to Merlin in the following chapters. Without dwelling on the modifications that allow the source text to be woven almost entirely into a new context, we would like to focus on a lexical difference between the two works that is symptomatic of a larger issue. The original text shows Merlin trapped in a cellar, which Apollinaire then transformed into a tomb. This change gives the term *enserrement* (being enclosed, trapped, or hemmed in) a commemorative value, and it also allows the paranomastic shift to its near-synonym, *enterrement* (burial). *L'enterrement* means placing someone under the earth, or in a burial vault; *l'enserrement* means compacting a body, squeezing it in, or confining it to an open, and hence long-lasting, grave. This grave consequently becomes a monument for public remembrance, one of the mnemonic sites to which

---

be the singer of Ahasvérus, or a humble investigator of Celtic antiquities? In truth, the latter person has not been slightly upset upon seeing his small and peaceful domain abruptly invaded to the sound of heroic fanfare. (1–3)

people can turn for their cultural traditions. The tomb is an emblem for the very role played by Philippe Le Noir's text in the system of intertextual references set up by *L'Enchanteur pourrissant*. It is the site for an intertextual reappropriation of legend and for its insertion into a literary lineage that is dominated by tradition.

In the book's conclusion, "Onirocritique," the issue of intertexts appears in another guise since it is no longer the story as a whole that is attributed to different authors, but particular figures for rites of passage. The critics Jeanine Moulin, Francis Carmody, and Marie-Jeanne Durry have traced borrowings in this chapter from, among other sources, Nerval's *Aurélia* or Rimbaud's *Illuminations* and *Une Saison en enfer*. Moreover, Durry considers the passage in which an omnipresent gaze captures the whole world to be a precursor to Eluard's poem "Les Yeux fertiles," a link that has been confirmed by Henri Meschonnic.[19] The reader can thus break up Apollinaire's text apparently at will and restore each fragment to its presumed owner. Nevertheless, if we go one step further than such commentaries, which only consider isolated figures (and then view them as offshoots not from the text itself but from other writings), we can find a unity underlying the book's final chapter—and for the simple reason that the poetic apocalypse it puts forward is situated outside the confines of any apparent reality. The dream that is named in the title, "Onirocritique," is a favorite place in earlier texts for seemingly chance encounters and pairings, such as Apollinaire's dawn that offers its hand to the tempest.[20] With this model established, Apollinaire engages in some risky hermeneutic exercises by using his storehouse of verbal associations and literary memories as both an organizing principle and a field to be disrupted. The preset itinerary that is made up of the usually frequented commonplaces becomes a disorganized meander and a means of access to poetry-as-prophecy, "proclaiming, in the style of Gauvain, a new destiny for humanity and a renewed spirit of adventure."[21] The process of turning

19. Henri Meschonnic, *Pour la poétique,* vol. 3 (Paris: Gallimard, 1973), 57, 119–43.

20. This is true for all the various possible meanings of the word *onirocritique*. It can be traced back to Baudelaire's "Oneirocritie," which is itself inspired by De Quincy's oneiromancy, or to Maeterlink's *Onirologie*. One can also detect a clear echo of Rabelais's character Artémidore Daldanios, in the eighteenth chapter of *Pantagruel,* who is described as an "absolute *onirocrite* and *oniropole*" (our emphasis). Even if the word *critique* has only a vague meaning in Apollinaire's title, it is still undeniable that the entire chapter appearing under this heading develops the implications of the word *dream*.

21. Michel Leiris, *Frêle bruit* (Paris: Gallimard, 1976), 340.

reality into fiction slots elements of the fantastic into literary molds, while
the poet, who is haunted by classical culture and quite literally a recluse
among his books, finds himself propelled into the artifice of a unified
verbal object that is crisscrossed by a variety of elements coming from
many different sources. In order to be meaningful, Apollinaire's continual
self-duplications can only come about through the widest possible grasp
of a closed world. Collecting and condensing the text's jumble of quota-
tions, Apollinaire thus finds a new organizing principle for his frag-
mented work. In other words, if he chose to shut himself up in a world
where elements of the fantastic were within a few words' reach, it was
because the only sure way of constructing a lasting image of self was to
group together this *vade-mecum* of relevant sayings. The writer's task
consequently broadens in order to take in the vast storehouse of texts
that serve as its operational guide. This technique of fabricating poetic
sequences out of elements from varied sources is confirmed by many of
the poet's works—a fact he readily admits in "Sanglots": "Or nous sa-
vons qu'en nous beaucoup d'hommes respirent / Qui vinrent de très loin
et sont un sous nos fronts" (Now we know that within us breathe many
men / Who have come from afar and have become one in our minds).

From its first to last chapters, the text of *L'Enchanteur pourrissant*
clearly exhibits the heterogeneous field on which all writing operates.
The procession of legendary, mythic, or fictional characters is first and
foremost a commemorative procession of time-honored works—even if
such a procession is tied to the well-established tradition of the *Prophetia
Merlini* or the *Orlando Furioso*. It is an intertextual celebration that glori-
fies its own links to the unified body of literature, or, as Apollinaire puts
it in "Cortège," "Tous ceux qui survenaient et n'étaient pas moi-même /
Amenaient un à un les morceaux de moi-même" (All those who hap-
pened to put in an appearance and who were not me / Each brought
fragments of myself). As a result, if Apollinaire lets himself get caught up
in another author's sentences, it is because his writing practice tends to
be exclusively schizoid. As Bataille surmised in his *Sur Nietzsche*, "it is
perhaps essential to man's growth that he only develop piece by piece.
Therefore we must never overlook the fact that ultimately we are dealing
with the issue of how synthetically man is produced."[22]

At this point in our analysis we can see how the archetypal symbol-
ism discussed at the beginning of the chapter has in fact absorbed the

22. Georges Bataille, *Sur Nietzsche* (Paris: Gallimard, 1945), 19.

principles of poetic productivity into a coherent allegory. The death-into-life symbol thus retraces the movement of a text's significance. Consequently, if the text is read as a breaking up of all its borrowings, it is because the deconstruction or *decomposition* of other texts is a necessary prelude to the fermentation, or synthesis, of this particular work. In *L'Enchanteur pourrissant* it is not the enchanter who is rotting (or *pourrissant*) but the text itself, which has become a potpourri of earlier readings. If there is some trace of a self in this work, then such a self is totally coextensive with this decomposing and recomposing, since it both gives rise to such a form of writing and is produced by it. In short, the self is the very substance of Apollinaire's text. To confirm this hypothesis about the primary function of language, we need only think of Bataille's dictum that "reading is rotting a little. Understand this well: *during one's whole life*, right up to the moment of collapse—your act of reading inexorably manages to taint you [so that you become] the one who is tainted" (39).

The three terms usually used to conceptualize Apollinaire's writing technique—*remplissement* (filling in), simultaneism, and librettism—point toward a poetics that gives precedence to the joining together of diverse fragments that are reordered and unified. By criticizing *L'Enchanteur pourrissant* for being "less an expression of an individually chosen aesthetics than a reflection of certain readings from which Apollinaire never managed to free himself," Pascal Pia misses the point, since the very aesthetics embraced by Apollinaire is one of rejuvenating borrowed texts, which both underscores the importance of tradition and gives the author a scriptural legitimacy.[23] By inserting himself into ready-made symbolic systems he sets himself up both as a figure of posterity and as a member of the literary community. By apparently rubbing shoulders with so many other authors Apollinaire may well have incurred the censure of his commentators, but this is precisely how his writing attracts our attention and parades its own modernity.

A poetics based on the reordering of citations is certainly what is referred to by the monster Chapalu's famous claim in *L'Enchanteur pourrissant*: "Celui qui mange n'est plus seul" (He who eats is no longer on his own; 86). Whereas Franz Hellens sees in Chapalu the quintessential image of the lycanthrope,[24] and others detect a reminder of Apollinaire's

23. Pascal Pia, *Apollinaire par lui-même* (Paris: Seuil, 1954), 45.

24. Franz Hellens, "Apollinaire avec le recul," *Europe* 451–52 (November–December 1966): 86–97.

legendary appetite,[25] it seems to us that in this compact passage, which groups together both the fragmentary and the multiple, there lies the inscription of a poetic practice. In support of this thesis one can point out the obvious reversed pun that is illustrated by the name Chapalu, and also the book by Méziriac (alias Maxime Planudes), *La Vie d'Esope*, which reminds us that the title of the review founded by Apollinaire, *Le Festin d'Esope*, refers to a form of consumption that is in no way down to earth.[26] These considerations are, in one sense, superfluous since we need only take the verb *to eat* as a metaphorical substitute for the verb *to read* and then discover the proposition, "He who reads is no longer on his own." It would seem that here we have a case of what Michael Riffaterre has called syllepsis, or a sign with a double meaning.[27] In the French sociolect, nourishment (*les nourritures*) can be terrestrial as well as spiritual, just as fragments (*les morceaux*) can be of bread, meat, or literary selections (*morceaux choisis*). Similarly, we can devour books just as we do meals, to the extent that our taste for reading (*notre appétit de lectures*) nourishes us with classical culture until we can take in no more. How can we avoid interpreting Chapalu in this way—a character who introduces himself as someone "looking for Merlin since he was wise and would have known how to make me prolific," and who, once his appetite has been satisfied, turns toward his shady enclave and says to someone behind the scenes:

> Je ne suis pas prolifique, c'est vrai, mais je possède un excellent appétit qui me met en contact avec d'autres êtres et je n'en de-

25. For a parody of the Apollinairean menu, see *Europe* 451–52 (November–December 1966): 103.

26. At the time of putting together the review, Apollinaire wrote to James Onimus (on 8 October 1902), "At the present time I'm flat broke," and according to André Salmon the entire period during which *Le Festin d'Esope* appeared was marked by difficult financial circumstances (*Souvenirs sans fin*, vol. 1 (Paris: Gallimard, 1955), 100–101), which makes gastronomic revelry most unlikely. In his article "Guillaume Apollinaire et *Le Festin d'Esope*" (*Europe* 451–52 [November–December 1966]), Pierre Adéma gives no reason for Apollinaire's choice of title for the review (78–86). We are therefore left with the double play on words in the title, which is based on the multiple meanings of eating and tongue. Aesop invites his guests to come and nourish themselves on tongue (language). This is the way that André Billy understood the title (in his book *Apollinaire* [Paris: Seghers, 1947]) since, as if to confirm our hypothesis, he mentions that Apollinaire had taken up the habit at this time of calling himself "the Polyglot."

27. Michael Riffaterre, "Interpretants," chap. 4 in *Semiotics of Poetry* (Bloomington: Indiana University Press, 1978). See also his article, "La Syllepse intertextuelle," *Poétique* 40 (November 1979): 486–501.

mande pas davantage. Au reste je suis mauvais ouvrier et si vous n'espériez qu'en moi, vous courriez le risque de périr d'inanition.

(I am not prolific, that's true, but I have a marvelous appetite that brings me into contact with other beings and I'm not asking for more. Besides, I am a poor worker and if you believed only in me, you would run the risk of starving to death.) (57)[28]

The status of the poet and that of poetic activity are blended in Apollinaire to form a never-ending process of logophagy, or word digestion.

For Apollinaire, the self that emerges out of a text's production is consequently the embodiment of freshly assimilated fragments of earlier works. This places Apollinaire's writing squarely within the field of semiosis, since the literary fragment contributes to the organization of a text that will in turn become a propitiatory fragment destined for another text, thus copying the indefinite referral set up within Peirce's triadic sign that moves between the representamen and the interpretant. The object and the natural world are precisely the things excluded from this semiotic transfer, which contributes to the overall effect of unreality in Apollinaire's text.[29]

28. If any confirmation were needed, both of the meaning and importance of Apollinaire's model for writing, one could cite Max Jacob's work "Le Siège de Jérusalem, grande tentation céleste de Saint-Matorel," *Saint-Matorel* (Paris: Galerie Simon, 1909), 101–210. This text is, in turn, both a plagiarized version of, and homage to, *L'Enchanteur pourrissant*. In his summary, moreover, Max Jacob explicitly directs to Apollinaire's work any reader who doubts the veracity of his book's subject matter, or who is looking for a guarantee of its "reality." In Jacob's version the monster Chapalu, whom Apollinaire had described as having "the head of a cat and the body of a horse," takes on a mythical form and becomes a unicorn. As in the original version, this animal seeks out shade. Jacob makes a direct reference to readerly bulimia:

[the unicorn]: Ho there, Lion, my secular enemy, wake up! Saint-Jerome's Lion! This little human is degrading us! Revenge! But you are not waking up. So be it! I'll drag him into my cave and tear him apart! I'll pull down whole walls of books upon his knees, I'll bury his stomach under my dictionaries! Watch out for me, Victor Matorel! (108)

The same verbal game is taken up again, in much the same way, in Yvan Goll's *Lucifer vieillissant* (*Oeuvres*, vol. 1 [Paris: Emile Paul, 1968]): "To eat, to grow out into a ball the way the earth does! To eat with one's mouth, one's nose, eyes, to eat through every pore of one's body, with all one's effort" (241–42).

29. It is probably Apollinaire's predilection for using the symbolic as his starting

The key scene in *L'Enchanteur pourrissant* involving the upside-down Christmas party with its voices that have come from many different bookish sources is a scene built on a polyphonic dialogism. But this principle does not lead the text to expand into some indeterminate netherworld since there is no chaotic fragmentation in the work. The text does not escape from the law of its own continuity, nor does it work against its own systematic unification. Quite the opposite, in fact, since the altered celebration of Christmas is an allegory for the reordering and reunification of themes and the interweaving of elements represented by the themes. It is not merely a catalogue of orphaned fragments but a systematic patterning of their echoes. Consequently, texts from various periods are grafted onto one another rather than simply juxtaposed. The references that Apollinaire introduces are the result not of a haphazard collage, but of a deliberate organization that involves reconstructing an individualized system of meaning and putting this new symbolic system to the test.

If there is any change in Apollinaire's writing strategy over the years it is to be found in the relation between parts and wholes throughout all the various forms of poetic sequence that he proposed: his "conversation-poems" (such as "Lundi rue Christine"), his poems with simultaneous time frames, texts where he uses the printed page to break up the basic constituents of language itself, or else his lyrical ideograms and calligrams. When Apollinaire composed *L'Antitradition futuriste, manifeste synthèse* for Marinetti in 1913, the work was not, as Michel Décaudin points out, "an indication of Apollinaire's conversion to Marinetti's movement, but rather one of playful congeniality."[30] What are missing in Apollinaire's "futurism" are the elimination of language, disorderly leaps of imagination, and the complete liquidation of literary tradition. Nevertheless, his writing does advocate the destruction of the standard literary self—namely, the mind or I that is generally assumed to constitute a text's unity. There is, however, another self produced by texts, according to Apollinaire, from which everything flows and to which everything returns, but it is a self produced by the ritualized economy that is none other than the mechanics of writing. As Jean Burgos has pointed out in

---

point that led the Peircean-inspired Semiotic Society of America to choose as the iconic logo for its review, *Semiotic Scene,* the portrait of Apollinaire by le Douanier Rousseau. This painting was completed in 1909, the same year that *L'Enchanteur pourrissant* appeared.

30. Michel Décaudin, "Chronologie," *Europe* 451–52 (November–December 1966): 326.

connection with "Onirocritique": "Even if they have no apparent refer-
ential continuity, the most unexpected images are nevertheless subject to
a continual control, with each one springing from the other in a way that
is seemingly delirious, and yet possessing an internal continuity."[31] In
L'Enchanteur pourrissant, moreover, the philosopher of the fragmentary,
Empedocles, receives no better treatment than his counterpart, Socrates,
the philosopher of unity. Put simply, this is because the way Apollinaire
organizes his fragments is not centrifugal but centripetal. It does not lead
to verbal dissemination but is rather a way of circumscribing, and hence
unifying, a familiar space of language.[32]

Michel Décaudin has often mentioned the sense of obligation that
is evident in Apollinaire's autobiographical writing. If we had to resort to
a conclusion based on genres, we would maintain that Apollinaire's use
of fragments, anachronisms, and semiosis all point toward the form of a
self-portrait. The goal of poetic activity is thus akin to Michel Leiris's in
Aurora or *L'Age d'homme,* especially in certain passages where poetic
technique and the code of self-understanding are one and the same. It is
also on a par with Philippe Lejeune's model of active reading (*la lisure*),
which uses Leiris's writings as a pretext for "self-reading" and for appar-
ently expressing things about the self that could not be stated more di-
rectly.[33] In this way the process of poetic production starts up all over
again and the textual self is being continually reconstructed from the
immemorial debris of other texts.

The genre of the autobiography is nevertheless dominated by a nar-
rative topos that is usually lacking in poems. The topos sets out to answer
the question, Who am I?—a query that Apollinaire occasionally sets forth
(as in "Cortège"), but without hazarding a reply. The visual self-portrait
that observers are offered in the calligram "Miroir" (Fig. 1) rearranges
the standard model of a self forever inhabited by a language in which it

31. Burgos, ci–cii. Michel Décaudin (*Le Dossier d'"Alcools"* [Paris: Minard, 1960])
maintains the contrary opinion when he argues, in connection with *Alcools,* that "in Apolli-
naire not only do the images spring forth independently of each other, so that not even the
most tenuous link can bring them together, but in addition they are grouped together in a
disorder that knows no bounds and that occasionally gives rise to the most jarring combina-
tions" (12).

32. See Chapter 2 for a development of these considerations on the literary frag-
ment.

33. Philippe Lejeune, in *Lire Leiris: Autobiographie et langage* (Paris: Klincksieck,
1975), writes: "Ma lecture de Leiris a été l'apprentissage de ce langage. *Leiris s'y lire*" (My
reading of Leiris has been an apprenticeship in this new language. *To read oneself in Leiris;*
181).

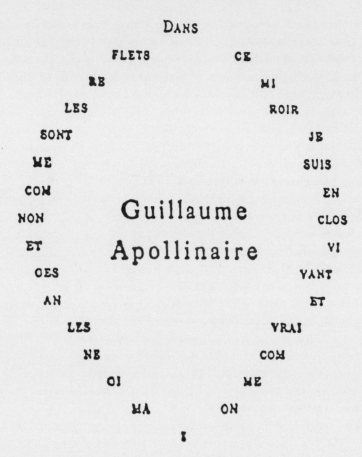

Figure 1

can read its own traces.[34] As a clockwise reading of the calligram points out, the life captured by the poetic self-portrait is a purely imaginative one, modeled on the textual immortality of figures born in literature (namely, angels). Consequently, if "Miroir"'s "enclosed alive" carries on from the "live entombment" of *L'Enchanteur pourrissant* it is for the simple reason that in both cases we find the same form of self-inscription whereby writing is authenticated by a series of displaced fragments that weave the verbalized subject into the encyclopedic memory of language

34. "In this mirror I am enclosed alive and real as you imagine angels and not the way reflections are: Guillaume Apollinaire." "Coeur couronne et miroir" (Heart crown and mirror), in Apollinaire's *Calligrammes (Oeuvres poétiques,* ed. Marcel Adéma and Michel Décaudin [Paris: Gallimard, Pléiade, 1965], 197).

itself. In such forms of poetic writing the unities of self and meaning are not guaranteed in advance but have to be constantly reworked through a never-ending recall of a culture's common legends. These legends set the machine of discourse in motion and also make *L'Enchanteur pourrissant* one of the most singular of all plurivalent texts.

two

"DADA MEANS NOTHING"

(TZARA,

ARAGON,

ET AL.)

"I kind of felt sorry for the monster."

—*The Girl* (*Marilyn Monroe*), The Seven-Year Itch

Every literary period has its monsters, and the tremors they produce often tell us more about the underlying displacements that make up the phenomenon of literature than the historical moments that literary historians dredge up in their search for a text's meaning. If the term *avant-garde* has any value at all it is not as a name for the passing phenomenon of "fashionable" texts, but instead as a symptom of certain theoretical and practical issues that push writing's potential to its outer limits. Dada plays just such a role by fathoming the deepest recesses of our modernity and bringing to the fore certain principles that writing continually refuses to avow. Dada still engages interest, seventy years after its passing, whereas simultaneism, futurism, unanimism, paroxysm, and ultraism (to cite only a few) have long since been relegated to the dungeons of literary history. This is because the Dadaist project illustrates two procedures that are fundamentally poetic: a recourse to the fragment form and a basic refusal of language's role as an organized system of intersubjective communication.

In order to set the following analysis in its proper framework, we begin by considering two issues that merit more elaborate treatment, as well as a broader application, than the one given here. Since this chapter is of a limited scope we shall merely propose them as practical axioms delineating the contours of a general argument that certain Dada texts serve to illustrate.

The first remark is that when dealing with Dada it is impossible to limit one's study to texts that are exclusively French. A few critical works have attempted to demarcate specifically national domains within the literary phenomenon of Dada—a phenomenon that is, according to its own principles, fundamentally international. Such a project deserves some praise and yet it soon comes to resemble attempts at squaring the circle, especially when the focus of the study shifts from historical aspects of the movement to the underlying principles that govern its texts' production. Dada always considered itself to be an international movement, even when its main protagonists were based in Paris. In his preface for Georges Hugnet's 1956 study of the movement, Tzara declared: "In Paris, DADA was antiphilosophical, nihilist, scandalous, *universal*" (our emphasis).[1] Moreover, in the preamble to his 1965 book *Dada à Paris,* Michel Sanouillet has to put forward a certain number of standard precautions in order to justify the national focus of his study:

> One of the particularities that distinguish the Dada movement from the other literary and aesthetic schools of this century is the fact that it was born simultaneously in Switzerland and in the United States and from there spread rapidly throughout the countries of both continents between 1915 and 1923. [...]
>
> It seemed to me, however, that the Dadaist phenomenon as seen from Paris could be detached from the rest since it constituted a significant chapter in the intellectual history of France, as seen through Dada's links with the various countries where the movement took hold or left its marks. [...This study] can be easily integrated within the movement's broader context as long as one remembers the parallel existence led by foreign groups whose importance was in no way less than that of the French branch. (iv)

Such well-intentioned nuancing was nevertheless unable to prevent the storm of criticism that greeted Sanouillet's geographical containment

---

1. Georges Hugnet, *L'Aventure Dada* (Paris: Seghers, 1957), 4.

of the Dada movement. The staunchest critics equated the project with an outright falsification of what Dada was all about. The lettrist writer Maurice Lemaître argued that the basic premises of Sanouillet's work revealed the author's complete misunderstanding of the movement:

Let's point out from the outset the *chauvinism* displayed throughout Mr. Sanouillet's "book": on p. 416 of the chapter on *Cahiers dada* we read that [...] "Certain [Dada] discoveries that had been, up until that point, at the embryonic stage were about to undergo a spectacular and unexpected development, *thanks to the methodical powers of the French mind*. When we consider that Dada, even in Paris, was made up principally of Jews and foreign aliens, of the likes of Tzara, Man Ray, Picabia, Arp, Dali, Mirò, Sophie Taeuber, Ernst, Janko, etc., we can only burst out laughing. (our emphasis)[2]

Although we do not wish to be caught up in this debate about Dada's unquestionably international status (which is marginal to the textual analyses we offer here), we have, nevertheless, chosen to discuss predominantly French texts. This is partly because the principles governing these texts prove quite clearly that the controversy surrounding Dada's "nationalism" is based on a fallacy. For if Dada questions language in general, it cannot really be concerned at all with a particular national language.

Our second preliminary remark is of a theoretical nature since it has to do with the sacrosanct linking of Dada to Surrealism. We are not at all convinced by this connection, imposed on the two movements by critics who have followed outmoded historiographical models. Mere habit has made natural a connection between two movements that is not at all obvious but instead demands close examination. After all, we cannot overlook the fact that, at the end of her study of Surrealism, Anna Balakian uses a noteworthy description of the Dadaists as "pilgrims of perdition,"[3] nor can we ignore Michel Sanouillet's remark that "we can at least be grateful to the Dadaists for having explored for us, and to their great peril, the unsure and forever receding frontiers of human intelligence" (56). Since both these comments suggest that the Dada enterprise reaches an outer limit of human experience, how can we then speak of a

2. Maurice Lemaître, *Le Lettrisme devant Dada et les nécrophages de Dada!* (Paris: Centre de créativité, 1967), 41.

3. Anna Balakian, *Literary Origins of Surrealism: A New Mysticism in French Poetry* (New York: New York University Press, 1947), 141.

"continuation" or "following up" of Dada in Surrealism? On the contrary, everything seems to suggest that, despite their historical resemblances, the two movements should be clearly differentiated. The more recent studies by Foster and Kuenzli and by Erickson fortunately move in this direction.[4]

From the passage in the first *Surrealist Manifesto* where Breton sets forth the image as the key to a new, yet still to be founded, aesthetics, Surrealism makes a complete break with Dada and offers a completely different view of literature. Between both movements there are clear divergences that cannot be covered up by hyphenation, or even a slash, but that appeal instead to the disjunctive *or*. From the standpoint of its symbols, Surrealism is obviously less experimental and less opposed to semiotic orthodoxy than Dadaism. It accepts as a starting principle the possibility of verbal symbols based on the conventional nature of communicative signs, and consequently it limits its innovations to redistributing semiotic properties via the transferal of figurative meaning. By contrast, what characterizes Dada and gives its apparently diverse projects an overall cohesiveness is the way it tears apart the basic pact of linguistic communication and then gathers the fragments together in a plan for a *protosemiotic* system that, by its very nature, challenges the convention-bound exchange of signs. The analyses that follow attempt to refine and support these general remarks on the Dadaist project.

DADA SAYS NOTHING

Our approach to the literary fragment owes much to the trails already blazed by Bataille, to Blanchot's untiring investigations, and, more obviously, to a rereading of Nietzsche. The latter plays a decisive role during the period examined here since the Nietzschean intertext constantly resurfaces in Tzara's arguments and writings—to such an extent, in fact, that Apollinaire gave him the nickname Tsara Thoustra.[5]

We must not forget that the technique of the fragment had been introduced, via collage, by Cubist painters and had then been fundamentally reworked by the Dadaists, who were followed in turn by their own

4. Stephen Foster and Rudolph Kuenzli, eds., *Dada Spectrum: The Dialectics of Revolt* (Madison, Wis.: Coda Press, 1979); John D. Erickson, *Dada: Performance, Poetry, and Art* (Boston: Twayne, 1984).

5. Tsara (*sic*). This pun is quoted by Max Jacob in *391*, 5 June 1917.

successors, called the "ex-dadas" by Yvan Goll,[6] who came to be known as Breton's Surrealists. It all began with the gluing of already-made items onto a flat surface—items such as newspaper cuttings, bits of card, metal, or wood, pieces of string, and so on. When painters adopted this technique it was to underscore the fact that their goal was no longer the creation of an artwork that copied reality in an idealized form. Hence the importance of a prefabricated fragment, since artists wanted to demonstrate that their work already used elements *from* reality, with the result that the frontier between art and reality becomes fuzzy. As Duchamp himself argued, the reason for this technique was primarily to deny the possibility of any autonomous function for art.[7]

The choice of fragments gradually moved from handmade objects to a selection of machine-made ones, as the taste for technology became part and parcel of the emerging Modernist movement in art, prophesied by Apollinaire's 1917 dictum that poetry should be "manufactured" in the same way that the world was now "manufactured."[8] Such fragments have the effect of erasing the original function of the object from which they came, since the text where they now figure is organized on a new symbolic pattern that is determined solely by the artist's choice. Breton was thus able to write, at a later stage, that "fabricated objects have been elevated to the dignified status of art, thanks to the artist's choosing."[9] Nevertheless, a key concept in this apparently random use of odd materials quickly emerged: chance. The artist's intervention became limited to selecting and arranging the individual elements. Such arrangements were further constrained by the fact that the strangeness of the juxtapositions, apparently caused by the capricious hand of chance, was precisely the desired effect. Consequently, the technique of fragmentation allowed the artist to deprive the assembled objects of any function whatsoever and instead offer us a picture of their apparent needlessness. What strikes us when we first see such works is both the fortuitous aspect of their ar-

6. Goll's comment is in the "Manifeste" published in *Surréalisme* no. 1, October 1924.

7. Duchamp quoted by Man Ray in William C. Seitz, *The Art of Assemblage* (New York: The Museum of Modern Art, 1961), 46.

8. "Conférence sur l'Esprit Nouveau" given on 26 November 1917 and published on 1 December 1918. Poets, argued Apollinaire, "want poetry some day to be manufactured in the way the world has been manufactured. They want to be the first to give a fresh lyricism to the new techniques of expression afforded by cinema and the phonograph, techniques that have brought movement into art."

9. André Breton, "Phare de la Mariée," *Minotaure* 6 (winter 1935).

rangement and also their provocative strangeness. The latter effect first of all confounds spectators who are used to a mimetic dimension in artworks. Moreover, such confusion cannot be dissipated by the spectator's attempt to reconstitute an image of daily reality from the symbolic (dis)order presented by the work in question. The spectator is then forced to bring into question his or her own habits of aesthetic appreciation, with the result that the fragment gradually undermines the standard notions of spectator and the surrounding world. A revealing comment by Udo Rusker shows the importance for Dada of these principles underlying the reception of artistic fragments. "Dadaism is a strategy," declares Rusker,

> in which the artist can impose on his fellow citizen a small degree of that inner disquiet which prevents the artist himself from dozing off under the influence of habit and routine. By means of external stimuli he can counterbalance the lack of fervor and vitality in his fellow citizen and lead him toward a new form of living.[10]

It is useful to introduce at this point an important distinction made by Michèle Duchet between what she calls *fragmentary* and *fragmental* works, which are two different ways for the artist to use sets of fragments within the fields of literature and the plastic arts.[11] The *fragmentary* technique clearly exhibits its gratuitous nature, as illustrated by Breton's comment from the early period of his own Surrealist venture: "We are even entitled to call a 'poem' the most gratuitous collections [...] of titles, or fragments of titles cut out from newspapers."[12] Fragmentary works always underscore the provocative aspects of their composition, and their combining of disparate elements simply highlights the haphazardness of the juxtapositions. In *fragmental* works, on the other hand, there is more than just a trace of systematic ordering in the text's overall significance. Indeed, the text's projected unity is iconically inscribed within its written form so that even if the material chosen for the work displays a fragmented form, this material is the opposite of a meaningless amalgam put

10. Udo Rusker, in Richard Huelsenbeck, *Dada Almanach* (Berlin: Erich Reiss Verlag, 1920), 15.

11. Michèle Duchet, "Fragments," *Les Cahiers de Fontenay* 13–15 (June 1979): 45–47. Duchet's investigation has as its object certain texts by Diderot, but her conclusions apply to a much wider field. As we will see, this theoretical distinction is particularly useful for an understanding of Dada.

12. Breton, *Manifestes du surréalisme* (Paris: Jean-Jacques Pauvert, 1962), 57.

together simply because of its strangely aberrant elements. On the contrary, the structure of a fragmental work is predicated on a hidden puzzle, so that little by little the reader uncovers a coherent utterance.[13] Two different techniques of text- and image-production flow from Duchet's contrasting terms: fragmentary works are akin to collage, whereas fragmental ones resemble a photographic montage.

Fragmentary and fragmental works do have one element in common, however. Both promote oblique meanings and consequently attack the predominance of literal, self-evident sense over all other acts of communication, a predominance that is evident in such diverse fields as everyday messages, the self-assured moralizing of fables, the preaching of doctrine, or the lyrical codas to narrative poems. Where the fragmental diverges from the fragmentary, however, is in the latter's espousal of the doctrine of art for art's sake, where provocation becomes an end in itself. For fragmental texts always invite their readers to retrace the thread that leads us back to an initial meaningfulness, with the result that we uncover something more positive than the nihilism of chance occurrence—namely, the uncanny necessity that is created by a system of significance.

It seems to us that the shift from fragmentary to fragmental works marked the end of Dada. If one examines the shift that takes place in either Breton's or Tzara's aesthetic pronouncements one finds the same blurring of the distinction between the fragmental and the fragmentary. Their later political stands and dogmas are in fact merely a symptom of this same shift. Without blinding ourselves to the diversity of the Dada movement, we can nevertheless detect a similar evolution in the other members of the group.[14] With the taste for excess lasting only a short while, the violent disintegration that characterized Dada's initial phase, along with the propensity for scandal, began to scare off quite a number of artists. Tatlin's constructivist principles attracted such defectors as Lis-

13. For the importance of the fragmental in connection with written self-portraits, see Michel Beaujour's "Autobiographie et autoportrait," *Poétique* 32 (November 1977): 442–58. The fragmental is also discussed as a writing model in Chapter 1.

14. Of course, the Dada movement included individuals who each had their own particular interests. One cannot ignore the fact, however, that the group's members had developed a high degree of conformity among themselves. The ideas put forward by one member were often taken up immediately by the others. Claire Goll has commented that they went out of their way to "ape one another," and later even Tzara was led to criticize the group's monolithic façade (*La poursuite du vent* [Paris: Oliver Orban, 1976], 150). "I think that the current stagnation that has been caused by trends, the mixing up of genres, and the substitution of groups for individuals, is more dangerous than a reactionary backlash," he wrote in a letter to Breton in 1922.

sitsky and Malevitch, while Eggeling's neoconstructivism enticed Hausmann and Schwitters. Arp and Richter rediscovered their taste for order through their work with geometry. Georges Hugnet aptly characterizes the movement's disintegration when he remarks:

> Moreover, the abstract painters, who were preoccupied with setting firm foundations for a new type of art that would be grounded in the modern experience—an art that would change the face of beauty and that would be in step with the return to simplicity that characterized the architecture of our times—these painters began to feel less and less comfortable within the Dada revolt, which was increasingly critical not only of the results that art had produced but also of the very notion of art itself.[15]

Even Richard Huelsenbeck, who had gained notoriety for his static poems ("Biribum bibibum saust der Ochs im Kreis herum . . .") and for his performances at the Cabaret Voltaire, quickly repudiated Dada along with his own pseudonym by becoming Dr. Charles Hulbeck, a fashionable New York psychoanalyst.[16]

As a result, the truly productive phase of the movement lasted only from the end of 1918—with Picabia's arrival in Zurich—to November 1919, when Flake, Serner, and Tzara published *Der Zeltweg,* the last major public statement by the Anonymous Society for the Development of Dadaist Vocabulary. Beginning with its transfer to Paris in 1920, Dada became a movement bereft of theoretical principles and its championing of fragmentary works was already being attacked, from within the movement, by adherents of fragmental art. In 1921 Picabia declared that Dadaism was "a sham," and even if in 1924 Breton continues to make a case for fragmentary principles, in order to set his own brand of Surrealism against Yvan Goll's Apollinaire-based Surrealism, and claims that he is not an "oracle," but that he prefers the sacred fever of poetic disintegration to any dictates of consciousness (*Manifestes* 60). It is clear that Breton has already found his place within *his own* movement, and that he has already started issuing papal decrees, along with merit marks or punishments for those who try to emulate him. By 1924 Breton is already writing from the standpoint of transparent meaning and overall meaningfulness.

15. Georges Hugnet, *L'Aventure Dada* (Paris: Seghers, 1957), 314.
16. Richard Huelsenbeck, *Almanach Dada* (Paris: Editions Champ Libre, 1980).

By taking the side of the fragment against the presuppositions of totality or plenitude, Dada inaugurated a deconstructive model that is predicated on incompatibility and that underscores the impossibility of any apparent unity. Such incoherence at the surface of the text finds its just desserts in the reactions it stimulates in the reader or spectator. Consequently, the reign of passive art consumption is broken, and the reader is shocked into an awareness of his or her own activity, which temporarily forestalls the "demise of intelligence" that Dadaists often predicted for humanity. Hugo Ball claims that in order to trigger this awareness in the reader, "a trench must be dug between the audience and the spectacle, with the latter becoming incomprehensible, and unjustifiable, to the extent that the spectator is cut off from all explanations and is forced to confront himself" (C. Goll 60).

Along with Dada's insistence on the fragment as a means of nullifying all semblance of systematic organization[17] came an attempt at dislocating language, in order to both liquidate its bad effects and build a new foundation. Such a strategy lends credence to the standard image for Dada activities—namely, a laboratory overflowing with a variety of experiments.[18] Many different workers, each with their own input, took part in these experiments and forged several new paths, but all of them were convinced that the universe was tottering on its old axes and that new horizons were about to be opened up, even if no precise directions or limits were imposed on the experiments. Writing thus came to be seen primarily as a territory to be explored via the destruction of old rules and the laying of new foundations. This viewpoint follows logically from the extreme vehemence that one finds in such pronouncements in *Dada Almanach* as, "Let every person shout out aloud: there is a great destructive and negative task to be accomplished. Sweep away, clean everything off!" (*Dada Almanach* 104).

All responsibility for the catastrophes that had swept down on humanity in the Great War was laid at the door of language, with the result that language itself was to be "cleansed" in Dada's great co-operative task. This is not as surprising as it seems when we consider that every

17. "I am against all systems," declared Tzara, "the most viable of all systems is the one that refuses on principle to accept any system" ("Manifeste Dada, 1918," reprinted in Tristan Tzara, *Lampisteries, précédées de sept manifestes Dada* [Paris: Jean-Jacques Pauvert, 1943], 29).

18. For the limited usefulness of the laboratory metaphor, see Steven Winspur's "Desnos' 'Coeur en bouche': Laboratory Catalyst or Surrealist Maze?" *Dada/Surrealism* 9 (1979): 102–14.

major upheaval in society begins in its early stages by breaking apart or even negating the codes and systems that channel the acts of intersubjective communication. Significantly Hugo Ball imputes language because it is a space of authority and he even attempts to refuse using it since, according to him, language functions by permitting the spread of capitalism (the buying and selling of actions) and by giving free rein to military discipline. "Words are responsible for war," he declares (C. Goll 60). In order to achieve a "higher" level of humanity, Yvan Goll asks people to express themselves solely through chuckles, onomatopoeias, and rumblings. Hence the famous phonetic poems such as "rhinozerossak hopsamen bluku terullaba blaulala looooo," or "trabatgea boroooooooooo oo-oooo . . . ," which were occasionally uttered in front of groups of "300 completely stupefied onlookers" (C. Goll 59). Dada says nothing, Dada phonetizes.

Once language had been deviated from its utilitarian function as a tool for communication there was still more work to be done on it since words had to become completely new objects, freed from all practical conventions. The program that underpinned this endeavor was nothing short of the inauguration of a new symbolic order that would respond to conventions that were as yet unknown, and that had to be discovered and tested through a permanent process of experimentation.

Although merely alluded to during Dada's earliest period, this program quickly came to the fore as a rallying cry for the group. Paul Eluard, who in 1919 was still within the Dada fold, gives an early description of the project in his preface to "Les Animaux et leurs hommes, les hommes et leurs animaux":

> Let's find out what we are capable of doing. Let's try, although it's difficult, to stay absolutely pure, and then we'll start noticing all the things we have in common [...]. As for that unpleasant language that is good only for gossiping, and that is as decrepit as the crowns on our foreheads, let's change it, pull it apart.[19]

As part of a reference to Apollinaire, he makes the same rallying cry in the first issue of his review *Proverbe* (1920): "O mouths! Man is in search of

---

19. Paul Eluard, *Oeuvres complètes,* ed. Marcelle Dumas and Lucien Scheler, vol. 1 (Paris: Gallimard, Pléiade, 1968), 37.

a new language about which the grammarians of all existing languages will have absolutely nothing to say!"

The revolutionary consequences of the enterprise are obvious since an open challenge is thrown out to the proponents of verbal style. It is not a question of merely altering some linguistic conventions but rather recasting all conventions and redefining language on the basis of new criteria. The speechifiers' Babel is cast aside and language is brought back to its minimal units. Sentences are broken up, words are scattered across the page, the alphabet takes on a material form, and letters are dispersed in long typographic strings made up of discrete units that are all sucked into the protosemiotic universe that characterizes this renewed form of writing.

DADA SEMIOTICS

Since the term *semiotics* takes on different meanings depending on the theoretical context in which it is used, we shall preface our analysis of Dada texts by mentioning that Saussure's definition of the sign is our starting point. More precisely, with the Saussurian sign explaining only what goes on *within* language, we have preferred to adopt a tripartite diagram that includes both a double linguistic component (the signified and the signifier) and an extralinguistic component (or referent) for which the sign serves as a stand-in (Diagram 1). The signifier is itself double since it includes both the phonetic and graphic aspect of the ver-

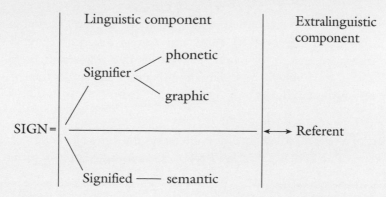

Diagram 1

bal trace. The signified constitutes the semantic aspect of the sign. Without wanting to prolong these technical definitions that are now part of linguistic orthodoxy, we still want to insist on the fact that the referent is situated outside the frame of language. Consequently, the sign is composed only of the signifier and signified, which together form the foundation of conventional linguistic communication.

Aragon's poem "Suicide" (1920) is one of the clearest examples of this principle whereby language is reduced to its basic units (Fig. 2). In the text the raw material of language is boiled down to its smallest elements. If we use the title as an interpretant we can certainly "explain" what follows. Words are ground down to the most elementary typographic distinctions, which, as Martinet pointed out, are always different from the basic units of meaning.

It is interesting to note in passing that the poem (which today seems emblematic of so many others) in fact played an inaugural part in the history of Dadaism. As Sanouillet has pointed out, the text's publication did not go unnoticed since it received a sarcastic welcome from the respected critics of the time. These critics saw it mostly as a gag or as a facetious example of playfulness. Indeed, in order to carry on the gag, one particularly skeptical critic published a counterpoem titled "Resurrection," in which the alphabet appeared in reverse order, beginning with the letter z.

From a semiotic standpoint, however, the poem's reductiveness remains ambiguous, since it maintains one of the elementary and conven-

---

SUICIDE

A b c d e f

g h i j k l

m n o p q r

s t u v w

x y z

Louis ARAGON

Figure 2

tional structures of language—namely, the alphabet itself. By giving us this structure without any apparent change in its order or form, Aragon still allows the reader to reconstitute from his alphabetic grid a number of linguistic signs that are socially acceptable. Aragon's text is therefore on the boundary line between semiotics and what we earlier termed proto-semiotics. There is certainly a reduction of language in the text, but it does not go as far as to dismantle the sign itself. This boundary line is where we find writing strategies that are peculiar to Dada, which will be examined in the following pages.

Of all the Dada works we examine, Raoul Hausmann's famous text "FMSBWT . . ." (1918) seems to be the furthest removed from the sign as a conventional unit (Fig. 3). Hausmann actually defended the "international" character of this work against Schwitters, who uses a similar verbal motif in his text "Ursonata" (1932), but gives it a decidedly German tone. The text's apparent internationalism is no doubt due to the fact that, as in Aragon's "Suicide," communication is reduced to its smallest units of meaning. Here we find a parodic destruction of language that comes about through an accumulation of discrete units (namely, letters) that are offered in a neutral graphic form, since they are all printed in the same typographic style. The text is generated by a punctual sequencing of letters in which all semantic markers are excluded. As a result, the text's signs are truncated and incomplete—all we recognize

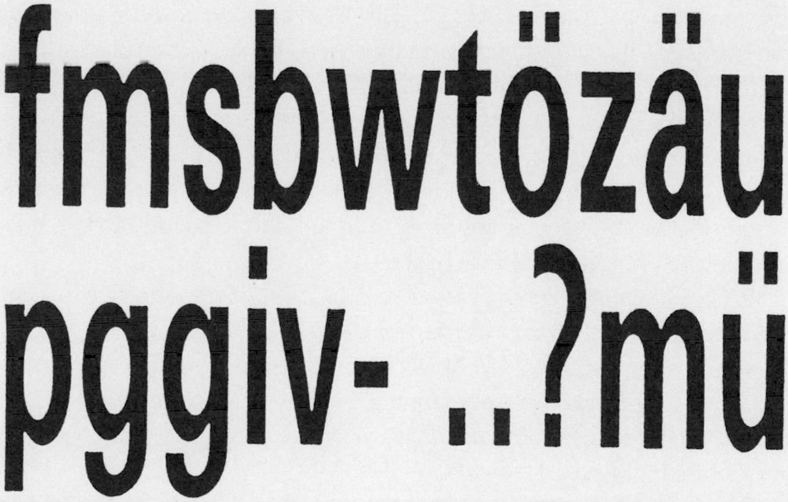

fmsbwtözäu pggiv- ..?mü

Figure 3

are signifiers. Moreover, in the opening, marked by the six initial letters, the signifiers are themselves unacceptable since the sequence of consonants is unpronounceable as it stands. Consonants, as their name tells us, must be accompanied by vowels in order to be spoken at all, and it is generally accepted that a sequence of three consonants deprives any statement of its phonetic dimension. We must conclude, therefore, that the structure of Hausmann's poem deprives the text of its voice, thus transforming it into an apparent code, with the result that its phonetic component can only be actualized at the risk of misinterpretation. (This is precisely the route chosen by Schwitters in his "Ursonata": wanting to turn the piece into a text for singing, he changes the sequence "fmsbwt" into "Fumm bô wô fa.") What we have here can be called a *protosign,* a sign stripped of its semantic dimension and in which the signifier itself lacks any conventional phonetic form. This neutral and evasive graphic text is linked to language as a whole only by means of its typographic form.

Pierre-Albert Birot's "Poem to be shouted and danced" (1924) also depends on the meaningless accumulation of discrete units (letters again), but instead it reinstates, and even gives precedence to, the phonetic dimension (Fig. 4). The text's phonetic aspect is apparent in the attempt at creating rhythmical sequences, so that, in line with the title, any linguistic value that the text may have is eliminated in favor of a musical effect. In other words, it is not the words that matter but rather the tune. Another example of this linguistic evacuation of a text is Schwitters's phonic poem (Fig. 5). Birot's text is more relevant to our argument since its typography is neutralized, no longer underlying any particular word (as the capital letters do in Schwitters's text). It is the lines themselves that stand out for Birot's reader, marking the text's rhythm and indicating that beneath the verbal layer there is an underlying order that dictates the seemingly random layout of graphic marks. A similar underlying order is apparent in Man Ray's pseudoverbal poem "Lautgedicht" (1924), from *391* (Fig. 6).

Whereas typography took over the function of the signifier in Hausmann's poem (the first text examined above), in Birot's poem phonetic value swamps the signifier—as does rhythmical order in Man Ray's piece. If we take at face value certain comments made by the *lettristes* Isidore Isou and Maurice Lemaître in 1967, it is precisely this technique that moves lettrism close to Dadaism.

The poem "Etyomons," published by Adon Lacroix in 1917, seems to come very close to Schwitters's texts insofar as it too is based on the

POÈME A CRIER ET A DANSER

Chant III

Figure 4

phonetic qualities of the signifier. And yet on closer inspection it turns out to be a hybrid text rather than a purely phonetic one (Fig. 7). The verbal sequences "not so," "I love you," and "marmelade" are interspersed within the text's phonic structure. The very title of the volume in which the poem appears—*Visual Words, Sound Seen-thoughts, Felt-feelings Though*—displays the rather eclectic choice of specialized vocabulary that gave rise to the text. The musical reference given at the end of the text ("mi o do ré mi mi o") nevertheless points the reader to the fact that the poem is also a *pseudo*verbal sequence governed predominantly by rhythm.

In Picabia's "Coeur de Jésus" (1920) the subversion of the linguistic sign is achieved by offering a parody of a standard poetic form—the stanza (Fig. 8). The parody works by mixing up signs ("me," "vide," "son," and so on) with nonsigns (for example, "cha," "gnée," and

Lanke trr gll

P P P P P

oka oka oka oka

Lanke trr gll

pi pi pi pi pi

züka züka züka züka

Lanke trr gll

rmp

rnf

Lanke trr gll

rmp

P P P P P

rnf

pi pi pi pi pi

Lanke trr gll

P P P P P

zi U J u

zi U Λ u

zi U J u

zi U Λ

Figure 5

"ndon"). Even if certain elements in the text can pass phonetically for French words, their lack of a conventional graphic form prevents them from taking on fully the role of signs. As with any parody, the obvious upturning and mirroring in the poem attest to there being a prior model

Figure 6

for this text that would be made up of authentic signs. Consequently, the text's mode of production implicitly underscores the presence of an underlying semiotic order.

To complete this overview of protosemiotic writing practices within Dada, and especially of those that stem from a foregrounding of the signifier's phonetic dimension, we now turn to "L'amiral cherche une maison à louer" (The admiral is looking for a house to rent), which was published in 1916 by Huelsenbeck, Janko, and Tzara (Fig. 9). This simultaneist poem in fact combines all the properties that have been noted in the previous examples, but in addition there is an overlay of sounds. This overlay has the effect of scrambling passages that, when read separately, appear perfectly clear. In its performed version the text consequently takes on the form of a sound collage, in which the work's overall noise submerges the fragments of conventional language that form its backdrop. The parasitic borrowing of fragments subverts any tendency toward communicating a message that the text might otherwise have. Nevertheless, since the text as a whole is built in part on passages that

ETYOMONS

not so
DA DI ME
OMA DO RE TE
ZI MATA DURA
DI O.Q DURA
I love you
PN
ZAZZ
O Ma QU
RRO RRO
RU K

TI MA TOITURA
DI ZRATATITOILA
LA LA LAR-R-RITA
LAR-R-RITA
LAR-R-RITA
ASCHM ZT
PLGE
ZR KRN NMTOTO
NM E SHCHU
KM NE SCU

mi o do ré mi mi o
« marmelade »

Figure 7

CŒUR DE JÉSUS

Jardi me cha vide

Plu cuses vi gent re

Jan este oses cine resses

Brûl ille mor gnée cui

Avo alon allu ndon

Cur emblés chi tite pord

Porch raient couro sotis chrét

Son terrés eff Teprie sa

Francis PICABIA

Figure 8

L'amiral cherche une

Poème simultan par R. Huelsenbeck, M. Janko, Tr. Tzara

HUELSENBECK / JANKO, chant / TZARA

Abol abol Des Admirals gwirktes Beiniglcid schnell rerfält the d
Boum boum boum Where the boomy suckle wine twrlea liseft arround common
débabila sa chair quand les grenouilles humidics

HUELSENBECK / JANKO, chant / TZARA

und der Conciergenblcuhe Klapperschlangengrün sind milde sch verzerrt in der
can hear wcopour will arround the hill c'est très inté
serpent à Bacarat ou dépendra mes amis dortnavant et

HUELSENBECK / JANKO, chant / TZARA

prrrza chrrrza Wer suchet dem wird Der C
mine admirably Grandmother aufgetan deux eléphants Journal de
pirrza comfortably Dimanche: said

Intermède rythmique

HUELSENBECK	hihi Yabomm hihi Yabomm hihi hihi hihiiii					
TZARA	rouge bleu rouge bleu rouge bleu rouge bleu rouge bleu					
SIFFLET (Janko)						
CLIQUETTE (TZ)						
GROSSE CAISE (Huels.)	000 00000 00000 0;0.000 0000 ọ u					

Figure 9. Detail

respect conventional words and grammar, a communicative semiotics has not lost all foothold here, even if it is undermined by traces of meaninglessness that make the sum of the fragments unacceptable.

A second protosemiotic strategy within Dada gave preeminence to the signifier's typographic component. Perhaps the most famous example of this tendency is Hugo Ball's "Karawane" (1920), in which each line offers a change in typography, thus varying the effects of the poem's phonetic elements (Fig. 10). The iconic value of the poem's form is controlled by the overall layout of the text, which corresponds to that of a traditional verse poem, with each line beginning at a common margin and ending at an apparently predetermined point. Such a parody of poetic form is perhaps the reason why so many commentators attempt to interpret this text and give meaning to the erroneous sense of familiarity that it suggests to them. In this respect the title acts as a switchman who points the reader in a number of wrong directions. Whereas the meaning of Aragon's sequences in "Suicide" is hard to channel into an interpretation of the poem as a whole (since this meaning is merely a pointer to the overall goal of the poet's project to use linguistic raw materials against the very notion of language itself), the term *karawane* (caravan) has been taken to be a thematic marker, which allows some critics to surreptitiously bring the primacy of the signified back into their reading of the poem. Because they detect the presence of *elephant* in "(j)olifanto," they turn the text into a representational sign for a column of thick-skinned mammals crossing the desert. The so-called lexical units in the text are thus interpreted as parts of a general attempt to achieve imitative harmony (Foster and Kuenzli 67).

If one were to discredit this type of interpretation because of its arbitrary way of grafting meaning onto the text, one would still not have pinpointed its main flaw—its incompleteness. For it does not tell us anything about the particular typographic form of each of the lines. What connection is there between this form and elephants? It seems pointless to look for an explanation in the poem's sound structure (even if Huelsenbeck reminds us that Ball used the poem phonetically), since it is the work's typographic strangeness that is immediately noticeable to the reader's gaze. It would therefore seem that the diversity of printed lines on the page is what constitutes the caravan named in the title. Such a reading would reinforce Ball's explicitly stated goal of liberating humankind from its "empty language," since the arbitrary aspect of signs would be abolished. This would come about not by a mimetic representation of

KARAWANE

jolifanto bambla ô falli bambla
grossiga m'pfa habla horem
·égiga goramen
higo bloiko russula huju
hollaka hollala
anlogo bung
blago bung
blago bung
bosso fataka
ä ää ä
schampa wulla wussa ólobo
hej tatta gôrem
eschige zunbada
wulubu ssubudu uluw ssubudu
tumba ba- umf
kusagauma
ba - umf

Figure 10

sounds (the apparent evocation of marching elephant steps), but by a
straightforward sampling of linguistic units as they actually are—a succes-
sion of material traces, in varied forms, that all operate on the same sur-
face level.

Hausmann's "Poem without a title" from 1919 provides us with
another typographic model (Fig. 11). Unlike our previous example, this

Figure 11

poem is a case of "type-speech." With the exception of the final line, where empty spaces introduce a rhythmical interval between the letters, the overall rhythm of the text—or, more precisely, its tonality—comes not from a scattered distribution of discrete neutral units but from the typographic accentuation that is applied to some of the marks.[20]

All the forms of writing discussed so far in this chapter undermine

20. For a discussion of the (typo)graphical games that characterize Dada and Surrealism, see Leroy Breunig's "Surrealist Alphabets," *Dada/Surrealism* 7 (1977): 59–65.

the signs that make up conventionalized communication by negating what is taken to be a required homogeneity between signifier and signified. The line drawn between these two halves of the linguistic sign is consequently used as a means of separation, since the texts we have examined activate the signifier to the exclusion of all traces of the signified and alternatively develop the typographic or phonetic component of the former. The substance of meaning is linked directly to linguistic materiality, with the result that the path toward interpretation is blocked—a phenomenon that criticism all too readily designates by the term meaninglessness. Nevertheless, even if it is true that such texts convey no obvious or literal sense, they do not cease functioning once their provocative effect has been noted. Each text is a system of exchange in which linguistic value is transformed, so that their non-semantically-oriented statements still belong to the field of significance.

Another principle of semiotic dissidence leaves the constituents of the linguistic sign untouched but instead deliberately opposes the conventional nature of the sign. It does so by questioning the sign's status as an arbitrary construction that is supposedly not motivated by any extralinguistic reality. In her contribution to Foster and Kuenzli's collection of essays, Mary Ann Caws writes of Dada "hieroglyphs" (224), and Rudolph Kuenzli reminds us of Ball's mystical project of recovering an original, Edenic language that would be purified of all compromises with human usage and where objects themselves would appear as they truly are, while at the same time also being within the verbal realm. The word and the world would thus find themselves reunified in a transcendent truth, with the inherent deception of social signs thus being wiped out.

Such analyses correctly identify a second antisemantic model that is present in Dada. According to this model, the goal is to find an adequation between the verbal medium and its extralinguistic referent. After a series of operations contained in the model, the sign apparently rediscovers its motivated, natural, and necessary form.

It seems to us, however, that when Dada began to move in this mimetic direction its subversive practices lost their innovative character. Instead they followed a long tradition that Gérard Genette studies in detail in his book *Mimologiques,* and that is encapsulated in the notion of salvation through writing rather than perdition. One example of this fixation with representational texts is Pierre-Albert Birot's "Offrande" from 1924 (Fig. 12). The text is similar to a calligram, a filiation that is confirmed by the explicit reference to Apollinaire that is contained within it.

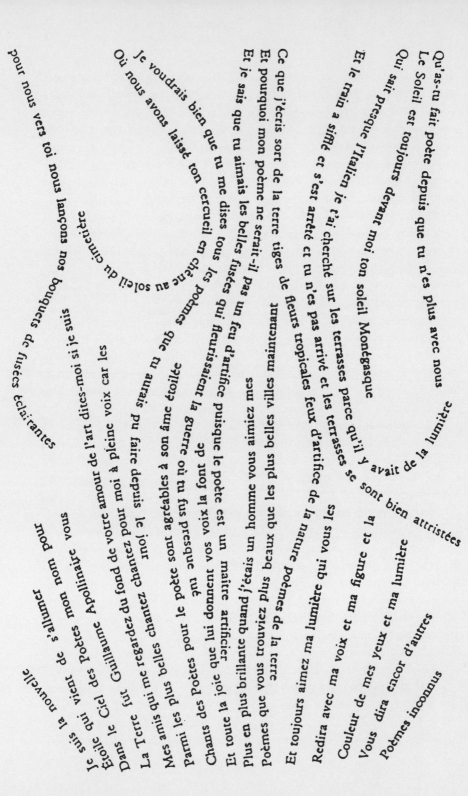

Figure 12

Moreover, this text-as-homage was published at the time when Birot stopped following the Dadaist line and joined the Apollinairians whom Yvan Goll had grouped together in his review *Surrealism* (1924). One can see how certain concrete poems by Garnier (published in 1968) are based on this model, even if they were typed and not printed. Despite the fact that certain critics have interpreted the poem as a pair of out-stretched hands to the Apollinaire-star, we avoid this overly simplistic reading of the poem's complexity and instead refer the reader to the multiple values possessed by the figure of the star in Apollinaire's poetry.

A second example of Dada's mimetic strain is extracted from Pica-bia's 1917 "Isotrope" poems (Fig. 13). Especially in view of its title (*iso-trope* originally meant "figure of the same"), the text seems to follow

Culbutés

Dislocation de l'eau immobile

Haricots

Opium

Explosion

Le signal des flûtes godille

A mes pieds.

Biscornus dans le pli de son hiéroglyphe

Enceinte

Ebréchée

Maison

Magiques enclos à midi

De tous côtés horizontal séjour

Née

La méthode à embrasser

Néant.

Figure 13

graphic onomatopoeia whereby the vertical axis is opposed to the horizontal one in an endless series of somersaults. Unlike the previous example, this poem does not offer an immediate representation of what the text denotes. The abstract concept designated by the title is put into effect by a typographic ordering that reproduces verbal dislocation while at the same time respecting the conventions of textual typography.

A final example is afforded by "Caricare," published by Zayas in 1917 (Fig. 14). The traditional frame surrounding a poem has been exploded once and for all. Nevertheless, due to their arrangement on the page, excerpts from conventionalized speech are spread out in an anthropomorphic shape that reinforces the meaning of each fragment while sketching out a simplified human form. The excerpt in the upper portion of the page deals with the mind and is followed underneath with the demonstrative pronoun *Ici* (Here), which introduces the eyes. Lower down still we find hands, and at the very bottom feet. Despite the fact that the real object is not clearly copied here, it can nevertheless be detected in the schematic ordering of its parts. This process is underscored by the poem's title since "caricare" is in fact the Latin word from which *caricature* is derived—the latter meaning "an approximate figure."

This brings to a close our typology of poetic forms that suggests some clear steps toward an understanding of Dada writings, which many scholars still believe to be a merely anarchistic and chaotic jumble of signs. It is true that Dada invites such labels as nihilism and gratuitousness through its attack on the authoritarian hold of conventional meaning. On closer inspection, however, it is clear that this attack pushes Dada writing into the realm of abstract symbolism, rather than conventionally motivated meaning, and so it weakens the movement's debts toward mimetic representation. The written text is defined instead as the domain of techno-ludic experimentation where the only things that matter are material inscriptions and a search for significance within the well-known realm of everyday, practical semiotics.

Returning to the semiotic diagram proposed earlier, it is now possible to place the examples we have discussed relative to one another and to the specific sign-components on which they depend (Diagram 2). Our descriptive analysis, even if it were exhaustive, would be of little value unless it helped us better understand the initial project of Dada's proto-semiotic endeavor, along with all the theoretical ramifications that such a project entails. For often the perplexed reader of such texts, even if he or she is aware of their innovative symbolic function, will view them merely as literary games, or exercises in futility.

La mentalité d'une femme   { Une femme est une cathédrale
en Art—en Science—en Amour   { nerveuse comme le grand sympathique

Ici il y a des yeux qui regardent des cons
et des chose sérieuses

Les mains
Diamants
Rubis
Emeraudes
Frs
$

Et des petits pieds
de curé espagnol

Figure 14

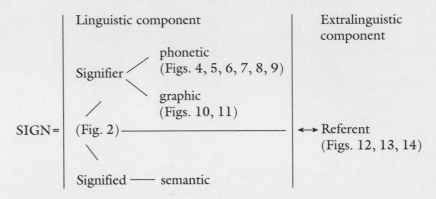

Diagram 2

The project is, however, a much more serious one and it goes back to the very foundations of interpersonal exchange. Umberto Eco has given the following provocative definition of semiotics: "Semiotics is in principle the discipline studying everything which can be used in order to lie."[21] The relevance of this definition for an understanding of Dada's epistemological implications is brought out in the remarks from Eluard's "Les Animaux et leurs hommes," which we quoted above and can now restore to their immediate context: "May we rediscover our strength *for honesty*, as some poets and constructors who lived young have already taught us to do. Let's find out what we're capable of doing. Let's try, although it's difficult, to stay absolutely *pure*" (our emphasis).

How can the ideals of honesty and purity be restored? According to Eluard and others, it is by refusing any offer of compromise from the falsifying language of fancy oratory. So Dada does not speak. Dada says nothing, and Dada means nothing. Consequently, it is an oversimplification to posit a political or social cause to Dada's revolt, or worse still, to discredit the movement with the derogatory label of nihilism. Dada aesthetics is the direct result of a *moral* uneasiness.

And yet even this statement deserves qualification. For there is nothing in common between Dada and a society characterized by conformity, in which the right to pronounce moral judgments has been lost, and where routine concessions are made to bolster the overall indifference that each individual feels. Dada refuses to give in to the imperial-

21. Umberto Eco, *A Theory of Semiotics* (Bloomington: Indiana University Press, 1976), 7.

ism of altered meanings and to be the blissful slave of the manipulative and deceitful process of naming. It is significant in this respect that the movement's grandiose "cleansing" project should first be applied to language itself, which symbolizes such a worship of convention, and a turning of conventions into the consensus of "what is naturally obvious."

As a closing comment, we could speculate on earlier movements of intellectual revolt in which the initial call for a tabula rasa is traditionally accompanied by the hope for a revelation of truth. In this respect, literature and moral philosophy share more than a passing resemblance. For is not the motto *Opus impendere vero* (To devote a body of writing to truth) one of the early definitions that was assigned to what we now call literature?

three

TOPOLOGICAL POETICS

(ELUARD)

> *On April 26, 1937, the German air force, acting under the orders of General Franco, bombed and almost destroyed the defenseless city of Guernica on a crowded market day. This first example of modern mass bombing, during the Spanish Civil War, was a grim foretaste of what would happen on a larger scale in World War II.*
>
> —*Anthony Blunt*, Picasso's Guernica

Of all the military atrocities perpetrated between the two world wars, the bombing of Guernica probably had the greatest impact on the writers and artists of that era.[1] Fixed in time:

> Le 26 avril 1937, jour de marché, dans les premières heures de l'après-midi, les avions allemands au service de Franco bombardèrent Guernica durant trois heures et demie par escadrilles se relevant tour à tour.[2]

1. See Marc Hanrez, ed., *Les Ecrivains et la guerre d'Espagne* (Paris: Panthéon Press, Les Dossiers H, 1975).

2. Paul Eluard, "Guernica," in *Poèmes retrouvés (Oeuvres complètes,* eds. L. Scheler and M. Dumas, vol. 2 [Paris: Gallimard, Pléiade, 1968], 913). Eluard wrote two texts on the subject of Guernica. "La Victoire de Guernica," analyzed in this chapter, was composed in 1937, at the same time as Picasso was working on his famous painting *Guernica*, which would be exhibited in the Spanish pavilion at the International Exhibition in Paris in 1937. The poem accompanied the painting. It was first published in *Cahiers d'art* 1–3 (1937):

(In the early afternoon of April 26th—market day—Guernica was bombed for three and a half hours by relays of German air squadrons under General Franco's orders.)

and in space:

> Guernica. C'est une petite ville de Biscaye, capitale traditionnelle du Pays basque. C'est là que s'élevait le chêne, symbole sacré des traditions et des libertés basques. Guernica n'a qu'une importance historique et sentimentale. ("Guernica" 913)

> (Guernica, a small town and the traditional capital of the Basque country. It was here that grew the oak of Guernica, sacred symbol of Basque traditions and Basque freedom. Guernica's importance is purely historical and sentimental.)

the reality of this event was bound to attract the attention of the author of *Les Yeux fertiles* and *Donner à voir,* who held that poetry should first and foremost reveal "le visage de la vérité" (the face of truth).[3] The event obviously lent itself to journalistic writing and was reported in great detail.[4] Nonetheless it was to this same event (perhaps better suited to the

---

36. The English translation by Roland Penrose and George Reavey first appeared in the *London Bulletin* 6 (1938): 7–8. The complete text of this poem and its translation appear at the end of the chapter. Any subsequent, and more literal, translations of the poems are by Terese Lyons.

In 1949 Eluard wrote "Guernica," from which the quotation above is taken. The text was meant to accompany Alain Resnais's film on Picasso's painting and was published in *Europe* 47–48 (October 1948): 47–50. All the quotations in this chapter are from the version of this poem published in *Cours naturel,* in vol. 1 of Eluard's *Oeuvres complètes,* 812–14.

3. Eluard, "Baudelaire," in *Poèmes retrouvés (Oeuvres complètes,* vol. 2, 912).

4. See the account given in *Paris-Soir* and in *The Times* (April 1937), which corresponds almost sentence to sentence with Eluard's version:

> Guernica, the most ancient town of the Basques and the center of their cultural tradition, was completely destroyed yesterday afternoon by insurgent air raiders. The bombardment of the open town, situated far behind the lines, took precisely three hours and a quarter, during which a powerful fleet of aeroplanes consisting of three German types, Junkers and Heinkel bombers, and Heinkel fighters, did not cease unloading bombs and incendiary projectiles on the town. The fighters, meanwhile, plunged low from above the town center to machine-gun those of the civilian population who had taken refuge in the fields. The whole of Guernica was soon in flames, except the historic *Casa de Juntas,* with its rich archives of the Basque race, where

grandeur of the epic form) that the poet turned for material that he would then exploit to symbolic effect. While removing the bombardment's referential value, this symbolic effect progressively drains the attack of its reality and transposes it into a system founded on universals of language that go beyond the journalistic facts that initially triggered off the poem's verbal system.

The mere name Guernica binds the text to reality since, as Derrida points out, it acts as a *monumémoire* (monumemory),[5] and is the label for a whole store of information related to one particular event. The place name is the most obvious aspect of "La Victoire de Guernica" to carry any referential value. This is not unique to Eluard's poem since, for there to be a referential side to any text, the referent (or excluded middle between signifier and signified) must be inscribed parasitically within the text. Consequently, its textual presence can act as an extralinguistic shifter—that is, as a sign speaking *about* reality and at the same time acting as a support for the other, purely symbolic elements within the text. The name Guernica is the poem's only historical emblem, marking the constraints of time and space that are imposed by history, and acting both as a milestone and textual boundary. Against this backdrop of reality the poem constructs an autonomous sign system of its own. Consequently, from the title onward, the exclusively referential value of the name Guernica is negated, since although the name designates an atrocious massacre, this effect is counterbalanced by its link with "Victoire"—and victory contradicts precisely those events in northern Spain that we have come to "know" through their reports in the press.

The system of bipolar opposition provides a preliminary model for the entire poem insofar as it is based on the principle of contradiction. Thus the referential presence underlined by the name Guernica has the sole purpose of allowing the opposite pole (indicated by *Victoire*) to be developed. So the denotation and connotations of the place name have no value in themselves, since Eluard is not concerned with constructing a pseudomimetic document such as those found in historical annals.

---

the ancient Parliament used to sit. The famous oak of Guernica, the dried stump that is 600 years old and the new shoots of this century, was also untouched. There the kings of Spain used to take the oath to respect the democratic rights (*fueros*) of Vizcaya, and in return received a promise of allegiance as suzerains with the democratic title of *Señor,* not *Rey Vizcaya.*

5. A portmanteau word coined by Jacques Derrida in *Glas* as a term for a *monument à la mémoire* (monument in memory [of someone or something]).

Nevertheless, one must acknowledge the particular function of the place name within the poem's bipolar system. As Benveniste has pointed out, the distinguishing linguistic feature of a proper name is its self-creating and self-referential status. Hence the special referential status of a text that is generated by this type of name. In an utterance such as *la victoire du génocide* (the victory of genocide) one could recognize a contradiction similar to the one expressed in *la victoire de Guernica*. There is, however, a fundamental difference between the two: *genocide* refers to an atopical and, alas, universal reality, whereas *Guernica* implicates the reader's encyclopedic knowledge—a type of knowledge that cannot possibly be ahistoric. The poem's contradiction, or in other words its meaning, of course becomes clear when the poem is read, since it is not solely limited to the title. Nevertheless, the way in which the event justifies the text in relation to a particular system of meaning in no way diminishes the event's role as a referential anchor, which is a trigger for the text rather than a matrix. This is demonstrated by the fact that when Eluard wants to commemorate the historical event, its site and its significance, he eliminates "Victoire" from the title (and along with it the principle of contradiction that the word provides), keeping only "Guernica." This transformation in turn alters the way in which the text is read, since what is elliptical, paratactic, and antithetical in the poem becomes direct, explanatory, and justificatory in the commemorative discourse:

On a tous lu dans les journaux en buvant son café; quelque part en Europe, une légion d'assassins écrase la fourmilière humaine. On se représente mal un enfant éventré, une femme décapitée, un homme vomissant tout son sang d'un seul coup. ("Guernica" 914)

(People have read all about it in the newspaper over coffee at breakfast: somewhere in Europe a legion of murderers had crushed a human anthill. It is hard to imagine a child disemboweled, a woman beheaded, or a man suddenly vomiting all his blood.)

Whereas the poem only exists by virtue of the tension created between a deceptively vague reference on the one hand, and a system of symbols that indicates a highly specific context on the other, the commemorative discourse refers only to the individual event. If one compares the two versions, written fourteen years apart, the differences between the two modes of writing are quite obvious from the very first verse:

Beau monde des masures
De la mine et des champs

(Beautiful world of hovels
mines and fields)

becomes in the second version

Les gens de Guernica sont de petits gens. Ils vivent dans leur ville
depuis bien longtemps. Leur vie est composée d'une goutte de
richesse et d'un flot de misère. ("Guernica" 914)

(The people of Guernica are humble folk. They have been living in
their town for a very long time. Their life is made up of a drop of
wealth amidst a flood of poverty.)

Although Eluard wrote in *Littérature* in 1919, "Let us reduce and
transform the displeasing language that satisfies mere chatter, language
that is as dead as the crowns which sit on our equally dead foreheads,"
and goes on to propose an aesthetics "aiming at an immediate rapport
between the object and the person who sees it,"[6] when he speaks of the
event itself, he cannot help developing an explanatory, metadiscursive
level of discourse. Even when interpolating fragments of the original
poem into the prose commentary he feels it necessary to modify them so
that the gap between the two not be too obvious. Hence

Ils vous ont fait payer le pain
Le ciel la terre l'eau le sommeil
Et la misère
De votre vie

(They made you pay for the bread
the sky the earth the water the sleep

6. "Le langage déplaisant qui suffit aux bavards, langage aussi mort que les cou-
ronnes à nos fronts semblables, réduisons-le, transformons-le (...) il y aura recherche d'un
rapport immédiat entre celui qui voit et ce qui est vu" ("Les Animaux et les hommes,"
Littérature 5 [July 1919], reprinted in *Physique de la poésie [Oeuvres complètes,* vol. 1, 37]).
See Chapter 2.

> and the misery
> of your life with your life)

becomes in "Guernica" (913):

> Ils vous ont fait payer le pain
> De votre vie
> Ils vous ont fait payer le ciel la terre l'eau le sommeil
> Et même la misère noire
> De votre vie
>
> (They made you pay for the bread
> Of your life
> They made you pay for the sky the earth the water the sleep
> And even the black misery
> Of your life with your life)

The repetition of "De votre vie" and the interpolation of "même" introduce a hierarchical distinction, whereas originally the mere juxtaposition and accumulation of words suggested equivalent, or at least similar, components that were all equally essential to the life of the "Beau monde." Bread becomes something one acquires, the result of work; sky, earth, water, and sleep are something given. "Même" is an inserted comment by the author since the adverb is both a reiteration and an amplification, with the result that "misère" functions almost as a superlative in relation to the other terms, a fact that is underlined by the addition of the adjective "noire." To use the terms of traditional rhetoric, one could say that whereas a metabole suffices in "La Victoire de Guernica," "Guernica" is more explicit and takes the reader methodically from one step to the next. And in case the reader or listener did not notice the shifts of meaning occurring in the poem, the prose commentary points them out quite unequivocally:

> Leur vie est composée de tout petits bonheurs et d'un très grand souci: celui du lendemain. Demain il faut manger et demain il faut vivre. Aujourd'hui, l'on espère. Aujourd'hui, l'on travaille. ("Guernica" 914)

(Their lives are composed of small joys and one great worry: that of tomorrow. Tomorrow they must eat and tomorrow they must live. Today they hope. Today they work.)

This type of discourse is quite foreign to that of our poem, since, as Nicole Charbois comments about the poem, "Eluard makes an utterance, then remains silent: no comment whatsoever. [...] Picasso conveyed violence by the shrieking and convulsed colors and shapes he used, but Eluard chose silence to make us aware of this violence. He holds in his cry, masters his language—but he says it all."[7]

There is no need for further demonstration since the examples given so far clearly prove the difference between the ways in which the poem and the commemorative text treat the referential event. The didascalic inscription differs too in each case. In the poem the symbolism generated by the referential trigger leads one to the text's meaning without there being any need for circumstantial reference. In the commemorative text, reference is the force that maintains legitimate meaning, and that controls its production through the text's underlying naturalism.

Consequently, a study of "La Victoire de Guernica" is also a study of a language system whose only postulate is to negate precise reference and endow it with a symbolic importance that transcends any mimesis of specific events, turning all imitation into a universal and transhistorical mode. We have already pointed out the antithetical character of the poem's title, and emphasized that the antithesis was not founded solely on the semantic qualities of the word Guernica, since this proper name retains its essential function as a designation and to read it means uncovering a set of extralinguistic connotations that are indissociable from its denotative function. Indeed it is this aspect that creates the poem's special status, and that has led us to place it in the category of *topological poetics*, since the fundamental trigger for enacting the poem's system appears as a sign-signal. This process is distinct from the poetic practice of opposing two verbal signs in such a way that each is deprived of its complete status as a sign. For example, when Michel Leiris writes "Etrusques aux frusques étriquées" (Etruscans in tight togs), "Etrusques" is used only so that it can appear as a portmanteau word that is a reverse contraction of "frusques étriquées."[8] Here language is only fighting with itself.

7. Nicole Charbois, "Eluard et Picasso," *Europe* 525 (January 1979): 188–207.
8. Michel Leiris, *Mots sans mémoire* (Paris: Gallimard, 1969), 127.

No extratextual reference is ever involved in this type of game, which never goes beyond the simple sign's specific properties.

It would not be rash to claim that, in "La Victoire de Guernica," once the title's emblematic effect and its value as a referential trigger are established, the poem's significance and its role as a "universal and atemporal monument" are created in a language that brings into play an exclusively verbal system. Extratextual reference plays only a minor role in relation to the poem's main preoccupation, which is to show language pitted against itself. Thus in topological poetics, the status of reference is that of a pretext which legitimizes and justifies the creation of a complex sign whose referent (the real world) is the excluded third component. Nevertheless, its impact is felt marginally all along the symbolic chain since, with the copresence of encyclopedic knowledge in each linguistic element's field, an allusion to the name Guernica—and, by the same token, to the referential context—can be attributed to each of these elements.

This explains how, in the first stanza, "masures," "mine," and "champs" (hovels, mine, fields) appear to offer a precise description of the lifestyle of Guernica's inhabitants, even though one would have to be sufficiently well-informed to assess the accuracy of such a statement—the task of a geographer or sociologist rather than of a literary commentator. In fact, "masures," "mine," and "champs" all serve as general signs for a hard and laborious life, and are used in order to contrast with "Beau monde," a fixed expression in French that usually designates the idle, elegant world of the privileged. The sole purpose of this antithetical disjunction is to herald a theme that runs through the entire poem—namely, that the little these people possessed was a "treasure" compared to their plight after the disaster. This theme of life as a treasure dependent on hope returns covertly in stanzas 5, 8, 9, and 12, and overtly in stanza 13 in a paradoxical formulation accentuated by the homophony of the two rhyming words: "Hommes réels pour qui le désespoir / Alimente le feu dévorant de l'espoir" (Real men for whom despair / Feeds the devouring fire of hope). The importance given here to "espoir" (hope)—and it is of some intertextual comfort to know that Malraux was later to choose it as the title of his own account of the Spanish Civil War—brings to the text a set of variants such as "feuilles vertes" (green leaves), "de printemps" (of spring), and "lait pur" (pure milk; stanza 8). Green is associated with hope in French, spring is the season of germination, milk is a metonym for motherhood and promise, and pure underscores the meliorative value of the figure by connoting natural innocence and fragility.

The thematic pole opposing this *beau monde* is obviously formed by the words "mort" and "vide" (death, void) in lines 6 and 7 ("Voici le vide qui vous fixe / Votre mort va servir d'exemple" [Here is the void staring at you / Your death shall be an example]). Both nouns transform "feuilles vertes (...) dans les yeux" (green leaves [...] in their eyes; line 20) into "roses rouges dans les yeux" (red roses in their eyes; lines 26–27). For "rouges" (red) is doubly overdetermined here: first by "sang" (blood), which follows it in line 28 and introduces violence into the field of utterance, and second by the fact that *rose rouge* is a metonym for extreme intensity and also the very end of a cycle.[9]

A metaphoric extension of this opposition between foliage and flower is embodied in the formula that contains the poem's exhortation: "ouvrons ensemble le dernier bourgeon de l'avenir" (let us open the future's last leaf bud together; line 35). "Bourgeon" (bud) refers directly to leaf, to green, and thus to hope, whereas in the flower system the precise term for bud would be *bouton* rather than *bourgeon*.

The asyndetic construction of the third stanza and of its first line ("Visages bons à tout") introduces a new cumulative series of notations that are presented as a figurative description not of a lifestyle, this time, but of the inhabitants themselves—though the description's naturalist flavor is again transformed into a negative value by an exclusively verbal semantic artifice. However, unlike the first stanza where the semantic opposition to the "beautiful world" was direct, disjunction now occurs within the syntactic framework, implying the restitution of the fixed expression "bon à quelque chose" (good for something) and indicating a positive value, good for action or a particular state. In line 3, "Visages bons au feu visages bons au froid" (Faces good for—or staunch in—the fire, good for the cold), "feu" and "froid" represent the entire paradigm of climatic conditions since they evoke its two extremes. Line 3 is thus the interchangeable equivalent of "good for all weather" as far as its meaning is concerned, but adds a certain concreteness to the utterance. The accumulation that follows brings together a group of negative elements—"refus," "injures," "coups" (refusals, insults, blows)—that, through analogical contamination, lead to "nuit," which is an a priori

9. Consider, for example, these famous lines by Malherbe in "Ode à Duperrier sur la mort de sa fille": "Et rose, elle a vécu ce que vivent les roses / L'espace d'un matin" (And as a rose, she lived what roses live / The space of a morning).

neutral element, a pejorative value similar to the one it will acquire in the penultimate line of the poem, "la couleur monotone de notre nuit" (the monotonous color of our night). Because it is usually laden with negative presuppositions, "monotone" confirms this value. The effect of semantic contrast relies, therefore, on the opposition between "bons" (good), which is considered to be positive, and the negative value of the terms to which this adjective is structurally attached, and which all indicate the natural or man-made atrocities that the townsfolk suffered.

This type of semantic dislocation of a fixed structure is used again in stanza 5, since the phrase "De votre vie" (Of your life) can be linked equally well to both the preceding nouns, "le pain / Le ciel (...) la misère / De votre vie" (the bread / The sky [...] the misery / Of your life), and to the preceding verb, if one allows for a stylistic inversion such as *Ils vous ont fait payer de votre vie le pain, Le ciel* (They made you pay with your life for the bread, the sky). In this case, the phrase would imply a simple quid pro quo, whereas the first structure would elaborate on the idea of treasure, by insinuating that "they" (*ils*) have so indulged in excess that they even put a price on the most complete destitution. This interpretation would concur with the statement "ils exagèrent" (they exaggerate) in line 18. It should be noted, however, that any partial interpretation matters little here since the dislocation of the syntactic structure reinforces the ambiguity of paying for one's poverty. Unlike the ambiguity we examined in the second stanza, where the ensuing disjunction concretizes the semantic opposition between the two poles of good and bad, the ambiguity in stanza 5 reinforces meaning to the point of redundancy, since the copresence of the two formulations serves to reinforce both of them and corroborate the figures of excess, and since these two formulations are themselves a type of "overflow" of meaning.

In both cases, the use of syntactic possibilities forces language into a state of internal ambivalence, and the resulting dichotomy removes any possibility of direct, unitary denotation. Instead it produces a meaning that establishes either redundancy or opposition, as the case may be. It seems clear, then, that referential mimesis, which is always based on an utterance's direct meaning, is overshadowed by a symbolic process that introduces a certain number of exclusively verbal distinctions that then proceed to take over.

The syntactic utterance in line 8, "La mort coeur renversé" (Death heart overturned), derives its force from the discovery of verbal effects at different levels. The absence of an explicit grammatical or semantic link between the two parts is naturally perceived to be a case of symbolic disorder, the precise nature of the relation depending on how the reader construes it. Yet one cannot overlook the well-known expression "coeur renversé," which adds to the physical description given in the line (a heart upside-down, upset, or even knocked over) a quite special psychological and figurative value akin to emotionally upset and overwhelmed. Such an interpretation would create a consecutive link between "La mort" (death) and "coeur renversé" (upset heart), implying that it is death that upsets. Yet "renversé" is also a synonym of "changed to the exact opposite," which is precisely what death has done in relation to the victims' former state. In this case "renversé" would simply appear to be an expansion of "La mort" with a more limited meaning focusing on the result of the latter. Naturally one would still have to explain its association with "coeur" since, given this meaning, "renversé" and "coeur" cannot constitute a fixed expression. However it is possible that the sequence "coeur renversé" (taken in the sense of upside-down heart), instead of being a pseudomimetic representation of the victims' situation, plays an emblematic role in relation to "La mort" and that both terms could be joined to make a heraldic description. If a beating heart is a symbol of life, "coeur renversé" would be the opposite, a blazon of death. The structure "La mort coeur renversé" would thus introduce the bearer (the enemy) and his sign, his "speaking arms." This brings us back indirectly to the original context of war, and it also introduces an adversary, the undefined "Ils" (They) mentioned in the fifth stanza. Here again meaning is a result of semantic compression and therefore cannot simply be reduced to a singular, unequivocal reference.

Just as the hovels, mine, and fields could be seen as referring directly to the real world of Guernica's inhabitants, so the characterization in the sixth stanza could make us think that these are fragments of a description referring metonymically to the chronicle's "Nazi pilots." In fact, the undefined "They" marks the moment at which the poem breaks loose from its specific frame of reference and introduces a generic dimension that is devoid of any specific situation. What appear are thus general qualities—hypocrisy, vanity, and avarice. The opacity of "They saluted the corpses" (*Ils saluaient les cadavres*) takes a semantic shortcut that plays on the choice of a term indicative of finality instead of something in progress or expected.[10]

10. See the French expression *cuire le pain* (baking bread), which is sometimes said

"Corpses" can refer just as well to "dead heroes" as to victims of military atrocities—but that is beside the point. What the expression "They saluted the corpses" does indicate is a fetishistic and ritualized salute to, or taste for, death, the complete opposite of life (as given in the fifth stanza) and thus of the positive pole presented in that stanza as the only remaining possession of Guernica's future victims. So it is that the overall effect of these connotations is to establish a semantic field based on the notion of excess. This is confirmed semantically in line 18 by "They persevere they exaggerate they are not of our world" (*Ils persévèrent ils exagèrent ils ne sont pas de notre monde*). "They are not of our world" doubly defines the unidentified oppressors since, over and above the opposition between life and death, the utterance also incorporates the opposition between excess and destitution that will be continued in the following stanzas. The "leaves," "spring," and "pure milk," in addition to their previously mentioned values, characterize women and children and so connote the victims' natural simplicity (their being real people), in contrast to line 15, for instance, where "a farthing" connotes a society that is organized and artificially based on monetary exchange. It is a society of convention, as the use of the verb "salute" had already indicated.

The antithetical formulation of stanza 11, "La peur et le courage de vivre et de mourir / La mort si difficile et si facile" (The fear of living and dying and the courage to do both / Death so difficult and so easy), could be put anywhere in the poem, and indeed in "Guernica" these words appear at the beginning of the text. The antithesis merely restates in an explicitly paradoxical and abstract way what the various concrete expressions have thus far underlined: namely, that living out one's daily life is a continual and hard-won victory, so precarious that at any moment it may be interrupted. Similarly, death, which is always easy and within reach the moment one gives up, is relentlessly deferred by effort and work. As they stand, these two lines apply not just to the inhabitants of Guernica but to many others as well. This explains our interpretation of "pariahs" (line

---

instead of *cuire la pâte* (baking dough), the process whose result is the making of bread. This contrast also occurs in the expression *percer un trou* (to drill a hole) versus *percer un mur* (to drill [a hole in] a wall). The predominance of verbal expressions favoring the result of an action over a filmic description of the action's course is often considered to be specific to French. Consider, for instance, the French translations of the following two sentences: "Stay off that ankle!" (*Ménage cette cheville!*), "The heavy book slipped off my knees" (*Ce livre trop lourd m'est tombé des genoux*).

36) in the final stanza as a term used to generalize meaning, which destroys once and for all the poem's specific reference by adding a collective dimension to each of its statements.

If it were still necessary to prove that stanzas 6, 7, 8, and 14 lead us to read the poem as a generalization, it would suffice to note that they are the only ones that do not appear in "Guernica." They are the sole stanzas excluded from the chronicle since, according to the rules of its genre, the latter is restricted to specific events in a particular space and time. This additional evidence is not essential, but merely a confirmation of what a close reading uncovers: namely, that through a *generalizing process* the poem frees itself from referential constraints. Indeed in each of the poem's sections one notices a type of formulation that makes retroactive generalization a model for language's function, thereby allowing the text to expel the real and the specific in order to attain the level of the universal. Each element of a paradigmatic series is picked up by a term that both resumes and contains the whole series. This term then comes to be regarded as a condensed version of the series and also appears, retrospectively, as a tautological expansion anticipating the series' closure. For example, "bons à tout" (good for everything) in line 5 picks up "bons au feu (...) au froid / Aux refus (...) aux injures aux coups (good for the fire [...] the cold / Refusal [...] swearing blows) in the two previous lines; "Ils vous ont fait payer (...) la misère" (They made you pay for [...] your misery) in line 11 picks up "ils vous ont fait payer le pain / Le ciel la terre l'eau le sommeil" (they made you pay for the bread / Sky earth water sleep) in lines 9 and 10; "Les femmes les enfants ont le même trésor (...) de durée" (Women and children have the same treasure [...] of lasting) in lines 19 and 21 picks up "De feuilles vertes de printemps de lait pur" (Of green leaves of spring of pure milk) in line 20; finally "la couleur / Monotone de notre nuit" (the monotonous color of our night) in lines 37 and 38 picks up "la mort la terre et la hideur / De nos ennemis" (death earth and the hideousness / Of our enemies) in lines 36 and 37.

Reading these lines, along with the poem's lists of juxtaposed terms, gives the impression that on a formal level the poem plays out the semantic value of the word "monotonous" in line 30, and consequently takes on the canonical structure that is typical of plaintive ballads traditionally used in tragic poems. The ensuing monotony is broken only by the collective appeal of the final line, "Nous en aurons raison" (We will overcome them), to which the poet associates his voice. This association of the poet and the collectivity is already anticipated by "notre monde" (our world) in line 18, "ouvrons ensemble" (let's open together) in line 35, and by "nos ennemis" (our enemies) in line 37. The use of the first person plural in these lines is yet another way of turning the specificity of "your life" and "your death" (which address Guernica directly in lines 12 and 7) into a more general symbolic statement. Moreover, one can hardly fail to notice that the exceptional quality of the last line conforms to the pattern of the *envoi* or coda, which is the traditional climax for such commemorative poems.

Eluard concludes his other text on Guernica by extending the lesson of this particular agony to other grimly remembered landmarks: "Guernica comme Oradour et comme Hiroshima sont les capitales de la paix vivante" (Guernica like Oradour and like Hiroshima is the capital of living peace; "Guernica" 917). The subject then broadens and Guernica returns as one of several examples of a pattern of conflict that transcends all particular circumstances: "Guernica! l'innocence aura raison du crime" (Guernica! innocence will overcome crime; 917). From this standpoint, the lessons of "La Victoire de Guernica" and "Guernica" are similar, but in the latter work Eluard is forced to explicitly abandon the work's chronicle form so that he can proclaim the event's universal and perennial quality. As a result, the referential model is suddenly stripped of its specific value and becomes confused with other Guernicas, thus losing the spatio-temporal characteristics that make it a unique place and subject in history. In "La Victoire de Guernica," however, the process of generalization is internal to the language of the poem itself since, by exclusively verbal operations, specific extralinguistic references are stripped of their naturalistic identity, and thus transform what is said into a victorious song of hope that is both plural and universal.

APPENDIX

La Victoire de Guernica (from *Cours naturel*)
Paul Eluard

> Beau monde des masures
> De la mine et des champs
>
> Visages bons au feu visages bons au froid
> Aux refus à la nuit aux injures aux coups

Visages bons à tout 5
Voici le vide qui vous fixe
Votre mort va servir d'exemple

La mort coeur renversé

Ils vous ont fait payer le pain
Le ciel la terre l'eau le sommeil 10
Et la misère
De votre vie

Ils disaient désirer la bonne intelligence
Ils rationnaient les forts jugeaient les fous
Faisaient l'aumône partageaient un sou en deux 15
Ils saluaient les cadavres
Ils s'accablaient de politesses

Ils persévèrent ils exagèrent ils ne sont pas de notre monde

Les femmes les enfants ont le même trésor
De feuilles vertes de printemps et de lait pur 20
Et de durée
Dans leurs yeux purs

Les femmes les enfants ont le même trésor
Dans les yeux
Les hommes le défendent comme ils peuvent 25

Les femmes les enfants ont les mêmes roses rouges
Dans les yeux
Chacun montre son sang

La peur et le courage de vivre et de mourir
La mort si difficile et si facile 30

Hommes pour qui ce trésor fut chanté
Hommes pour qui ce trésor fut gâché

Hommes réels pour qui le désespoir
Alimente le feu dévorant de l'espoir
Ouvrons ensemble le dernier bourgeon de l'avenir 35

Parias la mort la terre et la hideur
De nos ennemis ont la couleur
Monotone de notre nuit
Nous en aurons raison.

The Victory of Guernica
Translated by Roland Penrose and George Reavey

    High life in hovels
    In mines and in fields

    Faces staunch in the fire staunch in the cold
    Against denials the night insults blows

    Faces always staunch   ·   5
    Here is the void staring at you
    Your death shall be an example

    Death heart overturned

    They made you pay for bread
    Sky earth water sleep   10
    And the poverty
    Of your life

    They said they wanted agreement
    They checked the strong sentenced the mad
    Gave alms divided a farthing   15
    They greeted every corpse
    They overwhelmed each other with politeness

    They insist they exaggerate they are not of our world

    The women the children have the same treasure
    Of green leaves of spring and of pure milk   20
    And of endurance
    In their pure eyes

    The women the children have the same treasure
    In their eyes
    The men defend it as best they can   25

    The women the children have the same red roses
      In their eyes
        All show their blood

    The fear and the courage of living and of dying
    Death so hard and so easy   30

Men for whom this treasure was extolled
Men for whom this treasure was spoiled

Real men for whom despair
Feeds the devouring fire of hope
Let us open together the last bud of the future   35

Pariahs death earth and the vileness
Of our enemies have the monotonous
Color of our night
The day will be ours.

four

COMPETENCE AND RECOVERY

(JACOB)

We could have titled this chapter "On a sentence (or a verse) by Max Jacob" were it not for one problem. The sequence of words in question is, strictly speaking, neither a sentence nor a verse. Here it is:

L'enfant, l'éfant, l'éléphant, la grenouille et la pomme sautée.[1]

(The infant, the ifant, the elephant, the frog and the sautéed potato.)

In the section "Le Coq et la Perle" (The rooster and the pearl) in *Le Cornet à dés* this sequence of words is a discrete unit, separated from the other fragments in the section. Classical rhetoricians would consider it to

---

1. Max Jacob, *Le Cornet à dés* (Paris: Gallimard, 1945), 59.

be a *sententia maxima*—an expression that only a bad punner would translate as "a saying by Max."

The sequence as a whole appears to be an expandable list of determinate nouns, which discounts its being a sentence since the latter requires the binary structure of subject and predicate. The predicate function is created by a verb, which is lacking in the quotation above. From a strictly linguistic point of view, since this extract is not a phrase, we are dealing neither with syntax nor with parataxis (which is the absence of any link between prior syntactic units). Instead we are within a *synthematic* realm, if we understand theme in the context of the grammatical distinction between topic and verb, where theme is a name for the particular constitution of a topic. A synthematic distribution of words is, consequently, closer to a paradigmatic derivation than a syntagmatic one. The peculiar status of the extract above underscores the importance of these distinctions, since its value as a maxim highlights the uselessness of a syntagmatic reading, as well as the presupposition of narrative continuity that goes along with such a reading.

Viewed from another standpoint, the broken, jumbled, and apparently disoriented aspect of the statement increases its incomprehensibility and wipes out the traces of any code that might give order to its fragments. What is it talking about, what does it mean? we might ask. To give a commentary on the statement, one is initially confronted by what Tzvetan Todorov has called a "textual complication" (as opposed to a textual explication).[2] He introduces this notion as part of his reading of Rimbaud's opaque and apparently undecidable prose poems, the *Illuminations*. We can sense the disappointment that surfaces in his conclusion that "in principle [Rimbaud's poems] resist all explication" (244). Coming after Todorov's attack on the four dominant modes of Rimbaldian criticism (evhemerist, etiological, esoteric, and paradigmatic), this avowal of hermeneutic incompetence seems especially harsh. For Todorov's readers could well be excused for thinking that there is no meaning whatsoever to be recovered from Rimbaud's dysfunctional texts.

On close reading, however, Todorov's analysis reveals traces of an underlying obsession that belies the decisive tone of his conclusion. One could paraphrase this obsession by saying, "I know very well that an explication is impossible, *and yet* in principle nothing should be capable of

2. Tzvetan Todorov, "Une Complication de texte," *Poétique* 34 (1978): 241–53.

escaping explanation." We find elements of such an argument in passages where the critic discusses the apparent incoherence of Rimbaud's poems. This incoherence is never said to be total since Todorov shifts the focus away from the fragmentary nature of the poems' verbal sequences and suggests that a deliberate process of subversion is the cause. Hence the following question: "How should one react in the face of such incoherence, or such an appearance of incoherence?" (243)—the qualifier suggesting that all is not what it seems. Or: "We no longer have any means for stating the most striking aspect of this text—namely, its surface incoherence" (244). Even if the main thrust of Todorov's argument is aimed at preserving the initial feeling of inaccessibility that Rimbaud's reader experiences, one cannot escape the fact that by using the notion of a textual "surface" Todorov is implying that at a *deeper* level the incoherences in the *Illuminations* could be solved. It is precisely this presupposition of deep structure versus surface disorder that we would like to examine in light of Max Jacob's exemplary text.

At the outset it is worth remarking that Todorov's disappointment is due to the fact that the only critical model he uses in an attempt to deal with the text's linguistic structure is hampered by restraints that he himself has imposed on it. These restrictions were formulated in two earlier articles that Todorov had devoted to poetry. The first put forward the hypothesis that a poem affords no reading-construction for its audience. "There are several literary texts," Todorov tells us, "that lead to no construction of meaning whatsoever, namely, nonrepresentational texts. Among these one can pinpoint certain categories: the most obvious of these is what is usually called lyric poetry, and which describes no events, nor evokes anything that lies beyond its own confines."[3] The second article, on poetic discourse, is even more skeptical about reading competence, as is clear from the following statement: "It is precisely the implicit axiom of poetry's coherence that ought to be examined as a philosophical oversight. For what if the poetic text were not coherent, harmonious, unified, or repetitive?"[4] After reviewing and rejecting each of the four previously mentioned critical models, Todorov suggests indirectly that pragmatics may hold the right answer. This final recourse remains hypothetical, however, since the author avows that he can say very little about

3. Todorov, "La lecture comme construction," *Poétique* 24 (1975): 425.
4. Todorov, "Théories de la poésie," *Poétique* 28 (1976): 389.

the pragmatic approach, and that he is not aware of any instances of it in the field of literary interpretation. "Curiously enough," he writes,

> no study [...] has ever given a pragmatic definition of poetry—or, in simpler terms, has ever defined poetry in terms of the author's state of mind before the poem appeared, or of the reader's state of mind after its appearance. [...] One could easily imagine some revised pragmatic responses to the problem, and I am indeed surprised that none exists to my knowledge (which is probably due to my reading only one review). (385–86)

The field of criticism is in fact not as underpopulated as these comments suggest, for since the appearance of the article above a certain number of researchers have abandoned the areas of syntax and semantics in order to assist developments in pragmatics. It is not certain, however, that such recent activities supply us with the kind of linguistic answer to the problem that one might expect, nor that pragmatists' elaboration of "possible worlds" is of any value to poetics. Samuel Levin, for instance, aligns himself with Richard Ohmann and John Searle when he proposes in his article, "What Kind of Speech Act a Poem Is," that every poem be preceded by a hyperphrase that would translate the pragmatic force of the work. "Here is the statement that I take to be the hyperphrase that is implicit in every poem," argues Levin, "and which expresses the type of illocutionary force that should be recognized in the poem: 'I imagine, and invite you to conceive of, a world in which . . .'"[5] This initial pragmatic index seems to match the logic of certain poems, such as Baudelaire's "Correspondances":

I imagine, and invite you to conceive of, a world in which

> "Nature is a temple where living pillars
> Occasionally let out confusing words;
> Man wanders here amidst forests of symbols
> Which observe him with familiar glances."

5. Levin, "What Kind of Speech Act a Poem Is," in T. A. van Dijk, ed., *Pragmatics of Language and Literature* (Amsterdam: North-Holland, 1976).

But it is hard to see where it would lead us with Jacob's maxim:

I imagine, and invite you to conceive of, a world in which

"The infant, the ifant, the elephant, the frog, and the sautéed potato."

We are not trying to totally discredit the pragmatic approach (whose importance for literary studies we have shown elsewhere).[6] Instead we are merely pointing out that the introduction of a hyperphrase in fact accentuates the fundamental difference that distinguishes any text from a lived situation: namely, the autonomous functioning, within the text, of a particular symbolic system that depends on its own internal rules. This leads back to the more basic axiom whereby each text generates its own legibility. Before concluding that a text is indeterminable or undecidable (two obstacles to understanding that are not, logically, the same), we should not, therefore, be in a hurry to invoke such nonverbal components of the text as its source and its reception.

In Jacob's hermetic and fragmentary sequence of words the absence of structuring marks inside the statement (that would point to clearly separated grammatical and syntactic units) invites its commentator to make a metatextual detour that would add extra information to the verbal sequence. This procedure is based on a specialized linguistic competence that is first and foremost an encyclopedic memory. Through the processes of recall and anticipation, this memory restores the apparently missing elements and thus solves the textual riddle. Inevitably this results in the critical commentary's running parallel to, and at times interacting with, the text that is being analyzed. The commentary thus puts itself forward as the necessary context for calling up a body of external quotations. An intertext is formed through a series of borrowings that are transferred from this body of quotations to the work under study. Although similar in kind to the intratext that is produced by the work's own connected parts, the intertext depends on the commentary for its own existence. In the end, work, commentary, and intertext all fuse into

6. See Jean-Jacques Thomas, "The Paraphernal Pragmatics," *PTL* 4 (1979): 179–83; "Pragmatique et socio-texte," in *Sociocritique* (Paris: Nathan, 1979), 45–50; "Metasemantics," *Dispositio: Revista Hispánica de Semiotica Literaria* 4, no. 10 (1980): 140–66; and Steven Winspur, "Text Acts: Recasting Performatives with Wittgenstein and Derrida," in Reed Way Dasenbrock, ed., *Redrawing the Lines: Analytic Philosophy, Deconstruction, and Literary Theory* (Minneapolis: University of Minnesota Press, 1989), 169–88.

a unified discourse, and the endorsement of the commentary as an inter-
textual generator comes about when we consider, in the words of Michel
Charles, that the "[particular] text [studied] is a combination of earlier,
or contemporary, works; in other words, the text is a particular mounting
of quotations."[7]

When confronted by extremely hermetic literary works, one could
attempt an intertextual type of analysis based on the restrictions that are
internal to the stock of quotations within the reader's linguistic com-
petence. These quotations would help the reader restore the legibi-
lity of statements that are scrambled, overly dense, or lack overall direc-
tion.

To illustrate and refine this approach we start by examining some
possible linguistic transformations of Jacob's title, "Le Coq et la Perle"
(The rooster and the pearl). Here we have an elementary accumulative
structure, closed off by the conjunction *et* (and). The reader's memorial
competence immediately brings forth another verbal sequence starting
with *le coq et*—namely, *le coq et l'âne* (which translates literally as "the
rooster and the donkey"). This sequence then lends itself to various com-
binations (*le coq et l'âne, le coq à l'âne, le coq en l'âne*), depending on the
propositions in which it figures—*mêler/mélanger le coq et l'âne* (to mix
apples and oranges), *passer/sauter du coq à l'âne, saillir du coq en l'âne*
(to make a string of nonsense)—not to mention Desnos and Sollers's
easy paraphonic *coq à l'âme* variations (which one could render as "soul-
nonsense" in English). Inevitably this fixed expression brings along with
it the kind of semantic dissonance that it denotes. To do a *coq à l'âne*
means to skip from one topic of conversation to another without there
being any apparent link between them. French dictionaries call this prac-
tice a *cocasserie* (comical turn), the etymology of this word underscoring
the term *coq* that lies within the initial expression. This meaning actually
reiterates one of the dictionary definitions of *perle* (pearl) as an absurd,
and often hilarious, joining of two unrelated propositions. Without exag-
geration we can say that the sequence "Le Coq et la Perle" has a mimetic
relation to the word *perle*, since the very appearance of the word *coq* leads
our memorial competence to anticipate the word *âne*, whereas in fact it is
the partial synonym *perle* that takes over.

Such quotational competence is of equal importance for an overall
reading of the statement "Le Coq et la Perle," since this borrows from

7. Michel Charles, "La Lecture critique," *Poétique* 34 (1978): 129–51.

one of the titles in La Fontaine's *Fables.* Nothing inside Jacob's text points us toward such an intratextual reference, except for a vague thematic similarity in the bestiary form. Instead, it is in what Derrida calls the *hors-livre* or what is often referred to nowadays as the "paratext" (namely, a work's preface), that this extratextual link is endorsed. For in his 1943 preface Max Jacob gives the following sequence of events that led to his publishing "Le Coq et la Perle":

> Why don't you do a sequel to the *Cornet à dés?* [...] I began the task: one day, over the phone, I announced that I had 60 pages. Come for dinner! And bring the 60 pages. They were read enthusiastically, friends were phoned to come along and join us, and with each new arrival the pages were reread. After midnight I was driven by a chauffeur to 17, rue Gabriel, my lodgings, with my arms full of flowers. The smallest piece of silver would have seen me better off [*Le moindre ducaton aurait mieux fait mon affaire*]. (Jacob 17)

It is clear that the last sentence is an unannounced borrowing from the conclusion to the second stanza of La Fontaine's fable:

> Un jour, un coq détourna
> Une perle, qu'il donna
> Au beau premier lapidaire,
> Je la crois fine, dit-il;
> Mais le moindre grain de mil
> Serait bien mieux mon affaire.
>
> Un ignorant hérita
> D'un manuscrit qu'il porta
> Chez son voisin le libraire.
> Je crois, dit-il, qu'il est bon
> Mais le moindre ducaton
> Serait bien mieux mon affaire.[8]
>
> (One day a rooster uncovered
> A pearl that he gave
> To the first jewel dealer he saw.

8. La Fontaine, *Fables,* ed. A. C. M. Robert, vol. 1, bk. 20 (Paris: Etienne Cabin, 1825), 81.

"I think that it is a fine pearl," said the rooster,
"But the smallest millet seed
Would have seen me better off."

An ignoramus inherited
A manuscript that he took
To his neighbor the bookseller.
"I believe that it is good," he said,
"But the smallest piece of silver
Would have seen me better off.")

The use of the archaism *ducaton* in Max Jacob's extract only serves to underscore the intertextual link between the two works.[9] La Fontaine's fable is, moreover, a reworking of earlier texts, since A. C. M. Robert's critical edition of the *Fables* gives no less than twenty-nine transformed predecessors. If we adopt Philippe Hamon's argument in his article "Texte littéraire et métalangage," where fables are considered condensed statements, La Fontaine's "Le Coq et la Perle" would be an instance of an intertextual link within an intratextual framework. In such cases Hamon finds "a juxtaposition of two texts that mirror one another: the story itself (with animals), followed by its moral (where we recover traces of an *utterance* and of anthropomorphism). This moral serves as a paraphrase that makes a 'clear' reading of the fable possible."[10] In the case of this specific fable the large number of variants for the story is not surprising, since what La Fontaine transposes into a narrative, and what Jacob also underscores in his preface, is the nonequivalence of certain elements that are strictly complementary: a hen/a pearl (a seed of grain), an ignoramus/a manuscript (a silver coin), a penniless author/flowers (a silver coin). Both the fable and Jacob's borrowing exemplify a stringing together of verbal units from unrelated fields, which, by the same token, underscores a continuous development of unrelated parts.

As a title, Max Jacob's expression *le coq et la perle* consequently has a very rigorous significance, once its inner workings are restored via our memorial competence. At all the relevant levels—syntactic, lexical, and

9. The link is made even stronger by the fact that in his preface Jacob mentions his *émeraude* (emerald), which leads directly to the other title commonly used for this fable by La Fontaine: "Du coc et de l'Esmeraude" (*Ysopet* I). The term *émeraude* introduces the seme of "crafted artifact," which is absent in *perle*.

10. Philippe Hamon, "Texte littéraire et métalangage," *Poétique* 31 (1977): 261–84.

narrative—what becomes apparent is a structure that privileges incompatibility or discordance. When read along with the text beneath it, Jacob's title plays out its role as an emblem, since it both justifies and explains the body of diverse fragments that make up the work, and that one has to call a verbal jumble.

Before reading one of these fragments in detail, it is useful to define more clearly what we mean by a reader's memorial competence.[11] This expression might appear to be a tautology since competence is always a matter of memory, and in a linguistic sense, competence is always collective. It is a memory written into the system of a language, and hence a finite yet intangible body of rules. By definition, then, this competence cannot take on diverse forms, or be individually transformed. However, our use of the expression memorial competence is meant to designate another, yet related, type of memory. It is a set of specific discursive presuppositions that have been learned and that a reader can reactivate when trying to interpret a text (as long as these presuppositions seem warranted by words within the text in question). For instance, in the example above, the verbal sequence *le coq (et)* engaged a specific type of competence concerning syntax (namely, the presence of a pairing) and quotability (*le coq et l'âne*). It would appear that there is no structural distinction between the triggering off of linguistic competence and that of memorial competence, since both are copresent when a verbal sequence is read. The difference between the two is purely functional: whereas linguistic competence is necessary for any statement to be understood, memorial competence is optional. The separate functions of a primary pseudolinguistic system and a secondary framing system that groups together the literary, cultural, and intertextual aspects of a work, should not hide the fact that linguistic units are already culturally determined (as we demonstrate in Chapter 6). This presents no problem for a theory that respects the copresence of both linguistic and memorial competence. Thus, in French, a cultural difference is already embedded in the semantic system of *pot* and *vase:* however, a reader may remember that *pot* is the word used in the title of the famous fable by La Fontaine, "Le Pot de fer et le pot de terre." Once the two types of competence are conjoined, then their constant interaction, and indeed a type of reciprocal control, go without saying.

11. On the issue of memory and reading, see Michel Charles's article "Bibliothèques," *Poétique* 33 (1978): 1–27.

When interpreting poetry it is perhaps indicative of the importance we should attach to a reader's memorial capabilities that Michel Leiris calls one of his texts *Mots sans Mémoire* (Words without memory). It is in this work that Leiris tries to create highly personal linguistic sequences, where a certain "original innocence" is restored to words that the poet is attempting to rescue from an oppressive memorial competence.

Let us now apply these insights into the nature of a poeticized language to a specific work, and see if they help us resolve the textual complication that Jacob's saying initially evoked:

L'enfant, l'éfant, l'éléphant, la grenouille et la pomme sautée.

(The infant, the ifant, the elephant, the frog and the sautéed potato.)

From a simple descriptive standpoint, this sequence has both a morphological balance and a syntagmatic and denotative imbalance. The latter is caused by the anomalous last entry: "pomme sautée." Morphologically speaking, the masculine and feminine nouns are both in their own groupings. From a syntagmatic standpoint, as is the rule for any list, the last element in the sequence is introduced by the conjunction *et,* but, unlike the other terms, *pomme* is made more specific by a past participle functioning as an adjective, which leaves intact the core of its verbal force. On a denotative level, whether one approaches the basic semes or the secondary ones, *pomme* is an anomaly in the sequence. *Enfant, éfant, éléphant,* and *grenouille* are all marked by the seme [+ animality], whereas *pomme* lacks this seme. And yet it is also accompanied by *sautée,* a word that usually requires an animated subject. We can see, then, how this anomaly follows the kind of perturbations that were revealed by an intertextual analysis of the title "Le Coq et la Perle," since there too a scanning of the basic semantic components revealed the opposition between [+ animate] and [− animate].

We have not yet mentioned the phonological component since it is identical to the text's prosodic structure, and since the latter clearly has a determining role in the development of the verbal sequence in question. If the text is separated into metrical units, it conforms to the classical model of gradual enlargement, since there is the following succession of units: 2, 2, 3, 4, 4—namely, lã/fã, le/fã, le/le/fã, la/grə/nuj/jə, la/pɔm/so/te. This phonetic regularity is reinforced by the play of assonances in the sequence: fã/fã/fã/e/e. The metrical pattern here is far from complex since it is based on a simple arithmetic progression: 2, 3, 4. It is this progression that associates the text, through an intertextual borrowing, to popular songs, slogans, and more particularly, to children's rhymes. We find among this rhythmical grouping such examples as "Meunier, tu dors," the famous nursery rhyme, as well as various slogans that are built on the same model: for instance, the feminist catchphrase *Bo/lo/fa/cho—/les/sor/cières/ /au/ront/ta/peau.*[12]

The connection to children's rhymes is even stronger in the case of Jacob's statement since the latter not only shares with such rhymes a metrical structure, but also a common lexical field, in which "child," "elephant," "frog," and "apple" (*pomme*) recur frequently. We should not forget, moreover, that numerical rhymes that are used to usher commands or to name people in a certain way carry the colloquial, and much more quaint, title of "Pommes aux nombres" (Apples with numbers). Philippe Soupault's collection of French rhymes includes the following example, which has strong lexical and metrical links to Jacob's short text:

> Pomme bleue
> Pomme rouge
> Pomme d'acier
> Et pomme dorée
> alors, sortez![13]

> (Blue apple
> Red apple
> Apple of steel
> And golden apple
> so then leave!)

The final command "sortez!" is but one variant among a combination of other verbs that have the same syntactic form: *cherchez* (seek), *restez* (stay), *venez* (come), and of course *sautez* (jump). Since there is no phonetic difference in French between the *é* of the past participle and the *ez* of the imperative (both are transcribed as [e]), Max Jacob's sequence can

12. Quoted by Louis-Jean Calvet, *La Production révolutionnaire* (Paris: Payot, 1976), 85.

13. Philippe Soupault et al., *Comptines de la langue française* (Paris: Seghers, 1961).

thus be read as a type of rhyming game, which, according to Saussure's *Anagrammes,* is the guardian principle of all poetic language. From this angle we can explain the previously mentioned anomaly that occurs in the word *sautée,* placed after *pomme.* According to the genre's ludic form, after a list there should be an order—*sautez!* (jump).

Even if this intertextual reading of Jacob's text does not yet allow us to assign a meaning to the text, it does allow us to assign it a function—namely, that of a numerically formulaic sequence. This fact apparently underscores the sort of critical approach that is based on historical and biographical data (and that Michel Charles claims to be entrenched in the "realist's alibi"), since it is true that Jacob began his literary career by collecting popular rhymes and songs,[14] whose inspiration can still be traced in his books on his alter-ego, *Saint-Matorel.*[15] Nevertheless, up until now we have still not answered Todorov's claim that certain literary works lie beyond all possible attempts at explication, since no rule has been found to justify Jacob's replacing an imperative with a past participle *(sautée).* In order to tackle this problem we need to explore in more detail the memorial competence that lies at the root of the intertextual commentary we have just given.

We have already stated that on a linguistic level Jacob's short sequence can be considered a *synthème.* Generally speaking, synthemes result from either a condensing or an expanding of a statement's syntax, which leads to the suppression of a verb or of another grammatical element that is necessary for the meaning to be clear. Translated into rhetorical terms, a syntheme is an example of understatement, such as ellipsis, synthesis, zeugma, or anacoluthon. Such constructions are occasionally produced within the field of language itself, because of the tendency toward economy of expression. Such is the case, for instance, of words in apposition. If one were to write, "Fontanier, professor of literature in the Royal Colleges," one would be suppressing the verb *to be,* which in this case would simply be an implied syntactic copula. This meaning could be restored, however, and such a restoration would be governed by a linguistic semantics. The latter term is borrowed from Herbert Brekle, who distinguishes between a linguistic and a logical semantics—a distinction

---

14. Max Jacob, *Le Roi Kabil 1er et le marmiton Gauwain* (Paris: Picard & Kahn, 1904); *Le Géant du soleil* (Paris: Librairie Générale, 1904); *Saint-Matorel* (Paris: Kahnweiler, 1911); *La Côte: Chants bretons* (Paris: Chez l'auteur, 1911).

15. On Saint-Matorel, see Jean-Jacques Thomas, "Autel Matorel," in *Max à la Convergence* (Paris: Seuil, 1996).

of prime importance for an understanding of intertextuality.[16] As Brekle points out, linguistic semantics allows us to envisage cases of "chance semantic occurrences," where intertextuality can in fact come into play as a form of commentary.

Take, for example, the case of the following appositive synthemes:

Fontanier, the author of the *Figures of Discourse*
Fontanier, professor of literature
Fontanier, a man

Linguistic semantics allows us to restore the verb *to be* in each case. And yet this restoration does not come without a certain ambiguity, as we can see from a translation of the three propositions into their logical semantic form:

Fontanier *is* the author of the *Figures of Discourse*. (a relation of identity: $x = y$)
Fontanier *is* a professor of literature. (a relation of attributes: $x \in A$)
Fontanier *is* a man. (a relation of inclusion: $x \subset B$)

It is clear from this example that such formal operations within logical semantics exclude the possibility of redundancy, expansion, or condensation, and that they reduce every statement to a universal logic that lies outside the linguistic domain, strictly speaking, and outside the realm of textual (and hence intertextual) issues.

From the standpoint of semantic linguistics, then, our analysis of Max Jacob's extract rests on coreferences, or anticipatory and retroactive corepresentations that are much more diversified than any simple reduction to a single semantic unit. This underscores the fact that the elements within this intertextual field are linked by specific connections that the reader has to restore, rather than by juxtapositions that are simply due to chance.

L'ENFANT—L'ÉFANT

This grouping is justified from a phonological standpoint given the fact that it is what phonologists call a minimal pair: ãfã/efã. From a rhe-

16. Herbert E. Brekle, *Sémantique* (Paris: Armand Colin, 1974).

torical standpoint we are also dealing with an antanaclasis since there are two words with the same meaning and a similar sound. *Efant* is in fact a variant of *enfant* that Louis-Ferdinand Flûtre has traced in dialects from Picardy, Normandy, and Brittany. According to Flûtre, "[ã] often loses its nasal component to become [e] when concealed by a following nasalized syllable, as in *enfant—éfant,* or *Benjamin—Béjamin.*"[17] This fact would surely not be lost on certain biographical critics, as one presenter of the *Cornet à dés* points out, since it underlines Jacob's Breton roots and heritage.

Michel Leiris underscores the effect of this same word, *éfant,* when he sees in it the sign of a colloquial, if not familial, way of speaking.

> For example, when my father would call us, my brother and me, the "*éfants*" instead of the "*enfants,*" these were deliberate attacks against language, or word-games whose goal was [...] our own recognition as members of the same family.[18]

L'ENFANT—L'ÉFANT—L'ÉLÉPHANT

There is also a direct phonological association between [efã] and [elefã]. It is a minimal pair through syllabification, and classical rhetoric would classify it as an instance of paronomasia (a closeness in sounds but distance in meaning). The richness of the sound repetition brings this group of three terms very close to the two most often quoted sequences from Jacob's book: "Dahlia! dahlia! que Dalila lia / Cornet à dés: ADDE" (Dahlia! dahlia! that Delilah linked / Dice cup: ADDE). But the phonological coupling in *enfant—éfant—éléphant* is overdetermined by a double semic opposition of a metasemantic type. First *enfant* stands for youth and *éléphant* stands for old age, as is proven by the body of poetic references in French: "Ces éléphants gercés comme une vieille écorce" (Those elephants, cracked like an old bark), or "son corps / Est gercé comme un tronc que le temps ronge et mine" (his body / is cracked like a tree trunk that time is eating away and hollowing out).[19] By extension,

---

17. Louis-Ferdinand Flûtre, *Du moyen Picard au Picard moderne* (Amiens: Université de Picardie, 1977), 37.

18. Michel Leiris, *Biffures* (Paris: Gallimard, 1948), 189.

19. Leconte de Lisle, "La Forêt vierge" and "Les Eléphants" in *Poèmes barbares* (Paris: Lemerre, 1927). Even the sequence by Baudelaire in "Le Serpent qui danse" (The

the notion of age leads to that of everlastingness, whereas that of youth overlaps that of newness and all the associations linked to the latter word. We find this opposition between the freshness of youth and its everlasting surroundings in Mary Summer's *Tales and Legends from Ancient India*, specifically in her story "The Living Corpse" (which is transposed in Mallarmé's "Les Contes indiens"), where an "ivory bed" accentuates the beauty of the sleeping prince Chandra-Raja. The same contrast occurs in Leconte de Lisle's poem "Parfum d'Adonis": "Sur la couche d'ivoire où nous te contemplons / Eveille-toi toujours, Ephèbe aux cheveux blonds" (On the ivory bed where we gaze at you / Always wake up, ephebe with the blond hair). The connection between "ivory" and "elephant" is doubly justified to the extent that each is derived from the other via synecdoche, and lexically via etymology: "Elephant: [...] more popular form that also has the meaning of ivory (as in Latin and Greek)."[20]

A second semantic conversion introduces another binary link between *enfant* and *éléphant* based on the opposition between strength and weakness. Several literary extracts develop the matrix sentence "The elephant scares the child," as one can see from the following examples:

Et les éléphants font peur aux enfants

(And the elephants frighten the children)

Il fait peur aux petits enfants.
Qu'est-ce que c'est, c'est l'éléphant.

(It makes the small children scared.
What is it, it's the elephant.)

Serait-ce ce grand corps qui fait peur aux enfants?[21]

(Could it be this big body that scares the children?)

---

dancing snake)—"Sous le fardeau de ta paresse / Ta tête d'enfant / Se balance avec la molesse / D'un jeune éléphant" (Under the burden of your idleness / Your child head / Sways with the slowness / Of a young elephant)—confirms *a contrario* this semantic association since it has to introduce the notion of "jeune éléphant" in order to build the similarity between the child and the elephant.

20. O. Bloch and W. von Wartburg, *Dictionnaire étymologique de la langue française* (Paris: Presses Universitaires de France, 1960), 124.

21. Paul Fort, "Le Cirque," in *Ballades françaises,* vol. 2 (Paris: Flammarion, 1935); Georges Duhamel, *Voix du vieux monde* (Paris: Huegel, n.d.); La Fontaine, "Le Rat et l'éléphant," in *Fables* 8:15.

As is the case with all binary semantic oppositions, the two poles can be switched, so that *éléphant* becomes *enfant* when the seme [+ strength] is negated. In his poem "La Forêt vierge," for example, where he imagines the "destructive" toil of "man with the pale face," Leconte de Lisle turns the elephants that he had previously presented as "breaking the thickets which crumble under their force" into children:

> (...) tes plus forts enfants fuiront épouvantés
> Devant ce vermisseau plus frêle que tes herbes

> ([...] your strongest children will flee in terror
> From this earthworm that is more fragile than your grass)

In the same vein Pierre Ménanteau can write:

> Coltiner des fardeaux
> même déraciner les arbres les plus gros
> ce sont là jeux d'enfant pour l'éléphant.[22]

> (Carrying heavy loads
> or even uprooting the biggest of trees
> that's just child's play for the elephant.)

L'ÉLÉPHANT—LA GRENOUILLE

From an etymological point of view the connection between *éléphant* and *grenouille* (frog) is well established. It is a lexical derivation stemming from the original pronunciation for *éléphant,* "oliphant," which also took on the meaning of "ivory horn" by synecdoche (Bloch and von Wartburg 214). The sound made by the horn is a *graillement* (hoarse bellow), and it is from this type of sound that *grenouille* gets its initial *g*. Here is Bloch and von Wartburg's explanation: "Grenouille: an alteration from the older *re(i)no(u)ille,* from the popular Latin **ranuncula* [...], with a *g* that is probably due to the influence of certain words that imitate the cry of certain animals or the sound of a horn (hence the French *grailler*)" (297, 300).

---

22. Pierre Ménanteau, *Bestiaire pour un enfant poète* (Paris: Seghers, 1958). Incidentally, this book won the Prix Max Jacob for 1958.

This original etymological joining of elephant and frog in the same type of cry explains why in nineteenth-century French *éléphant* and *grenouille* were combinative variants in the expression "Pas piqué des grenouilles (des éléphants)" (the tapping steps of frogs [elephants]). This expression designated a style of oratory that was full of emphases and marked by an aggressive and occasionally overworked delivery.

LA GRENOUILLE—LA POMME

Here again, the semantic link between the terms, which is based on a derivation, becomes clear once we pass through the intermediary word *rainette* (tree frog or pippin apple):

> *Rainette:* 1425, "bush frog." Derived from Old French *raine*. [...]
> As the name of a variety of apple [...] also called *pomme de reinette,*
> from the sixteenth century (Paré), that the Littré dictionary still
> lists, it seems to be a figurative use of the *rainette* frog, since the
> spotted skin of this variety of apple resembles that of the frog.
> (Bloch and von Wartburg 524)

This lexical attraction is so strong that in two instances where modern writers have let language follow its own logic, as it were, the terms *pomme* and *grenouille* have generated each other.

First, Jean-Pierre Brisset, armed with his Science of God and his panglossary (which we should perhaps call his monster glossary), uses this lexical link to demonstrate how our "ancestors" were nourished:

> *J'ai un l'eau, je mans* [I have a the water, I ea(t)], which became
> *j'ai un logement* [I have a home], shows us that the first home was
> in water and that people ate there. *L'eau j'ai,* our ancestors were
> lodged (*loge*); *l'auge j'ai* = I have my *auge* (pig trough). The first
> trough was a pond (*mare à boue* [mud pond] or *marabout* [Moslem saint]), which became the first site for worship. *A l'eau berge*
> (at the water bank; also, at the inn [*à l'auberge*]), on the bank of
> the waters; *dans les eaux t'es* (in the waters you are) = *dans les
> hôtels* (in the hotels). [...] Consequently, our ancestors lived in the
> waters, ponds, and marshes. Since *grenouille* and *reinette* are but
> one and the same (*reinette:* little queen of the water banks) it has to

be (*il faut* = *il f'eau* = *il f'aux* = [I am lying]: such is the subtlety
of the lying ancestor: when he wanted to pounce on his victim, he
pretended to eat a tree-frog—*reinette*—which gave him confi-
dence) that *grenouille* and *pomme* come together in a sauce: *en
sauce y étaient* (in sauce were they), they were in society (*en société*)
[...]. The two fishermen wanted it that way, the big men (*les gros-
nouille*) used to eat the small ones (*reinette*) and good folks con-
tinue to celebrate this fact: "pomme de reinette et pomme d'api"
(pippin apple and lady apple). *Api*, just like a *grenouille tapie* (a frog
hiding) in the waters and waiting for its victim.[23]

The second example comes from Raymond Roussel's *Les Impressions
d'Afrique,* which Laurent Jenny has called a "potpourri of literary cul-
ture."[24] In the following brief passage we find *pomme* and *rainette* placed
almost side by side:

> —pour un jonc chic à pomme,
> la canne en l'air sautant; pour
> l'échelle où s'assomme
> la rainette à bocal.

> (—for a bulrush, smart for apples,
> with the stick jumping in the air; for
> the ladder where the frog
> under a glass bowl is beaten.)

Here *rainette* has to be understood as the semantic equivalent of *gre-
nouille,* as is suggested by the related terms *échelle* and *bocal.* We can
nevertheless retrace the semantic overdeterminations that lead to the ap-
pearance of *rainette* rather than *grenouille. Jonc* (bulrush) establishes the
transition from an initial thematic context (of canes and wands), while at
the same time introducing the implied meaning of frog, since one of the
standard literary periphrases for this animal is "the bulrush People" (La
Fontaine). Moreover, the word *pomme,* which modifies *jonc* in the cliché
and catachresis "jonc à pomme" (branch with fruit), brings the seme of

23. Jean-Pierre Brisset, "Où a commencé la vie des ancêtres," in *La Science de Dieu
(La Grammaire logique* [Paris: Tchou, 1970]).
24. Laurent Jenny, "Structure et fonction du cliché," *Poétique* 12 (1972): 511.

fruit into the statement, and *pomme* becomes *pommelé*, which generates the hybrid word *rainette*, in both its animal and fruit usage.

In the same extract one also finds the verb *sauter* (to jump). This is not surprising since just as *coq* generated *l'âne*, the intertextual presuppositions of frog include jumping. In most of the standard traditional French grammar books that offer literary examples as illustrations for cases of grammar, the example of the infinitive construction in French is a borrowing from La Fontaine's "Le Lièvre et les grenouilles" (*Fables* 1:36): "Grenouilles aussitôt de sauter dans les ondes" (The frogs immediately jumped into the waves). This results in a particular cultural linking of *la grenouille* and *le saut*, which turns the former into a verbal trigger for the latter.

POMME SAUTÉE

In general, cookbooks give at least five ways of preparing sautéed potatoes: "with savory herbs, with goose oil, with lard, in the Lyonnaise or the Provençal style."[25] It is not, however, the only segment of coded discourse that uses *pomme* as its lexical core, since one could also cite the case of *pomme-vapeur* (boiled potato). In the present case the adjective *sautée* is justified, as mentioned above, since the probability of its occurrence is relatively high after the word *grenouille*. Here again, because it makes sense in two lexical groups (jumping frogs and sautéed potatoes), *sautée* is the adjective that appears rather than any other one. What we have, then, is the systematic buildup within Jacob's extract of a sequence of linguistic semantics.

What separates *la grenouille et la pomme sautée* from a sequence such as *le cheval et la pomme vapeur* (which repeats the same logical structure in the final term) is the fact that the recovery of implied semes that is triggered off by the nouns in Jacob's extract is more dense than in the second example. One should also add that the morphological forms are different in both examples, so that the second one has less cohesiveness than Jacob's extract.

If we now return to this extract as a whole, it would seem correct to conclude that what dictates the appearance of the first three terms is a structure that is openly governed by a play on assonance. Metric and

25. See, for example, Raymond Oliver, *La Cuisine* (Paris: Bordas, 1967).

semantic rules nevertheless introduce constraints that reinforce the poetic consistency of the sequence and set the stage for the predominance of semantic constraints in the second half of the extract. These constraints turn the term *sautée* from being apparently the most unexpected word in the text to being, in fact, the most overdetermined one, since the extract ends with a grammatically fixed expression: *pomme sautée*. That explains why the verb *sauter* takes on the form of a past participle rather than an imperative, while its seemingly fortuitous appearance at the end of the list of nouns is actually predetermined on a functional level, as was shown earlier, by the form of rhyming game that Jacob's text imitates.

Our intertextual wanderings have allowed us to "explicate" Max Jacob's statement. What the author has demonstrated in this short maxim, as he does in several others, is that, quite unlike the surprising verbal mixture that apparently comes about whenever the dice of words are cast, there is a rigid framework that determines the creation of new meanings. The clash of incongruous terms, which sends off echoes from the tentative commentaries that every reader begins to lay out, confirms that even the most surprising linkages are probable, and always capable of being rewritten.

It is no doubt possible to have some reservations about the fact that this intertextual metalanguage is but a form of critical discourse that is mimetically parallel to the object that it studies. Moreover, it seems to ignore the issue of which interpretation is verifiable, and instead belies a mere fascination with literary phenomena. And yet our goal was to demonstrate that when commenting on particularly dense (or opaque) poeticized texts the phenomenon of undecidability forces the reader to build supplementary frameworks for meaning, and that these frameworks are nothing but the intertextual web that supports the text in question. Can we generalize this approach and offer it as a model for commentaries of more readable and clearly directed poems? We are unable to answer this question, but we do believe that a de facto exclusion of these issues, and their relegation to the realms of either fiction or scriptural derivation, hinder any attempt at giving them a sound theoretical basis. Fortunately, the language of poetry and the joys that it conveys are there to remind us that the recovery of linguistic intertexts through literary analysis is perhaps not merely a secondary bonus that comes from critical study, but in fact the essence of such study.

five

THE THING-IN-ITSELF

(DEGUY,

BONNEFOY,

SAINT-JOHN PERSE,

PONGE)

Modern poetry is an objective poetry.

—*Roland Barthes,* Le Degré zéro de l'écriture

This remark by Barthes echoes one of the dominant critical common-places concerning French poetry since World War II. Sartre had put it in the following way: "in one fell stroke the poet has discarded the concept of language as a tool; he has chosen once and for all the poetic attitude that views words as things and not as signs."[1] Coming from the author of *Being and Nothingness,* this statement is perhaps not surprising. The world of signs for Sartre is of less interest than the phenomenological world that reveals humankind's ever-changing links to being. Yet when we find the antisign doctrine of the thing-in-itself occurring in a pioneering semiotic study, the paradox becomes evident. In *Mythologies,* Barthes notes that modern poetry "attempts to recapture an infrasignification, a presemiological state of language" and that it tries to reach "a sort of

---

1. Jean-Paul Sartre, *Qu'est-ce que la littérature?* (1948; reprint, Paris: Gallimard, Idées, 1976), 18.

transcendent quality of things."[2] Now if the central message of *Myth-ologies* is that every aspect of cultural life (including literature) is orga-nized as a sign system, then it is an obvious contradiction for Barthes to claim that modern poems operate at the "*pre*semiological" level of "the thing itself" (220).

It would appear that Barthes is momentarily won over by the pro-fessed aim of such poets as Char and Bonnefoy, which is to reach a realm beyond any system of semiotic convention. He is not alone in this respect since we find Jean-Pierre Richard also insisting in his study of postwar French poetry that the poets discussed "have been grasped at the level of an original contact with things."[3] How can one account for "poetry's commitment to concreteness," as Susan Sontag has called it, from *within* a semiotic theory?[4]

If one were unable to do so, the very axiom of semiotics that con-cerns the omnipresence of signs in culture would have to be revised in order to allow for certain exceptions. One would also have to allow the validity of Barthes's paradoxical proposition that "objective" poetry such as Char's puts itself forward as an "anti-language" (*Mythologies* 220). It is clear, however, that whatever else poems may be, they are first and fore-most linguistic entities. The problem to be solved is therefore: how does the poem's linguistic structure create the appearance of being its exact opposite—an ideal, or Kantian, object that is uncontaminated by lan-guage?

In order to analyze some of the linguistic mechanisms that produce this illusion of the thing-in-itself, we turn to the work of four poets—Saint-John Perse, Francis Ponge, Yves Bonnefoy, and Michel Deguy. We believe, however, that the principles underlying these poems are to be found in many other works (and not only French) that are commonly grouped under such headings as objective poetry. For instance, William Carlos Williams's credo "No truth but in things" and Wallace Stevens's poem "Man on the Dump" reveal a similar preoccupation with poetic thingness in the American tradition.

In his poem *Vents* (Winds) Saint-John Perse characterizes the poet as one who deals in "non point l'écrit, mais la chose même. Prise en son vif et dans son tout" (not writing, but the thing itself. Grasped in all its

---

2. Roland Barthes, *Mythologies* (1957; reprint, Paris: Seuil, Points, 1970), 220.
3. Jean-Pierre Richard, *Onze études sur la poésie moderne* (Paris: Seuil, 1964), 7.
4. Susan Sontag, *On Photography* (New York: Farrar, Strauss, and Giroux, 1977), 96.

life and wholeness).[5] The opening line of Yves Bonnefoy's first poem, *Anti-Platon,* also proclaims this return to things: "Il s'agit bien de *cet* objet" (It's all about *this* object).[6] Moreover, in a later essay, Bonnefoy considers this return to be symptomatic of much of modern poetry. Concerning poets since Baudelaire and Rimbaud, he writes: "They have [...] re-created the few elementary gestures that unite us with things."[7] Michel Deguy's preoccupation with this question is clear from the moment when he asks rhetorically in *Actes* (Acts), "How can things be made to talk about themselves?"[8] From Francis Ponge's declaration (which reverses Paul Valéry's famous first sentence in *Monsieur Teste*), "Les idées ne sont pas mon fort. (...) Les objets du monde extérieur au contraire me ravissent" (Ideas are not my strong point. [...] By contrast, the objects of the external world enchant me"),[9] one can judge the vital importance of thingness in his writings too.

In the analysis that follows we concentrate on three aspects of the poetic code of the thing-in-itself: (1) the thing-in-itself described as an ideal poem that cannot be written, (2) the possibility of reaching essential thingness through a theory of naming, and (3) the link between things-in-themselves and the myth of a fictional origin to language.

UNTRACEABLE POEMS

One of the poems from Michel Deguy's collection *Ouï dire* (Hearsay) ends with the following lines:

> Toutes les trois heures un poème
> Devient nouveau puis se ternit
> Sous la lecture Recroît dans le silence[10]

> (Every three hours a poem
> Becomes new then is tarnished
> In the act of reading Rises up again in silence)

5. Saint-John Perse, *Oeuvres complètes* (Paris: Gallimard, Pléiade, 1972), 229.
6. Yves Bonnefoy, *Poèmes* (Paris: Mercure de France, 1978), 11.
7. Yves Bonnefoy, "L'Acte et le lieu de la poésie," reprinted in *Du mouvement et de l'immobilité de Douve* (Paris: Gallimard, Poésie, 1978), 200–201.
8. Michel Deguy, *Actes* (Paris: Gallimard, 1966), 174.
9. Francis Ponge, *Méthodes* (1961; reprint, Paris: Gallimard, Idées, 1974), 25.
10. Deguy, *Ouï dire* (Paris: Gallimard, 1966), 42.

Here a special sort of poem is described since it exists not so much when it is read (reading in fact tarnishes it), but when it is left in silence. Rather than come to life as a text—whose existence depends solely on the act of reading—it exists only when the text ceases to be.[11] Deguy is therefore referring to a poem that is not a written text. Yet how can there be such a self-contradictory entity? There cannot, but the illusion that there is, is what concerns us here.

A poem not trapped in a text is also the dream of the narrator in Saint-John Perse's *Exil*. At the end of the fourth canto of that poem we find the following statement: "me composant un pur langage sans office, / Voici que j'ai dessein encore d'un grand poème délébile (composing for myself a pure language without any function, / The idea still comes to me to write a great delible poem; *Oeuvres complètes* 129). Writing presupposes the creation of a durable inscription or monument—a text that by definition must survive the moment of its tracing. In other words, writing puts in place a system of indelible marks that, although empirically erasable (since texts may be destroyed), are logically required to last. This is because if meaning is to be conveyed at all, there must always be a text surviving indefinitely and independently of its author, in the form of a monument that awaits a potential reader. Yet it is this a priori indelibility of the text, excluded by Perse's ideal "great delible poem," that would appear to be an inscription capable of erasing itself the very moment it is written. The strangeness of such a poem is underscored by the usage of the rare adjective *délébile* whose meaning rests squarely on its more common contrary term *indélébile*.

The reason for such a hankering after impossible poems becomes clear in the light of a quotation from Yves Bonnefoy's *Du mouvement et de l'immobilité de Douve*:

> Présence exacte qu'aucune flamme désormais ne saurait restreindre; convoyeuse du froid secret; vivante de ce sang qui renaît et s'accroît où se déchire le poème. (40)

> (Exact presence that henceforth no flame could hold back; purveyor of the cold secret; alive with that blood that is born again and is growing where the poem is torn apart.)

---

11. Recent commentators of Deguy's poems still accept the illusion of an ontological realm beyond the space of language. See, for instance, Michel Collot's "Une Phénoménologie de l'espace poétique: Deguy et Merleau-Ponty," *Le Poète que je cherche à être: Cahier Michel Deguy*, ed. Yves Charnet (Paris: La Table Ronde/Belin, 1998), 62–72.

What is this presence that tears the poem apart? In an essay titled "Les Tombeaux de Ravenne" (The tombstones at Ravenna) Bonnefoy offers an answer. "The palpable object is presence," he writes, and he goes on to give the example of a torn ivy leaf, as opposed to the purely intellectual concept or sign *leaf of ivy.* "This torn leaf, green, black and soiled, this leaf that through its wound reveals all the depth of what exists, this infinite leaf is pure presence," he affirms, "and is, consequently, my salvation."[12] Rephrasing this point in a less poetic manner we can say that presence is the leaf as a specific object as opposed to the conceptual word *leaf* that could be applied to any number of referents. Presence is the object uncontaminated by language or, in other words, the thing-in-itself. This is why presence can be reached only when a poem is "torn apart," as Bonnefoy's text states, since it is only beyond the written text, where words come to an end, that the thing-in-itself can be made to appear.

Perse's delible text, Deguy's silent one, and Bonnefoy's writing that is torn apart are therefore all versions of the same ideal poem that exists in the absolute silence or fictional limit of language—the ideal point where words can cease and things can appear as they really are. The question, of course, arises: Can such a poetry really be classified as objective poetry, since what Deguy, Perse, and Bonnefoy are writing is not poems that show us things, but rather texts *about* utopian poems that would ideally reveal things? It is our contention, however, that such indirectness is inevitable since no poem can reveal things directly. A poem is always a verbal entity and never presents its reader with a referent; it can only replace the referent. Consequently, thingness can only be an illusion whereby the text strategically leads its reader to believe that its periphrastic substitute for the referent is not a substitute at all but the real thing.

Such an effect is created by Francis Ponge's short prose text from *Proêmes* (Proems) titled "De la modification des choses par la parole" (Concerning the modification of things by speech). The prose poem is built on a comparison whereby cold air is to a wave of water what words are to things:

> Le froid (...) entre à l'onde, à quoi la glace se subroge.(...)
>   Cela est le résultat d'une attente, du calme (...) en un mot, une modification.

12. Bonnefoy, "Les Tombeaux de Ravenne," in *Du mouvement et de l'immobilité de Douve,* 35–36.

A une, de même, onde, (...) peut entrer ce qui occasionne sa modification: la parole.

La parole serait donc aux choses de l'esprit leur état de rigueur.[13]

(Cold [...] enters the wave, for which ice becomes the substitute. [...]

This is the result of a period of waiting, of calm [...] in a word, a modification.

To one, similar, wave, [...] can enter what brings about its modification: speech.

Speech would therefore be for the things of the mind their indispensable state.)

Here the figure of comparison (which is a blatantly linguistic one, since it is through verbal associations that any x can be compared to a y) accomplishes a remarkable feat. For Ponge has used it to argue that certain uses of language (comparison included) do not merely alter connections between words, but also *modify things themselves*. How is this apparent sortie into the world of things accomplished by the linguistic mechanisms underlying Ponge's comparison? First, it is important to notice the ambiguous expression "things of the mind" in the last sentence, for it is used in the poem to designate not only things, understood as external objects, but also material upon which the mind operates (sensations, images, and so on). This subtle shift from external object to a form of perception is helped by the text's second paragraph (which was omitted in the above quotation):

De même (que l'onde) les yeux, d'un seul coup, s'accommodent à une nouvelle étendue: par un mouvement d'ensemble nommé l'attention, par quoi un nouvel objet est fixé, se prend.

(In the same way [as the wave] eyes, within a split second, adjust themselves to the sight of a new body: through a coordinated movement called attention, which allows a new object to be fixed, to take shape.)

13. Ponge, *Le Parti pris des choses, suivi de Proêmes* (Paris: Gallimard, Poésie, 1975), 122.

The form of things, according to these lines, is dependent on the physiological activities that allow a person to see them.

Although this claim is usually put forward in support of idealism (which makes the thing-in-itself secondary to the thing-as-it-appears for each observer), Ponge uses it to lend weight to his text's basic comparison: just as water changes state under the effect of cold (and eyes change when looking at different things), so things change under the effect of different words. The upshot of this comparison is, in fact, a radically materialist doctrine whereby there is no difference in nature between objects, temperatures, minds, and words; all are configurations of matter that change form whenever they touch one another.[14] By using "the wave" (*l'onde*) as his example of thingness, Ponge makes the comparison between words and objects even more convincing, since apart from its meaning as a body of water (used in the first paragraph of the text), the word also designates particles of light or sound as they are perceived by sense organs (such as the eyes in the second paragraph). Like "the things of the mind," the wave is consequently both an external object and the means by which this object is perceived. More importantly, these double meanings help Ponge redefine the thing-in-itself. Only language (and, by extension, the mind) is capable of capturing the thingness of an object, he claims, since language and the mind are made of the very same stuff as things.[15] We thus have the impression that his poem is talking about objects, when in fact it is simply drawing on the resources of comparison and semantic ambiguity.

The strategy whereby a poem in turn describes another ideal yet impossible poem is a very effective one in the case of many contemporary texts. Most readers of Perse and Bonnefoy, for instance, are taken in by this strategy of indirection, and are led to confuse the ideal poem with the text they are actually reading. The clearest example of such a mis-

14. See Ponge's comparison of *Le Parti pris des choses* to Lucretius's poetic rendition of the Epicurean theory of atomism: "Je voudrais écrire une sorte de De natura rerum (...) ce ne sont pas des poèmes que je voudrais composer; mais une seule cosmogonie" (I would like to write a sort of De rerum natura [...] it's not poems that I would like to compose; but a single cosmogony; 177).

15. "La parole est vraiment un matériau" (Speech is really matter), writes Ponge in *Comment une figue de paroles et pourquoi* (Paris: Flammarion, Digraphe, 1977), 35. It is an argument that he had developed in his poem "Notes pour un coquillage" (Notes for a shell-creature) where human speech is compared to a mollusk's secretions (*Le Parti pris des choses* 76–77). In the former book Ponge justifies his notion of the mind as a physical organism when he writes that "the mind has nothing better to do than this. To place itself in the world. To admit the existence of whatever offers it any resistance" (31).

reading occurs with Saint-John Perse's *Exil,* for most Persean scholars have considered the text itself to be "the great delible poem" of which Perse writes.[16] This is a blatant impossibility considering the logical indelibility of any text. Nevertheless, such misreadings (or rather, *correct* readings according to the strategic framework of the poem) do highlight the indirect method by which the thing-in-itself is brought into existence in poetry. Consider, for example, these lines from Perse's *Amers,* addressed to "la chose même" (the thing itself):

> Nous t'invoquons enfin toi-même, hors de la strophe du poète. Qu'il n'y ait plus pour nous entre la foule et toi, l'éclat insoutenable du langage. (*Oeuvres complètes* 378)

> (We invoke you finally as you are, outside the verse of the poet. Let there no longer be for us, between you and the crowd, the intolerable glare of language.)

The poet seems to be addressing the thing-in-itself from outside the margins of his poem, but we must remember that such an outside is a fiction, not a reality, since it only exists, like the thing-in-itself, within the space of a written text.

NAMING THINGNESS

A second component of the poetic code of the thing-in-itself is a theory of naming. As in the case of the hypothetical poem without words, a naming theory lends credence to the illusion of an outer limit to language where words cease and things appear.

Names seem to have privileged links to their referents because, unlike common nouns, they are used to particularize certain entities. It is this particularizing function that has created the myth of a proper name, according to which certain words are reserved solely for naming supposedly unique and individual referents. Such a view is a myth since no words in fact function in this way. As Saussure argued, language is not a nomenclature but a system of interrelated signs. Even so-called proper

16. See, for example, Roger Little's introduction to Perse's *Exil* (London: Athlone Press, 1973), 14; and Arthur Knodel's comments on the poem that are quoted in the notes to Perse's *Oeuvres complètes,* 1119.

names are signs, for if they were not then how could the name John Doe
have its meaning as Mr. Anybody?

The fact that language is a sign system does not create any prob-
lems concerning the designation of particular objects. We have signs that
are reserved for this task, such as demonstrative adjectives or personal and
demonstrative pronouns. Take, for example, the sentence "It's all about
this object." It is clear that even if you hear the sentence out of the blue,
with no idea what object is being referred to, you can still recognize the
sentence as a particularizing one. In other words, the utterance has
meaning independently of its referent, and so words such as *this* do not in
fact function as names. The objective poetry of Perse and Bonnefoy dis-
torts this linguistic fact, however, and gives the impression that partic-
ularizing signs such as *this, here,* or *now* are names of an unattainable
absolute—the thing-in-itself or missing referent. This impression is cre-
ated by separating such signs from their normal contextual functions so
that they appear to be pointing to an inexpressible something-or-other.

Here is the beginning of Bonnefoy's poem *Anti-Platon:*

> Il s'agit bien de *cet* objet: tête de cheval plus grande que na-
> ture où s'incruste toute une ville, ses rues et ses remparts courant
> entre les yeux, épousant le méandre et l'allongement du museau.
> (*Poèmes* 11)

> (It's all about *this* object: a horse's head larger than normal
> where a whole town has become encrusted, its streets and ramparts
> running between the eyes, following the meandering and elongated
> muzzle.)

These lines appear meaningless unless the reader, following the instruc-
tions of the opening phrase, attempts to imagine or picture its supposed
referent in all its uniqueness. Yet how does one imagine it? Its description
is apparently self-contradictory. For how can a horse's head be so large as
to encompass a whole town? Either the town is a metaphorical descrip-
tion of the lines, veins, and bumps of a horse's head, or else the head
must be a metaphorical description of a town (as seen, for example, from
a bird's eye view or on a map). Yet a metaphorical description can be
given of *any* town or horse's head, and so the text alone seems unable to
convey the specificity of the referent. The reader has to rely on the open-
ing words of the poem ("It's all about *this* object") in order to be reas-

sured that the strangeness of the subsequent description is due to the poem's attempt to evoke a unique, and hence indescribable, referent. It is the invitation to take the italicized word "*this*" as a name for the ineffable that helps create the illusion of the thing-in-itself for Bonnefoy's readers.

Taken to its extreme, as in the examples we are about to give, such a distortion of the function of particularizing signs has the effect of turning certain poems into long vocative statements that are apparently directed to an essential thingness beyond their own confines. In Bonnefoy's poem *Dans le leurre du seuil* we find the following series of pointers: "Par hier réincarné, ce soir, demain, / Oui, ici, là, ailleurs, ici, là-bas encore" (By yesterday reincarnate, this evening, tomorrow, / Yes, here, there, elsewhere, here, over there again; 327). The critic John E. Jackson, sucked in by the appearance of pure denotation, characterizes these lines as one of Bonnefoy's most "direct and immediate" forms of naming.[17] In Saint-John Perse's *Exil* we find the same strategy at work: "la simple chose, la simple chose que voilà, la simple chose d'être là, dans l'écoulement du jour" (the simple thing, that simple thing over there, the simple thing of being there, as the day wears on; *Oeuvres complètes* 127).

Rather than function as names reflecting the thing-in-itself, such deictic markers as *that, there,* or *now* are therefore contributing to the illusion of its existence in the poems we have examined. Detached from any contextual or pragmatic role, they are an example of the machine of language going wild, or, as Wittgenstein put it, the moment when "language goes on holiday."[18] They point toward something that is not there and which could not be there, but by doing so they lead us to believe that it could be somewhere—namely, at the fictional outer limit of language that is the only inhabitable terrain for the thing-in-itself.

LOST ORIGINS

The third aspect of the poetic code of the thing-in-itself that we examine is the quest for a lost origin of language that runs throughout the poetry of Perse, Bonnefoy, and Deguy. In Saint-John Perse's *Exil* the quest for the thing-in-itself coincides with the narrator's attempt to give expression to the original breath of life that started all creation: "Que

17. John E. Jackson, *Yves Bonnefoy* (Paris: Seghers, 1976), 90.
18. Ludwig Wittgenstein, *Philosophical Investigations* (Oxford: Blackwell, 1974), paragraph 38.

voulez-vous encore de moi, ô souffle originel? Et vous, que pensez-vous encore tirer de ma lèvre vivante?" (What do you want of me, original breath? And you, what do you think you can still draw from my living lips?; *Oeuvres complètes* 127). Like the breath of life that animated Adam in Genesis, this "original breath," because it is at the origin of all history, marks the fictional point of contact between language (which is coextensive with human history) and the prelinguistic world.[19] If there were no origin to language, no absolute beginning, then language would have no boundary limits through time. There would always be words, as far back as we could go, and consequently there would be no way of reaching a chronologically original world that would be independent of any sign system. Ever receding epochs of language would cut us off from the realm of things-as-they-are.[20]

This form of radical linguistic exile is sketched out in Perse's poem, "Le Livre" (The book):

> Et quelle plainte alors sur la bouche de l'âtre, (...) remuait dans ton coeur l'obscure naissance du langage:
> ". . . D'un exil lumineux—et plus lointain déjà que l'orage qui roule—comment garder les voies, ô mon Seigneur! que vous m'aviez livrées?" (*Oeuvres complètes* 20)

> (And then what groaning at the mouth of the hearth, [...] stirred up in your heart the obscure birth of language:
> ". . . From a luminous exile—and already farther back than the storm that is gathering—how can I preserve the ways, my Lord, that you had given to me?")

Here the dream of an origin to language comes to the poem's subject as a way of overcoming the exile to which he alludes. In other words, the hypothetical beginning of language lends credence to the belief that

19. For a detailed discussion of the importance of origins in Perse's poetry, see the first two chapters of Steven Winspur's *Saint-John Perse and the Imaginary Reader* (Geneva: Droz, 1988).

20. See Michel Pierssens, *La Tour de Babil: La Fiction du signe* (Paris: Minuit, 1976), for an analysis of this view and of its contrary—an Edenic theory of language based on "the pure nowness of presence, the gods' temporality, the time of the divine Word, of instantaneous creation after which everything will be adrift or fallen" (113). See also Chapter 2, where we discuss Hugo Ball's mystical project of recovering an original, Edenic language of the thing-in-itself.

there are indeed things-in-themselves, or a world of truth that lies be-
yond semiotic conventions. To posit an origin, of course, is to posit God,
the only being capable of overcoming the ontological impossibility of
creating something (subsequent to the origin) out of nothing (prior to
the origin). This is why Perse's poem is called "Le Livre," and by perus-
ing the divine book of origins the poem's protagonist prepares himself
for the revelation of God:

> alors, ouvrant le Livre
> tu promenais un doigt usé entre les prophéties, puis le regard
> fixé au large, tu attendais l'instant du départ, le lever du grand vent
> qui te descellerait d'un coup, comme un typhan, divisant les nuées
> devant l'attente de tes yeux. (20)

> (then, opening the Book
> you ran a worn-out finger between the prophecies, and then
> with your gaze fixed on the open sea, you awaited the moment of
> departure, the rising of the great wind that would unseal you all of
> a sudden, like a typhoon, parting the clouds before your expectant
> eyes.)

Saint-John Perse is not, however, a religious poet in the mold of
Paul Claudel or Pierre Emmanuel. We are suggesting that it is his desire
to reveal "things as they are" that makes his poems borrow elements
from a theocentric discourse of origins. The code of the thing-in-itself
uses religious terms for its own ends, as Perse himself suggests when he
writes in a letter to Claudel of the "search for the 'divine' in each thing
that has been the secret tension of my entire pagan life" (1019–20), or
as Bonnefoy points out in his remark that "the difficulty with modern
poetry is that it has to define itself at one and the same moment
through Christianity and against it" (*Du mouvement et de l'immobilité
de Douve* 201).

Bonnefoy's own search for "a dazzling brilliance in ancient words"
(*Pierre écrite,* in *Poèmes* 221) reaches its climax in a later collection of
poems titled, significantly, *L'Origine de la parole* (The origin of speech).
Here things-in-themselves are described as ideal essences inhabiting a
prelinguistic utopia:

La lumière était si intense! (...) les essences seules à être dans
leur ample bruissement clair d'air qui monte en vibrant au-dessus
d'un feu.

Et je comprenais que l'*été est le langage*. Que les mots naissent
de l'été, comme laisse un serpent derrière soi, à la mue, sa fragile
enveloppe transparente.[21]

(The light was so intense! [...] the essences alone existed in
their clear rustling, as of the air that rises, throbbing above a fire.

And I understood that *summer is language*. That words are
born of the summer as, at the beginning of the moulting season, a
snake leaves behind him his fragile clear envelope . . . that words
were invented, and through them absence.)

If, as Deguy writes in *Actes*, "poetry would be the *origin of language*"
(269), what is the nature of this origin? As we have demonstrated, it is a
poetic hypothesis put forward as one way of justifying the search for an
outer limit of language, which is the only habitable terrain for the thing-
in-itself. No text can actually reveal the moment of origin when words
were on the point of being formed. Poems such as those quoted in this
chapter are linguistic constructs creating the fiction of a poetic realm that
is prelinguistic. "Everything began we know not how," admits Deguy in
his book, *Fragment du cadastre*. "We search for the origin. / There's
nothing but the inaudible panting behind / the beginning that is reced-
ing more and more."[22]

Like the hypotheses of a poem beyond words or a poetic name
hailing its referent, the origin of language is a poetic ideal existing only as
a dreamed alternative to the actual workings of language. Such hypoth-
eses seem to undermine (and yet their textual nature only confirms) the
axiom that the limits of language can exist nowhere except as an effect of
language itself. It is now possible to understand the intricate connections
between metaphysics and the poems discussed in this chapter. It is not a
question (as Barthes suggests) of modern poetry merely taking over the
"essentialist system" of philosophy (*Mythologies* 220); instead it concerns
the operation by which the rhetorical structure of poetry turns back on

21. Bonnefoy, "L'Origine de la parole," *Récits en rêve* (Paris: Mercure de France,
1987), 202.
22. Deguy, *Fragment du cadastre* (Paris: Gallimard, 1960), 22.

itself and (rhetorically) posits the possibility of a nonrhetorical discourse. This bending-back of poetry on itself is justified by Michel Deguy in the following terms:

> Modern poetics does not admit that philosophy or any outside knowledge holds the key to its intelligibility [...], it tries *on its own* to go backwards toward the line of demarcation between [...] poem and prose. Swimming upstream in this way, to the uppermost head waters of language [...] it tries to perfect itself by rethinking the original metaphoricity of which speaking consists—and this is how poetry is able to estimate with increasing precision the unavoidable complicity between metaphysics and poems . . . a complicity that overwhelms it.[23]

Yet very often poetry's attempt to work against its own rhetorical nature produces the noncontextual, and apparently arhetorical, language of philosophical absolutes such as the thing-in-itself.

23. Deguy, *Figurations* (Paris: Gallimard, 1969), 187–88.

six

IMAGE AND FORMULA

(BONNEFOY,

MESCHONNIC)

This chapter outlines two distinct definitions of metaphor, summed up by the terms *image* and *formula*. After conducting several close readings of poems by Yves Bonnefoy and Henri Meschonnic we became convinced that, beyond some obvious stylistic and thematic differences, there is a fundamental contrast between the two types of discourse that the poets use. It would be pointless, for example, to try and interpret Meschonnic's poems by means of certain linguistic mechanisms that are characteristic of Bonnefoy's writing. This might seem odd to specialists of contemporary French literature since it has often been said that intellectually, at least, both poets are similar insofar as they are the heirs of Paul Eluard. Biographical details would also seem to link them since they are both poets and theoreticians of poetry. Bonnefoy used to hold the chair of poetry and poetics at the Collège de France (1981–93), while Meschonnic directs one of the most stimulating seminars on poetics at the University of Paris (Paris-VIII). However, a casual glance at their poems is sufficient to indicate that the discursive function of metaphor is central to the basic contrast between the two writers.

Before discussing their poetry we begin by situating the definitions of image and formula within the critical debates about the nature of metaphor. There has been an abundance of technical work done on metaphor over the last two decades and this work follows four major lines of research:

1. Developing an adequate taxonomy, which would identify, and then classify, different types of metaphor
2. Determining the process of metaphorical invention, which links Quintillian's "mechanics" of metaphor with Aristotle's views on a metaphor's "mechanism"[1]
3. Studying metaphor's social dimension, or how a metaphor comes into being with the interaction between presuppositions and the responses of a reader or listener
4. Examining metaphor's underlying function: put simply, does it belong to the field of argumentation or stylistics?

By necessity, these four approaches tend to be subsumed under whatever unified theory of metaphor is put forward, since the four aspects they examine can be found in any metaphoric utterance. It is possible, however, to isolate them, and indeed to detect a hierarchy among them. An individual researcher might, for example, base his or her taxonomy on one of the three aspects listed, and indeed a description of the metaphorizing process can stem from an exclusive study of either aspect 3 or 4. It is therefore legitimate in studying metaphor to distinguish these four aspects from one another and to indicate which one is the focus of the analysis.

The present chapter limits itself to the fourth aspect of metaphor given above (metaphorization). It is our contention that any metaphor in a text can be assumed to have one of two functions—either that of an image or that of a formula. This distinction explains the specific nature of the utterance in question, as well as the choice of its linguistic components. The distinction helps us tackle problems concerning the presuppositions that are implied by the stating of a specific metaphor, and prob-

---

1. See Samuel R. Levin, *The Semantics of Metaphor* (Baltimore: Johns Hopkins University Press, 1977), 86.

lems that arise with interpreting metaphors. It has the advantage of explaining why specific poems by Bonnefoy and Meschonnic cannot be approached from the same theoretical viewpoint, cannot be read in the same way, and, more importantly, why they should be viewed as stemming from two opposing notions of how language works.

We begin with Aristotle's standard definition of the trope. It can be found in chapter 21 of the *Poetics* at section 57b10 where we read that "metaphor is the transference (*epiphora*) of the name (*onomatos*) of a thing to something else (*allotriou*)." This statement has been the subject of countless glosses and interpretations. *Onomatos* can be translated as "word," "signification," "meaning," or "name"; *allotriou* as "strange," "foreign," or "uncanny," among other things; and *epiphora*, which contains the prefix *epi-* and is related to a similar word in the sentence beginning with the prefix *meta-*, has been translated as "a bringing to," "a bringing upon," or "an application to," depending on the translator (see the versions by Fyfe in the Loeb Classics, Ingram, Bywater, and Forster, to mention only a few of the best known English versions; the same can be said about the terminology of the many translations of Aristotle's *Rhetoric*—by Cope, Sandys, Roberts, Stanford, Freese, and others). Our translation of the passage is simply the English version most commonly accepted by contemporary linguists when they analyze Aristotle's *Poetics*.

However, we would like to stress that when working on Aristotle's theories in an era such as ours that is dominated by the pragmatic approach, it is essential to bear in mind that, despite the seminal value of Aristotle's treatise for future definitions of metaphor, *the central purpose of his study was to establish a general theory of argumentation*. Thus, Aristotle takes great care to differentiate between comparison and metaphor. He even coined his own term, *parabolé*, to name a specific figurative process that is more clearly defined than the general *eikôn*, a term referring to a comparative image. The distinctions he introduced between *parabolé* and *metaphora*, or between comparison and metaphor, can only be understood in the context of a theory of argumentation or a speech act theory of discourse.

"Achilles leapt at the foe *like* a lion" is a comparison. Because the two terms in a comparison are present, the intellectual reasoning of the speaker is brought to the fore and the audience can immediately grasp the extent of the argument. However, in a metaphoric utterance such as "The lion leapt at the foe" the first term (or so-called tenor) remains unknown and the audience has to retrieve it. In fact, this hidden reference may sometimes never be found. Consequently, metaphor should not be considered as part of a proof, but as one of the many means of achieving *liveliness* in a discourse. In short, whereas "The lion leapt at the foe" is a metaphor, "Achilles leapt at the foe like a lion" is not.

For Dumarsais and Fontanier, the most productive and respected rhetoricians within the French tradition, Aristotle's original distinction between comparison and metaphor is no longer relevant, nor is it taken into consideration. Although Fontanier mentions the figure of similitude and places it in the nontrope category whereas metaphor is put in the trope category, Dumarsais ignores the distinction completely.[2] If one takes a leap through the centuries and examines more recent studies of metaphor, it is clear that, since Jacobson established the opposition within language between metonymy and metaphor, the distinction between comparison and metaphor has become less important, to the point where one often finds comparison (or simile) grouped simply as a subcategory of metaphor. Metonymy and metaphor mobilize different operations of language competence.[3] Metaphor is a paradigmatic process, or transfer, based on semantic similarity, whereas metonymy is a syntagmatic process, based on syntactical addition or subtraction. One result of this polarization might be that, because metaphor and comparison both involve a paradigmatic process (of selection), the need to consider them as opposites has become less urgent.[4] For some scholars it is maybe even more to the point to simply consider them as one and the same.

If the placing of metaphor and comparison in the same category makes sense within current linguistic and rhetorical frameworks, it is too simplistic to allow us to distinguish between image and formula. For the purpose of our analysis it is essential to understand that metaphor is a figure with only one term. In the corpus of works by the two poets under consideration any statement that displays concurrently two terms joined by a figurative meaning (e.g., "Achilles is *like* a lion") will be excluded from the realm of metaphor. Consequently, the distinction that we draw

2. Classical rhetoric tended to distinguish tropes from figures on the basis of the following criterion: a figure is an utterance in which the literal meaning of each term is maintained (e.g., the comparison "Time destroys everything like a scythe"); a trope is an utterance in which the literal meaning of some terms is canceled out and "turned"—according to the etymology of *trope*—into a new, figurative meaning (e.g., "the scythe of Time").

3. Roman Jakobson, *Fundamentals of Language* (The Hague: Mouton, 1956), 146.

4. See Tzvetan Todorov, "Synecdoques," *Communications* 12 (1970): 24–35.

between an image and a formula involves only metaphoric constructs with one term.

It is inevitable that requiring metaphor to be a figure with only one term has repercussions when one tries to give a linguistic description of the uses of metaphor. The most important repercussion from a pragmatic standpoint is that it is impossible to consider metaphor exclusively as a phenomenon of language use, a simple embellishment. To do so would be to exclude the particular semantic operations at work when metaphors are coined.

Since the work of I. A. Richards in *Principles of Literary Criticism* (1925) and the ensuing analyses by Max Black in *Models and Metaphors* (1962), it has been assumed that a study of the semantic components in the production of metaphor should focus on the dynamic process of interaction. Metaphors reorganize the semes that are conventionally attached to a lexeme, so that the metaphor process is one in which some semes are selected and emphasized while others are deemphasized or repressed. If we analyze the semantic field (or *denotatum*) of the lexeme *lion* in Aristotle's example, "The lion leapt at the foe," we can isolate the following semantic features (or semes): [+ natural], [+ animate], [+ mammal], [+ quadruped], [+ male], [+ furry], [+ predatory], [+ strong], [+ courageous], and so on. In Aristotle's sentence not all the semes are activated, since [+ quadruped], [+ furry], and so on, can be considered irrelevant to our assertion. In any case, the meaning of the sentence is the product of a metalingual operation. In order to interpret it, we have to select from the semantic features that belong to the semantic field of the word *lion*. The trace of this selection process is an integral part of the utterance and it informs the reader.

The fact that in Aristotle's example "lion" is the *vehicle* (or frame, in Black's terminology) for the *tenor* (or focus) "Achilles" is only inferred from the physical proximity of the two words in the context-at-large of the literary work. But the sentence itself can be used in any kind of context where the text calls for a fight or a battle in which one of the protagonists is physically engaged. The sentence could therefore apply to any situation of hand-to-hand combat and, as such, it has only a generic value that can be applied to any contextually close character whose qualities of strength and courage have to be emphasized.

To understand how the semantic mechanism of interaction that is involved in the metaphor process allows us to distinguish between the figures of image and formula we now turn to extracts from Yves Bonnefoy and Henri Meschonnic. For the sake of clarity we analyze the different linguistic levels in these examples separately. What will emerge is the fact that the internal coherence of an image and that of a formula rest on totally opposite principles, thus revealing two different conceptions of the nature of language and its use.

The first extract is an example of an image and it is the concluding sentence to Bonnefoy's 1958 essay, "L'Acte et le lieu de la poésie":

Ne suffirait-il pas d'apercevoir, au flanc de quelque montagne, une vitre au soleil du soir?[5]

(Would it not be enough to catch sight, on the flank of some mountain, of a windowpane in the evening sun?)

Our example of a formula comes from one of Henri Meschonnic's poems:

Nos séparations sont l'antichambre où nous nous préparons
Nous entrerons ensemble
C'est notre répétition.[6]

5. Yves Bonnefoy, *Du mouvement et de l'immobilité de Douve* (Paris: Gallimard, Poésie, 1970), 234. This brief quotation exemplifies the structure of many other similar extracts from Bonnefoy's writing. As a result, our analysis can also be applied to the following passages (all taken from the collection *Poèmes* [Paris: Mercure de France, 1978]): "Le temps dort dans la cendre du feu d'hiver / Et la guêpe qui heurte la vitre a cousu / Beaucoup déjà de la déchirure du monde" (Time is sleeping in the ashes of the winter fire / And the wasp that knocks into the windowpane has sown / Already much of the world's tearing; "L'épars, l'indivisible" [The scattered, the indivisible], 321); "On dirait que le temps va faire halte / Comme s'il hésitait sur le chemin, / Regardant par-dessus l'épaule terrestre / ce que nous ne pouvons ou ne voulons voir" (One could almost say that time is going to come to a stop / As if it were hesitating along its path, / Looking back across the terrestrial shoulder / what we cannot or do not wish to see; "Deux barques" [Two boats], 263); "Un langage se fait, qui partage le clair / Buissonnement d'étoiles dans l'écume" (A language is being made, which divides the clear / burgeoning of stars amidst foam; *Pierre écrite* [Words in stone], 171).

6. Henri Meschonnic, *Dédicaces, proverbes/Dedications, Proverbs* (Paris: Gallimard, 1972), 68. Here again the verbal sequence has been chosen from a series of similar extracts that all illustrate the properties of a formula: for example, "nous avons notre voyage nous n'avons / même que nos chemins / où étais-tu demain / quand on ne se voit plus présents" (we have our journey we even have / nothing but our paths / where were you tomorrow / when we no longer see each other present; *Voyageurs de la voix* [Voice travelers] [Lagrasse, France: Verdier, 1985], 22); "on se voit à se faire mal / tant on est / ensemble" (we see one another until the point of doing ourselves harm / so much we are / together; 72); "Aujourd'hui nous sommes plus jeunes que nous-mêmes / parce que nous sommes l'un l'autre / le regard avec l'instant" (Today we are younger than ourselves /

(Our partings are the antechamber where we get ourselves ready
We shall enter together
It is our rehearsal.)

The semantic decomposition of each lexical element in Bonnefoy's sentence shows that all four nouns, "flanc," "montagne," "vitre," and "soleil," have the semantic feature [+ concrete] or [+ physical]. This feature is syntagmatically governed by the verb "apercevoir," which designates an operation of the senses and, as such, requires objects that are semantically characterized by a seme expressing their concreteness. It is also remarkable that "flanc," "montagne," "soleil," and "soir" have the semantic feature [+ natural]. "Vitre" is the only odd element in this respect since it is an artifact. However, from the standpoint of their concreteness, these elements can all be seen. Because of the ever-present seme of concreteness in this group, the reader considers the text to be a discursive expression of a visual perception, or a visualization, to use Philippe Hamon's term from his *Introduction à l'analyse du descriptif*.[7] The reinforcement of this illusion of representation is also accomplished by the presence at the semantic level of a seme that has to do with the very action of seeing: "vitre" has the seme [+ transparency], "soleil" the seme [+ light], and "soir" the seme [+ darkness]. As we indicated, this overwhelming presence of semic components related to concreteness or to light is made credible by the verb "apercevoir." It is also interesting to note that this verb is the one that Hamon claims to be the most likely verb to induce the effect of referentiality in the reader.[8] Hamon indicates, moreover, that this verb is generally reinforced by lexical items belonging to what he calls a topographical grid—words such as *left, right, below, above,* and so on. In Bonnefoy's sentence this function is fulfilled by the word "flanc" (flank). Although the topographical reference is indirectly indicated here by use of a figurative form (the flank of a mountain), it is nevertheless present. In fact, it can be argued that abstract formulations of topographical representation would have been ill-suited for a context that is marked by a high degree of concreteness. The overwhelming effect

---

because we are each other / the gaze with the moment; *Nous le passage* [We the passing] [Lagrasse: Verdier, 1990], 9); "une distance / remplace / une voix / un monde inconnu / commence" (a distance / replaces / a voice / an unknown world / begins; *Nous le passage* 55).

7. Philippe Hamon, *Introduction à l'analyse du descriptif* (Paris: Hachette, 1981).
8. Hamon, *Introduction*, 194.

of concreteness is reinforced, at a morphological level, by the predomi-
nant noun structure in the sentence (Fig. 15).

On the basis of this analysis, we can suggest that the image type of
metaphor is characterized, at a semantic level, by an isotropy of semic
features that have to do with concreteness and visual representation. This
claim simply reformulates in linguistic terms the definition given by such
empiricists as Berkeley and Hume, and according to which an image is
nothing more than a conscious impression whose components we could
recognize in the real world. The more difficult task is to demonstrate why
Bonnefoy's example is a metaphor. It is true that when taken out of its
context (which, in this essay, concerns the status of poetry), this sentence
can be read quite literally, and indeed there is no apparent clue to signal
the fact that what is said is not exactly what is meant. There is no sugges-
tion that a second term or domain should be introduced to interpret the
sentence properly. However, this is not a difficulty since we argued earlier
that metaphor is a one-term (and not a two-term) figure. What has to be
shown is that Bonnefoy's example includes a conjoined assertion and pre-
supposition, and also that the assertion is accurate.

The second requirement is met by the image's visualization aspect
discussed above, which Hamon defines as a "make-believe" reproduction
of something we know we can recognize in the real world. Hamon's
definition of semiosis is, nevertheless, unsatisfactory in that it ignores the
importance of presuppositions, and so for our present purposes we use
Charles S. Peirce's famous remark that "semiosis is, or involves, a cooper-
ation of three subjects such as a sign, its object and its interpretant, this
tri-relative influence not being in any way resolvable into action between
pairs." Defined in this way, semiosis plays an important part in our under-
standing of the metaphor as image, since the presupposition implied in
any metaphor is, in semiotic terms, an interpretant.

In the case of Bonnefoy's sentence, the interpretant signals that the
lexical items cannot be read literally and that they belong to a figurative
construction. Moreover, the interpretant implies the presupposition that
these lexemes are characterized by a marked semantic field. This mark-
ing, which extends to all the words ("montagne," "vitre," "soleil,"
"soir"), is that of poetic usage. An exhaustive quantitative search carried
out on the lexicon used by nineteenth-century poets (especially Baude-
laire, Rimbaud, Verlaine, and Mallarmé) confirmed this lexical overlap,
and even pointed to poems where there is a tight grouping of Bonnefoy's
very words: for example, Rimbaud's "où le soleil, de la montagne fière, /

Table 1

Ne	suffisait	il	pas	d'	apercevoir	au	flanc	d'	une	montagne
[+neg]	[+verb] [+ 3rd pers] [+ sing]	[+pers pro] [+ 3rd pers] [+ sing] [+ impers]	[+neg]	[−]	[+verb] [+ inf]	[+prep][+det] [+ sing]	[+noun] [+ sing]	[−]	[+det] [+ sing] [+ indef]	[+noun] [+ sing]
	[+ abstract] [+ adequation]				[+ sense perc.] [+ process] [+ visual]	[+ location]	[+ concrete] [+ natural] [+ physical] [+ location]			[+ concrete] [+ natural] [+ thingness] [+ massivess]

une	vitre	au	soleil	du	soir
[+ det] [+ sing]	[+ noun] [+ sing]	[+ prep] [+ det] [+ sing] [+ def]	[+ noun] [+ sing]	[+ prep][+det] [+ sing] [+ def]	[+ noun] [+ sing]
	[+ concrete] [+ artificial] [+ transparency] [+ light] [+ reflection]	[+ location]	[+ concrete] [+ natural] [+ light] [+ warmth] [+ color]	[+ time]	[+ concrete] [+ natural] [+ time] [+ darkness] [+ end]

Figure 15

luit" (where the sun, from the proud mountain, / shines), or "Quand la flamme illumine, claire, les carreaux gris! (...) Puis, petite et toute nichée dans les lilas noirs et frais: la vitre cachée qui rit là-bas" (When the clear flame lights up the gray windowpanes! [...] Then, small and completely lodged between the fresh, dark violets—the hidden pane that laughs over there).[9]

Moreover, when read in the context of the closing paragraph of "L'Acte et le lieu de la poésie," Bonnefoy's sentence takes on its role as part of an extended metaphor that has begun six sentences earlier: "La poésie moderne est loin de sa demeure possible. La grande salle aux quatre fenêtres lui est toujours refusée" (Modern poetry is far from its possible dwelling. It is still barred from the big four-windowed room; 214). By concretizing the metaphor "poetry's home," Bonnefoy has earlier established a contrast between two types of abode—an orange-greenhouse where all stands clear in the sunlight (192–93), and a darker building that is full of shadows. Whereas the former is a metaphor for classical poetry like Racine's, whose clarity lies "open to the sun of being" (193), the latter is used by Bonnefoy to metaphorize the poetry of Rimbaud and Baudelaire, which he considers to have mapped out a new direction for future poets (196–98). When placed in this context, the evening light reflected in a windowpane (as in the extract quoted above) becomes a

9. Through a computer search on the ARTFL (American and French Research on the Treasury of the French Language) database at the University of Chicago, we found out that the words used by Bonnefoy occur much more frequently in the corpus of nineteenth- and early twentieth-century poems than the average frequency for nouns. For example, all five terms occur in Rimbaud's poetry (see "Les Réparties de Nina" and "Le Dormeur du Val"), whereas in the same corpus none of Meschonnic's terms appears. In Mallarmé, there are 30 appearances of *flanc, soir, soleil,* and *vitre,* whereas only 1 case in which Meschonnic's term *ensemble* appears. There is also an important grouping of *soleil du soir* that reappears in Mallarmé in various forms (e.g., "Par le carreau qu'allume un soir fier d'y descendre, retourne vers les feux du pur soleil mortel" [From the windowpane lit up one proud evening part of the pure mortal sun returns toward its flames]). In Charles Cros's collection of short verse and prose texts (*Le Coffret de Santal*), there are 63 cases where *flanc, soir, montagne,* and *soleil* occur and none in which Meschonnic's terms appear. As for Apollinaire's *Alcools, côté, montagne,* and *soleil* occur 61 times. The contrast between Bonnefoy's and Meschonnic's lexicons is less striking when one considers Eluard's *Donner à voir,* since there are 43 appearances of *montagne, soir, soleil, suffit, vitre,* and *apercevoir,* while also 7 of *entrer* and *ensemble.* One of the latter group has quite clear intertextual connections with Meschonnic's poem, for in it we read: "Nous deux, j'insiste sur ces mots, car aux étapes de ces longs voyages que nous faisions séparément, je le sais maintenant, nous étions vraiment ensemble, nous étions vraiment, nous étions, nous" (The two of us, and I emphasize these words, since at each stage of those long journeys that we used to take separately, I now know that we were truly together, we were truly, we were, we).

signpost to poetry's future home, a flash of brightness in the shadows.[10] Such light-within-darkness is also a standard metaphor for hope, so that the rhetorical question in the extract under examination ("Ne suffirait-il pas d'apercevoir [...] une vitre au soleil du soir?") closes the demonstration that is announced at the outset of Bonnefoy's essay: "Je voudrais réunir, je voudrais identifier presque la poésie et l'espoir" (I would like to reunite, I would like to almost identify, poetry with hope; 185).

Two reasons compel us, then, to call a certain type of metaphor an image: its value as an icon for other literary extracts, and its connection to particular semes producing an effect of concreteness. If we consider the latter reason more closely, it becomes apparent that, because of its attempt to create a symbolic visualization, an image relies on a mode of discourse that foregrounds special attributes usually attached by a community of readers to the specific semic components of a lexeme. During the interpretation, no reference to the extralinguistic world has to be called forth, for such a connection is already explicitly inscribed within the text. Such ready-made linguistic references trigger the illusory impression that this type of metaphor has a metalingual value and that a seemingly direct contact with life, or with the world, has been established.[11] As a result, the reader has the impression of being confronted with an already familiar element of reality.

10. For an important analysis of the reflected light metaphor in Bonnefoy's poetry, see chapter 4 of Anja Pearre's *La Présence de l'image: Yves Bonnefoy face à neuf artistes plastiques* (Amsterdam: Rodopi, Chiasma, 1995), 60–76.

11. Such a "return" to a "writing of the world" is at the core of a recent book by Jean-Claude Pinson, *Habiter en poète* [Living as a poet] (Seyssel, France: Champ Vallon, 1995), which calls for the rehabilitation of a neolyric form of poetry. He writes thus: "on voit aujourd'hui s'affirmer un souci nouveau d'ouvrir d'avantage le poème sur le 'hors-texte,' de renouer une 'nouvelle alliance avec le monde.' (...) De nombreux poètes n'hésitent plus, en effet, sinon à sacrifier au 'reportage' tant décrié par Mallarmé, du moins à faire du poème le lieu d'un dire du monde" (today one can spot a new desire to open the poem 'beyond the boundaries of the text,' to build a 'new alliance with the world.' [...] Many poets no longer hesitate, if not to renew those 'journalistic chronicles' so ridiculed by Mallarmé, at least to return the poem to its role as 'chronicle of the world'). In Pinson's book, Bonnefoy is put forward as a hero of contemporary antitextualism. Pinson writes: "L'originalité de la poétique d'Yves Bonnefoy tient en l'affirmation d'un double primat (*sic*): d'une part celui de l'existence sur le logos, de l'habitation sur la formulation, du vivre dans l'écriture; d'autre part celui de la recherche du sens sur le plaisir illusoire de la 'dérive des signifiants' (Bonnefoy's poetics is original in the sense that it is clearly based on two priorities: first, valorizing existence over language, the poet's dwelling over formulations, and underscoring the part of life in writing; and second putting the search for meaning ahead of the illusory pleasure of wordplay). For a more detailed study of these questions, see Chapter 11.

It is possible, however, that the poet is the first one to fall victim to his own language-cloaking device with this type of image, since it can be argued that it is not the poet who has selected a certain number of words with which to build the metaphor, but rather the sociolect that has solidi-fied the special attributes attached to the semic properties of the lexeme. The poet simply validates the use of the lexeme with its ready-made pre-suppositional values.

Metaphor is not built on any apprehension of reality, and so it is wrong to consider it in terms of any immediate mimesis. However, be-cause metaphorizing is a discursive process involving a semiosis, it is es-sential to recognize the fact that it establishes a *fiction of reality*. As War-ren Shibles puts it, "When the metaphor is created to give insight into a concept, we have a clear case of language preceding thoughts, and at the same time of language partially constituting reality."[12] Metaphor's capac-ity to constitute reality in this way is, in part, due to the fact that it is built on an assertive pattern. The presuppositional component is the one that institutes the impression of quasi reality.

Certain proverbs are the ultimate illustration of how this image type of metaphor becomes solidified. They offer examples of discourse where not only is there a permanent metalingual selection attached to a lexeme, but the conjunction of a presupposition and its attached assertion is also widely preserved. This, in turn, determines the syntagmatic selection of the relevant semes that are present in the semantic field surrounding each lexeme in the sentence. As proverbs amply illustrate, any metaphor can therefore function only in a truth-suspending mode that does not really tell us much about an extralinguistic reality. Hence the obvious fact that one proverb can cancel out another, without an external reality interven-ing as a tribunal to determine the truth value of either proverb. "A bird in the hand is worth two in the bush" cancels out "Fortune favors the bold and the brave" and vice versa.

Finally, as an icon of other literary texts, an image metaphor presup-poses a collateral acquaintance with the culturally marked character of the lexeme. According to Peirce's claim, this collateral acquaintance is based on habits, and therefore introduces a relation that is, in his terms, "imageable."[13]

12. Warren A. Shibles, *Analysis of Metaphor in the Light of W. M. Urban's Theories* (The Hague: Mouton, 1971), 82.

13. Charles S. Peirce, *Selected Writings* (Cambridge: Harvard University Press, 1958), 395.

Meschonnic's example of metaphor is of an entirely different type.

Nos séparations sont l'antichambre où nous nous préparons
Nous entrerons ensemble
C'est notre répétition. (*Dédicaces, proverbes* 68)

(Our partings are the antechamber where we get ourselves ready
We shall enter together
It is our rehearsal.)

After a preliminary analysis, it can be said that the different lexemes do not presuppose a collateral acquaintance with a prior literary corpus that marks them and functions as the interpretant of the sentence. Here again, an extensive analysis of the canonical works of late nineteenth-century poetry proves that, with the exception of the word "ensemble," there is no lexical overlap. Meschonnic's words are simply not present in Rimbaud, Baudelaire, Verlaine, or Mallarmé. This lack of literary iconicity perhaps explains why Meschonnic's work is often dismissed as too "different" or too "difficult." In approaching it, the reader is disoriented and does not have the familiar impression of déjà vu or *déjà lu*. He or she does not recognize a poem by Meschonnic as being a "latticework of other texts,"[14] so that any intertextual factor remains inoperative.

Because the presuppositional component of the metaphor cannot be found in the sentences' iconic reference to other texts, we should be able to find it in the semantic organization of the sentences themselves (Fig. 16). As an analysis of the sentences' semantic features reveals, the seme [+ abstract] replaces the semes [+ natural] and [+ concrete] that we found in Bonnefoy's extract. We also cannot fail to remark that, in Meschonnic's example, the feature [+ action] is overwhelmingly present in the verbs as well as in the nouns, and is reinforced at the morphological level by the high frequency of verb forms. Moreover, the semantic isotropy that is established by the mark of the first person plural is present in the adjectives "nos" and "notre," the pronoun "nous," and the verbs "préparons" and "entrerons." The first person plural value of the ending *-ons* homophonically and rhythmically spills over to the nouns "séparations" and "répétition." Other internal isotropies link together several constituents of the sentences: location ("antichambre," "en-

14. Michael Riffaterre, *Semiotics of Poetry* (Bloomington: Indiana University Press, 1978), 191.

Table 2

Nos	séparations	sont	l'	antichambre	où	nous	nous	préparons
[+ adjective]	[+ noun]	[+ verb]	[+ det]	[+ noun]	[+ pro]	[+ pron.]	[+ pronoun]	[+ verb]
[+ poss]	[+ masc]	[+ present]	[+ fem]	[+ fem]	[+ relative]	[+ personal]	[+ personal]	[+present]
[+ plural]	[+ plural]	[+ plural]	[+ sing]	[+ sing]		[+ plural]	[+ plural]	[+ plural]
[+ 1st pers]		[+ 3rd pers]	[+ def]			[+ 1st pers]	[+ 1st pers]	[+ 1st pers]
								[+reflexive]
[+ sev. possessors]	[+ abstract]	[+ state]		[+ concrete]		[+ je + tu]	[+ je + tu]	[+ process]
[+ possessions]	[+ action]	[+ identity]		[+ location]	[+ location]			
	[+ partition]			[+ anterior]				[+anterior]

nous	entrerons	ensemble	c'	est	notre	répétition
[+ pron]	[+ verb]	[+ adverb]	[−]	[+ verb]	[+ adjective]	[+ noun]
[+ personal]	[+ future]			[+ present]	[+ poss]	[+ fem]
[+ plural]	[+ plural]			[+ sing]	[+ sing]	[+ sing]
[+ 1st pers]	[+ 1st pers]			[+ 3rd pers]	[+ 1st pers plur]	
[+ je + tu]	[+ process]	[+ plurality]		[+ state]	[+ sev. possessors]	[+ abstract]
	[+ movement]	[+ (re)union]		[+ identity]	[+ one possession]	[+ action]
	[+ change]					[+ anterior]
	[+ passage]					[+ unfinished]
						[+ iteration]

Figure 16

trerons"), anteriority ("préparons," "répétition"), and then the central opposition of separation and togetherness ("séparations," "ensemble").

The figurative value of Meschonnic's extract is therefore largely derived from the particular combination of semes that are attached to each of its elements, and that lend force to the metaphor's paradoxical assertion that "Our partings are the antechamber where we get ourselves ready." Consequently, the presuppositional structure of the extract is closely dependent on the statement's predicative form, and thus underscores the linear direction that discourse follows. Extending this principle to the field of poetry as a whole is precisely what Meschonnic suggested when he put forward his slogan "Non mots mais phrases, poésie" (Not words, but sentences, poetry).[15]

In Bonnefoy's image each individual word acquires its metaphoric value through solidified metalingual semantic features and an intertextual presupposition, but at the same time the words do not have any necessary semantic connections between them.[16] In Meschonnic's example the lexemes semantically corroborate each other and establish an ad hoc presuppositional pattern that is internal to the extract and accredits its assertion. The result is a formula that can only be understood on its own terms, within the discrete boundaries of its own figurative formulation.

15. Meschonnic, "Non mots mais phrases, poésie," in *Pour la poétique II* (Paris: Gallimard, 1973), 47–151.

16. As will be shown in Chapter 11, in their defense of a contemporary neolyricism, both Pinson and Jean-Michel Maulpoix (in his study *La Poésie malgré tout* [Poetry despite all else] [Paris: Mercure de France, 1996]) favor the image as the core of a renewed mimesis. Their definitions of image are more general than ours and encompass more than metaphor production. In each instance, nevertheless, the definition involves a construction of reality in language. Pinson goes so far as to suggest that metaphor could be the specific discursive device best suited to restoring "life" to a poem: "Il y a mimésis et mimésis. On l'a longtemps comprise en termes de copie reflétant, selon une logique de la signification réaliste, un réel déjà donné. Paul Ricoeur a montré qu'il pouvait s'agir de tout autre chose: de l'invention d'une forme verbale (d'une chaine métaphorique, par exemple, dans le cas de l'énoncé poétique), susceptible, dans le suspens de la référence première du discours, de libérer 'un pouvoir de référence de second degré'" (There is mimesis and mimesis. For a long time it has been understood as a copy of a preexistent reality. Paul Ricoeur has demonstrated that the term can be understood in a totally different way: it can be the invention of a new discursive sequence (a metaphoric chain, for instance, in poetry), which would suspend the primary reference of the text and thus favor the emergence of "a second-degree level of reference"; *Habiter* 54).

seven

BODY-SPEAK

(RISSET,

NOËL,

CHEDID,

JABÈS)

Our two previous chapters examined ways in which poems by Bonnefoy, Perse, Deguy, and Ponge create the effect of confronting objects, and thus turn structures of language into the appearance of their opposite: extralinguistic epiphanies. Now we turn our attention to a recent set of works by younger poets whose expressed aim is to give voice to the human body. Instead of discovering a "new" language of the body, as some of these writers have claimed to do, the poets examined here have redirected their attention to dimensions of everyday language whose poetic effects are often overlooked. One of these dimensions—the performative structure of utterances—has allowed several contemporary poets to apparently bring poetry closer to the body by redefining both of these as centers of action. Words-in-action (performative utterances) thus become privileged signs for bodily actions, and the resulting effect is poems that seem to express life directly. To uncover some of the mechanisms underlying this effect we examine in turn works by Risset, Noël, Chedid, and Jabès.

In 1991 when Jacqueline Risset published *Petits éléments de physique amoureuse* (Small elements of amorous physics) the opening poem of the collection, "Corps étrange" (Strange body), seemed to offer a new language for the human body. Defining the latter as "ce corps qui est gigantesque" (this body that is gigantic),[1] Risset goes on to characterize the experience one has of one's own, and another's, body when one is in love:

> Le corps aimé est corps épars
> je le touche en touchant par exemple la table
> (...)
> Ou encore
> à l'inverse
> boulevard
>
> soleil de face
> vêtu de noir traversant vite
> entouré de lumière
>
> entouré d'or
> alors:
> ce lieu-ci ce corps-ci
> (...)
> ce corps
> et pas un autre
>
> pas un seul autre
> sur la planète assez légère
>
> (26–27)

> (The loved body is a scattered body
> I touch it when, for example, I touch the table
> [...]
> Or again
> the other way around
> city street

---

1. Jacqueline Risset, *Petits éléments de physique amoureuse* (Paris: Gallimard, L'Infini, 1991), 26.

facing the sun
dressed in black crossing quickly
framed in light
framed in gold
then:
this particular place this particular body
[...]
this body
and not another

not a single other
on the planet that is now quite light)

These renewed feelings of joy (that come from touching a familiar object, and seeing one's lover crossing the street) are put forward by Risset as examples of "amorous physics." Before discussing the implications of this scientific metaphor, the present chapter examines the place occupied by language in such poems as Risset's where prominence is given to the body. The redefined human body that appears in recent poetry is an effect produced by systematically altered syntax and the transferal of vocabulary associated with minds to descriptions of bodies—or so we hope to prove. These linguistic changes affect, among other things, the particular register in which poems are written, and also the ways in which readers identify with the text. (For instance, in the extract above the use of parataxis beginning in line 3 and of deictic signs such as "this body" give the impression of an on-the-spot account whose veracity is based on an apparent immediacy in the act of reporting.) What is important here is that a particular philosophical lexicon, belonging to idealism, is altered and poeticized in such a way that the same lexicon seems to describe idealism's converse: bodily facts.

The interconnections between amorous physics and the basic organizing principles of poetry are acknowledged by Risset herself when, in the introduction to her book, she mentions approvingly the fact that for medieval troubadours "loving" and "singing" were synonymous verbs (9). Bodily acts and poetic ones meet in the linguistic gesture of giving praise. Another place where bodies and poems conjoin is in certain homophones within Risset's poetry. In the final text from *Petits éléments*, titled "Promenade M." (Walk M.), the narrator describes stepping outdoors to find that everything around her "s'échange et se parle" (changes

places and speaks to everything else; 124). The next line indicates famil-
iarity with such a dialogue between objects—"je vous connais, les signes"
(I know you, signs; 124)—but the familiarity is in fact grounded in
wordplay and intertextuality. For the "signes" (signs) addressed here are a
homophone for *le cygne* (swan) that is mentioned on the poem's opening
page, in a deliberate rewriting of Baudelaire's poems "Correspondances"
and "Le Cygne":

> je me promène à mon aise
> dans ce bosquet de symboles
> je sais qu'ils s'échangent
> (...)
> j'assiste
> à ce ballet caché
> Pensant à ton beau cygne
>
> (119)

> (I take a walk for pleasure
> in this thicket of symbols
> I know that they are changing places
> [...]
> I look
> at this hidden ballet
> Thinking of your beautiful swan)

By turning Baudelaire's "Le Cygne" into its homophone, the narrator
stresses that the unity of all things in nature is not so much a hidden
spiritual truth (in line with the doctrines of early Romantic poets) as a
poetic effect produced by the constant deferral of meaning between "les
signes noirs" (the black signs, or in other words, letters) of a printed
poem (124). Each thing that the narrator notices on her walk calls forth
another thing in the same landscape, and the poem re-creates this copres-
ence of interdependent signs by retracing an intertextual network that
points the reader simultaneously back to other texts (by Baudelaire then
Verlaine) and forward to the end of the poem being read. As we discov-
ered in Chapters 3 and 6, it is often through such intertextual referrals
that poems produce the effect of reuniting their readers with an appar-
ently extratextual world.[2]

2. Another example of the homophonic blending of the space of language with

To understand in more detail how this apparent contact with the lived body is created in certain contemporary poems, we turn now to works by Bernard Noël, Andrée Chedid, and Edmond Jabès.

Noël's 1954 poem "Contre-mort" (Anti-death) provides one illustration of the shift in register that occurs in body poetry. Overturning the intellectualist associations that come with the reading of poetry, one section of this seven-page text affirms:

> les yeux regardent à travers le seul oeil
> et dans l'épaisseur de midi
> les choses entrent dans mon corps
> (...)
> alors
> la grâce fait caca dans la cervelle   5
> et la convexité du corps
> touche à celle du ciel
> et je dors
> comme un dieu remonté dans la gorge du père
>
> il faut dire   10
> non à non et non à non non
> il faut retraverser la peau et vider dehors tout ce dedans
> (...)
> JE SUIS BIEN QUE JE PENSE
> et que je me regarde penser
> en m'obligeant de me chier moi-même dans la merde   15
>   de ma pensée
> au lieu de rayonner
> immobile
> tel le soleil[3]
>
> (eyes look through the only eye
> and in the thickness of noon
> things enter my body

---

that of the body is in the poem "Une Île" (An island) (31–34). Here the title alerts its readers to the central metaphor of the poem: the body of a beloved (an *il*, or a "he") described as a volcanic island. We are grateful to Mark Hall for alerting us to this homophone.

3. Bernard Noël, "Contre-mort," *Poèmes I* (Paris: Flammarion, 1983), 17–18. Unless otherwise indicated, all subsequent references to Noël's poems are made to this edition.

> [...]
> then
> grace makes poop in my brain   5
> and the convexity of the body
> touches that of the sky
> and I sleep
> like a god who has climbed back into the father's throat
>
> one must say   10
> no to no and no to no no
> one must go back through one's skin and empty out all those
>   insides
> [...]
> I AM EVEN THOUGH I THINK
> and though I see myself think
> forcing myself to shit myself into the shit   15
>   of my thought
> instead of radiating
> motionless
> like the sun)

There are four figures of spiritual illumination that are reworked in this passage. "The thickness of noon" in line 2 negates the brightness of the midday sun, which is a standard hyperbole in French poetry for a moment of intellectual awakening (as, for instance, in the opening stanza of Valéry's "Le Cimetière marin" [The graveyard by the sea]). This same hyperbole for mental purity is rejected in the last five lines where the activity of thinking is compared to defecating, rather than the radiating of sunshine. Similarly, when we read that "the convexity of the body / touches that of the sky," we understand, through metonymy, that the human realm has attained the outer reaches of the divine. Finally there is the turning of Descartes's famous cogito ("I think therefore I am") into "I am even though I think," which effectively reverses philosophical idealism by defining existence as a bodily state independent of thought. As a result of transforming all these figures for thought, Noël's poem invites its readers to continue the attack against idealism by "go[ing] back through one's skin and empty[ing] out all those insides"—that is, by expelling the imaginary "inner life" of thought and uncovering instead the true inside of our bodies (the sensations, pulse, and other physiological functions that bind us to matter). Once this transformation of language is achieved, words of the gods will cease being disembodied thoughts and return to their source—the human larynx (line 9).

Noël's poem is not merely designed to shock poetry lovers; it redefines both the style and object of poems. For since the seventeenth century in one way or another poets have always respected the Cartesian separation of the mind from the body. The latter was allowed entry into poetry only on condition that it be represented by the proxies of thought or figurative language—and lyric poetry from Lamartine's *Méditations poétiques* up to Eluard's *Capitale de la douleur* tells us much about these proxies. For when the body is mentioned in these poems it is filtered through an imaginary figure, whether it be an absent beloved (as in Lamartine) or dreams and a vocabulary of the subconscious (with the Surrealists).[4] Poetry thus remained a type of writing that was addressed to the intellect, with mentions of sexuality and other bodily feelings meant to alter the reader's understanding not of the body, but of the *mind* and its various faculties (imagination, memory, and so on). With "Contremort," however, it is the body that Bernard Noël addresses, and he does so in a deliberately nonintellectual way.

What type of body is it, precisely? Quite obviously it cannot be the one that traditional poetry has made known, which has always been derived from its imaginary double, thought. As Noël himself remarks, "it's as if language had always been reserved for an aristocracy, which is the mind, and a bourgeoisie, which is the body—or the appearance of body." He goes on: "When one wants to lend words to what is going on inside, to everything that is organic, one cannot; it gargles, makes noises, but not words. Our organic side is like an illiterate proletariat."[5] Giving words to the body is therefore a process of linguistic reeducation. Not only are metaphors for thought overturned (as in the lines quoted above), but descriptions apparently reach their outside limit, with the rediscovered body identified by the simple deictic sign "THAT," or else compared to an unidentifiable life-form:

de la bouche de la bouche de la bouche sortent les
mille petites pattes invisibles de CELA

4. There are some notable exceptions to such idealizing of the body—Baudelaire's "Une Charogne" is one. Yet even in this poem one finds that the description of bodily decay is subordinated in the last stanza to an idealist lesson: "j'ai gardé la forme et l'essence divine / De mes amours décomposés" (I kept the form and divine essence / Of my decomposed loves).

5. Bernard Noël, *Treize cases du je* (Paris: Flammarion, 1975), 113.

de cela qui perpétuellement coule dans le creux de mon
     contre-corps
pour agglutiner mon temps et mon je

                              ("Contre-mort" 20)

(from the mouth the mouth the mouth come the
     thousand tiny and invisible paws of THAT
of that which is forever flowing in the hollowness of my
     anti-body
in order to bind together my time and my I)

Insofar as these invisible paws are issuing forth from the narrator's
mouth, it is permissible to interpret them as sounds, or as the yet uni-
dentified units of a new language that names Noël's "anti-(idealist)
body."

     This interpretation is lent weight in Noël's later collections of po-
etry *Bruits des langues* (Noises of languages) and *La Chute des temps*
(Times' falling), in which strange sound combinations gradually give rise
to groups of rhymed words whose phonetic pattern (rather than their
shared semantic features) is the basis for the emergence of meaning. The
first poem in *La Chute des temps,* called "Contre-chant" (Anti-song), ex-
ploits this same technique in order to derive a criticism of metaphysics
("le grand patatras de l'au-dela" [the great crash of the beyond]) from
the following:

                    langue pâlotte
                    étroit de la glotte
                    vers l'extrémité
                    cherche l'achevé
                    mais la tête trotte[6]

                    (sickly-looking language
                    narrow in the glottis
                    near the extremity
                    looks for what is completed
                    but the head is scurrying)

6. Noël, *La Chute des temps* (Paris: Flammarion, 1983), 31.

The title "Contre-chant" follows the same logic as "Contre-mort" and "Contre-corps" used in the earlier collection. Just as the first poem we examined was an attack against an idealist notion of the body, and hence an attack against the figurative death to which bodies have been confined in standard literature, so "Contre-chant" offers a struggle between "what is completed" (namely the fixed forms of traditional lyricism) and a constant shifting of meaning that characterizes language in action. "La vie est trop pleine / de postérité" (Life is too full / of posterity), we read later in the poem, "puisque l'appris pue" (since things learned stink; 36). Unlearning what the language of traditional poetry has taught is, consequently, what "Contre-chant" helps us do, and it sets to work on quotations from Mallarmé, Valéry, and many others:

> celui qui médite
> passe la limite
> ni vu ni connu
> il revient repu
> mais sa chair est triste
> d'être idéaliste
>
> (34)

> (he who meditates
> goes beyond the limit
> neither seen nor known
> he returns satiated
> but his flesh is sad
> to be idealistic)

The strategy of upending intertexts is, however, not the only organizing principle used in *La Chute des temps*. In an interview with the critic Hervé Carn, Noël pointed out that his text was constructed on the basis of the number 1,111, which he had divided into two times 333 (cantos 1 and 3), two times 111 ("Contre-chants" 1 and 2), and one 223 (canto 2). When one also considers that almost all the titles of Bernard Noël's books have fifteen letters in them, one begins to understand the importance of numerical constraints in his writing. It is not that these numbers have a hidden meaning; quite the contrary, like the noises from which the sounds in a language are built, these numbers have no meaning but they do have a *form,* and it is on the basis of this form that the poems are

structured. Numerical form thus replaces the semantic matrix as genera-
tor for the poem (a procedure we examine closely in Chapter 8), with the
result that the poems' words themselves have body and give expression
to the poem's form rather than to putative thoughts in a narrator's mind.
One of the first steps in creating a new poetic language for the body is to
redirect the reader's attention to the corporeality of sounds that lies at
the basis of all languages. In a manner akin to the Dadaists we examined
in Chapter 2, Noël is poeticizing not the semantic features of French but
the materiality of its signifiers, considered independently of a given sign
system.

It might seem that Noël is inviting his readers to espouse an ele-
mentary type of materialism whereby every human action, including
speech, could be explained in terms of physical or anatomical transforma-
tions. He writes in "Contre-mort," for instance, that "strange machines
appear in my body" (15), and yet, far from leading to an organic mate-
rialism (whereby flesh would simply replace the mind as the center of
motor activity), the "strange machines" surpass any simple opposition of
body and mind. For if the body revealed in "Contre-mort" were just to
take over the authority that one normally ascribes to the mind, the nature
of this authority (and its repression) would in no way change. The terms
body and *mind* would simply have switched places. In order to free
readers from the "aristocratic" system that controls a person's interac-
tions with others, and with her- or himself, Noël has to go beyond both
idealism and a simplistic definition of the body as matter. He does so by
equating the body with a network of forces.

In a short text from 1956 he calls this network "la situation lyrique
du corps natural" (the lyrical situation of the natural body).[7] This natural
body resonates with its own life. Each of its gestures intensifies the reso-
nance while at the same time erasing the distinction between the inside
and the outside. "The inside equals the outside. And inside the inside
there is the outside. Was I eight or a thousand years old yesterday? Per-
haps both. Too many circles inside my bones, too many numbers on my
tree" (26). By measuring his age not on the basis of his developed "skele-
ton" (26) but from the metaphorical "circles" that accumulate on his
body after doing each action, the narrator in this prose poem is defined
as an intensity that is always in the process of moving toward others, and
is a field of potential acts that "call out for another body." The equating

7. Noël, "La Situation du corps lyrique," *Poèmes I* (Paris: Flammarion, 1983), 23.

of this potential to act to a body's "lyrical situation" gives a radically different goal to lyric texts from the one that readers are accustomed to find. Instead of having the purely descriptive function of expressing emotions, lyric poetry according to Noël is part of the field of action in which a body vibrates and lives. On the level of a poem's words, this amounts to replacing the descriptive statements inside a text with what J. L. Austin termed performative utterances—that is, statements whose meaning is grounded not in what the words say but in the pragmatic effects that they accomplish for their audience.[8] This shift was already noticeable in the sound experimentation in *La Chute des temps*, discussed above, and it governs the poems in *Bruits des langues* (1980), where what at first appear to be jarring meaningless sounds prompt each reader to construct a meaning as he or she proceeds through the text. Such poems act on their receivers and, when successful, lead the latter to act on them in return. They reinvigorate language by teaching readers how to make their own speech do something (for example, establish a human bond of compassion or friendship with an interlocutor), instead of merely report facts. In this way such poems lead their readers to refashion their links to the other speakers around them.

Noël's collection of one-page passages titled *Extraits du corps* (Extracts of the body) explores further "the never-mentioned gearing" that makes up each body's network of acts (19). Destroying the mentalist "mirage of self in me" (58), *Extraits du corps* focuses instead on what various parts of the body can do: "gestures filling up the whole body" (58). One of these actions is the ability to turn oneself inside out:

Né du trou. Bâti autour du trou. Je suis une organisation du vide. Ainsi mon oeil est-il toujours creux de mon non. Ainsi puis-je me retourner comme un gant. (59)

(Born out of the hole. Built up around the hole. I am organized around emptiness. In this way my eye is always a hollow of my no. In this way I can turn myself inside out like a glove.)

---

8. J. L. Austin contrasts performative utterances that accomplish actions (e.g., "I name this ship 'Good Hope!'" when pronounced by a dignitary at a launching ceremony) with constative utterances that describe a state of affairs (e.g., "It is raining outside"). See his *How to Do Things with Words*, 2d ed. (Cambridge: Harvard University Press, 1973), 3–7.

As creatures who emerge through mothers' vaginas, and who construct themselves in large part from what comes out of their own mouths, people are indeed fabricated out of hollowness.

More than the results of past actions, however, people are engaged in an on-going self-creation through present and future choices that add new bodily layers to their original emptiness. Noël has compared these layers, in a passage quoted above, to the rings of an ever-expanding tree trunk, and elsewhere he calls them "the snow of gestures" (82) or "a flock of habits" (80). In a poem from his 1967 collection *La Face de silence* (The face of silence) he describes the way in which a person's identity-through-action can turn back on itself:

> ô fini
> toujours bouclant sa boucle
> et jamais finissant
>
> le fleuve coule aussi vers sa source
> et se nourrit de soi
>
> je peux naître en aval
> devenir qui je suis
>
> (88)
>
> (oh finite creature
> always relooping its own loop
> and never finishing
>
> the river also flows toward its source
> and draws nourishment from itself
>
> I can be born downstream
> and become who I am)

Through such bendings back on oneself it is possible to discover the limits of one's own identity, limits that are not given once and for all, but that will continue to change for as long as one goes on living. The "finite" entity of the body-in-action can therefore undergo an indefinite number of transformations, and the "loops" that it traces when it bends back on itself contribute to this perpetual change. Nevertheless, the more one acts, the more the limits to one's identity take shape, in the same

way that the age circles in a tree begin, after a certain time, to copy out
the same irregular design on an ever-enlarging scale. These limits, or
traces of action, point toward an identity that is about to be "born down-
stream," and that can only be called a "source" if the term is understood
as a state that one discovers while in the process of making it (rather than
a half-hidden origin that would precede our actions). In short, to "be-
come who I am" means gradually discovering through one's acts and
projects the *lived body* that one is.

Andrée Chedid's long 1973 poem "Prendre corps" (Taking body)
charts a similar process of self-discovery.[9] Written in twenty sections, the
poem details the coming into the world of a force addressed as "you,"
and the first seventeen sections of the text end with the statement "tu
viens" (you are coming). Here is the opening section:

> HORS DU VENTRE
> Avec sang et cris
>
> Tu rejoins ce monde
> Tu t'enfonces dans le jour
>
> Arraché au silence
> à l'eau sans épine
> aux plages assourdies
> à la forge sans feu
> au cercle humide et pourpre
>
> TU VIENS[10]
>
>
> (OUT OF THE BELLY
> With blood and cries
>
> You rediscover this world
> You plunge into the daylight

9. The analysis that follows of Andrée Chedid's poems owes much to detailed
discussions that one of the authors had with Anne F. Carlson and to reading her article, "La
Poésie dynamique d'Andrée Chedid," in *Andrée Chedid: Chantiers de l'écrit*, ed. Sergio
Villani (Toronto: Les Editions Albion Press, 1996), 23–35.

10. Andrée Chedid, "Prendre corps," *Poèmes pour un texte (1970–1991)* (Paris:
Flammarion, 1991), 157. Subsequent references to Chedid's poems are made to this edi-
tion.

> Plucked from silence
> from water without thorns
> from the muffled beaches
> from the forge that has no heat
> from the humid and purple circle

> YOU ARE COMING)

Although this force is later addressed as "Enfant de l'orgueil et des sources" (Child of pride and from the source), this is clearly a metaphorical designation, since the force in question has capacities beyond those of a newborn, or of any child:

> Plus fertile de chaque graine
> Plus dense de chaque chagrin
> Tu afflues vers les terrasses
> Tu surplombes les frontières
>
> (168)

> (More fertile from each seed
> More dense from each chagrin
> You flow toward the terraces
> You hang over the frontiers)

The first and third lines above give important clues as to the identity of the text's addressee. Insofar as the addressee gains fertility from seeds, spreads across cultivated terraces, and, as we are told later, "builds up a tree shoot" (174), it can only be life itself, a principle underlying all growth and change in the world. "Ainsi la Vie parla" (Thus life spoke; 176), we read in the poem's penultimate section, and this personified living force expresses itself in the form of various bodies:

> La Vie s'insurgea
>
> Elle prit voix elle prit gestes
> Prit viscères et prit sang
> Prit visages et mains
> Prit coeurs et puis regards
>
> (175)

(Life flared up

It took on a voice, it took on gestures
Took on intestines and took on blood
Took on faces and hands
Took on hearts and then looks)

"Taking body" is thus a phrase that Chedid uses for all the various ways that life acquires form. Body is consequently an ambiguous term in her writings since it designates both the experience of physiological sensations ("Captifs de l'étrange machine / Qui nous mène de vie à trépas" [Captives of the strange machine / That leads us from life to passing away]; 229), and also a general form-giving principle that, as we will demonstrate, is closely linked to the language of poetry.

This ambiguity is most apparent in her collection *Epreuves du vivant* (Trials of the living person). Using the same type of syllepsis as Bernard Noël in his *Extraits du corps*—whereby "extraits" (extracts) and "épreuves" (trials or proofs) simultaneously name areas of the body and sections of a printed text—Chedid's title establishes a basic similarity between body and writing. Taking on form, in these poems, is both an anatomical and a textual process. Setting out to explore "Tant d'inconnu / Dans ce corps reconnu" (So much unknown / In this well-recognized body; 83), *Epreuves du vivant* asks:

Qui
Se tient
Derrière le pelage du monde?

Quel visage au front nu
Se détourne des rôles
Ses yeux inversant les images
Sa bouche éconduisant les rumeurs?

Quel visage
(...)
Nous restitue
Visage?

(185)

(Who
stands there
Behind the world's fur?

What face with a bare forehead
Turns away from roles
Its eyes inverting images
Its mouth dispensing with rumors?

What face
[...]
Gives us back
Our face?)

The type of body that is indicated by these rhetorical questions is not a public persona, put on to fulfill the "roles" or project the "images" that the impersonal gaze of society requires. Instead it is a face that is not made up, nor clothed, in any way. Moreover, its mouth cuts through the gossip that gives the illusion of substance to so much daily conversation (and that also turns the faces of gossips into featureless talking heads). In short, it is a real body who, in looking at us, restores our own capacity to see, and acknowledge, others. Such a body emits light in which one can "discover the beauty of things / Obstinately intact under the exfoliation of unhappiness" (199). This last metaphor, which is a continuation of the one used in the passage quoted above, equates sorrow with growths that cover the body, whereas happiness is achieved by removing these coverings. Only then can each body take on its particular form, and joy.

In "La Table des poussières" (The table of dust) Chedid describes writing in the same terms—a scratching through surfaces that precipitates the ongoing appearance and disappearance of form. While the poem's title literally designates the sands on which ancient people would inscribe their signs and pictures, the poem's syntax is organized around imperatives that address present readers:

Inscris
Le poème doublé de nuit
Le poème drapé du linceul des mots
(...)

Inscris

    Le poème s'étirant dans les blés
    Le poème s'allongeant vers les sphères
    (...)
    A présent

Efface

    Que le poème retourne à la poussière
    Qu'il supprime toutes paroles
    Qu'il t'annule à ton tour

                    (207–8)

(Inscribe

    The poem replaced by night
    The poem draped in the shroud of words
    [...]

Inscribe

    The poem unwinding itself in the wheat fields
    The poem stretching out toward the spheres
    [...]
    Now

Erase

    Let the poem return to dust
    Let it suppress all words
    Let it annul you in turn)

Giving body to the poem (by inscribing it on the ground) means pulling out of limbo the words in which it is shrouded and the landscapes that inspire it. Yet it also means that the poet and reader acquire body through the inscription and reading of the text, so that when the poem is wiped out the vague notions that the reader has of her- or himself are wiped out with it. These notions are metaphorized as the items listed in a book's table of contents (*table des matières*).[11] Consequently, the turning of a *table des matières* into a *table des poussières* goes hand in hand with the shift from a bookish definition of humankind to a lived one. "La Table des poussières" ends with three imperatives that apply to the

11. For a discussion of Chedid's figurative use of *table des matières* in other contexts, see Maurice Delcroix, "Un poème d'Andrée Chedid: 'Solfège du squelette,'" *Travaux de littérature* 1 (1988): 253–63. We are grateful to Anne Carlson for bringing this article to our attention.

blending of the reader's own form with that of the written text: "Efface
et puis / Renais / Sur la table rase / Inscris . . ." (Erase and then / Be
reborn / On the tabula rasa / Inscribe . . .; 208). Chedid calls this bodily
identification between reader and poem "embrasser la poésie au plus
large" (embracing poetry in the widest way; 200), and it has the follow-
ing result:

> Alors (la poésie) devient 'acte,' elle devient 'oeuvre.'
>   Poésie pénétrant à pleines mains, à plein regard, à plein souf-
> fle, dans la vie; pour mieux l'appréhender, pour bâtir autrement.
> (201)

> (Then [poetry] becomes 'act,' it becomes 'artwork.'
>   A poetry that penetrates life deeply, with its hands, its gaze,
> and its death. It does so to grasp life better, and to construct differ-
> ently.)

Constructing "differently" should be understood both in a literary and
ethical sense, since poems not only reveal new structures in the language
they poeticize, but also lead their readers to redefine their own actions,
and hence themselves. The intransitive use of the verb *bâtir* in the pas-
sage above reinforces this ambiguity, and allows us to understand that
what are constructed are not just texts, but also lives. By giving language
new foundations, poetry teaches its readers to reinvent their speech acts,
and in so doing to reinvent themselves, through changing their patterns
of action toward others. "It's the 'making, un-making, re-making,' the
movements of life itself, that are important to me," declares Chedid near
the middle of *Epreuves du vivant* (206). "How can life be drawn / out of
all its jails?" asks the narrator rhetorically in "Regarder la vie" (Looking
at life; 215). Reconnecting readers to the performative power of words is
one key way, and Chedid achieves it through metaphors and syllepses
that redefine a standard vocabulary of books (*épreuves, table des matières,
inscrire*) in terms of organic life. Poeticizing language, for Chedid, in-
cludes remetaphorizing some of the basic terms of poetry writing.
    This constant transformation of "living proofs," which are both
texts and stages in the construction of a body-in-action, is not the private
property of the author but is shared by writer and readers alike. Indeed,
if, as noted above, we can "regain face" only by recognizing another's

true body (185), then an understanding of life is predicated on the very principle of sharing:

> Il nous faut le partage
> Il nous faut l'incendie
>
> Pour que s'amorce la source
> Pour que vive la vie.
>
> (43)
>
> (We need sharing
> We need the fire
>
> So that the source comes alive
> So that life can live.)

Such shared understanding comes through poetry. "En ce monde / Où la vie nous fuit" (In this world / Where life escapes us), writes Chedid, the poet

> Invente le poème
> Ses pouvoirs de partage
> Sa lueur sous les replis.
>
> (192)
>
> (Invents the poem
> Its powers of sharing
> Its light under the folds.)

Edmond Jabès's *Le Livre du partage* (The book of shares) contains a series of extended meditations on the ways in which poetry brings its readers to acknowledge their own, and others', life.[12] First of all, the author stresses that the human imperative to act and to change oneself (which is the basis of the lived body for Chedid and Noël) is common to all people. In "L'Héritage, I, II, III" (The heritage), Jabès characterizes it as a legacy that does not belong to anyone. A wise man in a later text puts it to his students thus:

12. Edmond Jabès, *Le Livre du partage* (Paris: Gallimard, 1987).

> "La question à ne jamais se poser est celle-ci:
> *Qu'est-ce qui m'appartient?*
> (...)
> Mon bien est davantage le vôtre que le mien." (58)

> ("The question to never ask oneself is this:
> *What belongs to me?*
> (...)
> My wealth is more yours than mine.")

According to "L'Héritage, I," the legacy that life offers is not a thing that can be possessed, but instead the capacity (as well as the necessity) to absorb and surpass misfortune:

> Lutter contre chaque ombre, non pas en les affrontant mais en les assumant.
> Tourner adroitement la difficulté.
> Déjouer leurs manoeuvres. (25)

> (To struggle against each shadow, not by confronting them but by taking them over.
> To skillfully turn difficulty around.
> To dismantle their maneuvers.)

Indeed, this capacity is one trait that gives humankind a certain power over God who, by definition, is above all misfortune. "In creating humanity, did God know that He would never manage to make a person," asks Jabès rhetorically, "since only the latter has the power to become a person through his or her own actions?" (41).

Two characteristics of such self-making stand out in *Le Livre du partage:* a new definition of the future, and a deeper understanding of our bonds to others. Since life teaches a person to absorb change and adapt to the unpredictable, the future is not written out ahead of time, but is instead a by-product of the actions and choices that each person makes. "Rien n'est parfait. Tout est à parfaire" (Nothing is perfect. Everything remains to be perfected; 57), comments Jabès about the ethical necessity to constantly improve the models for action (be they written or lived out) that we give to others. By following this impulse, we stop being mere pawns in a future that has nothing to do with us, and instead come to taste "the peaceful joy, for oneself, of henceforth having nothing to expect of the future" (123). In this way we can count on the future, once we recognize its dependence on us and leave behind "the slow agony of a vainly entertained hope" (31)—namely, any hope that a particular thing will come to pass, which draws us into a series of self-centered calculations to ensure that it does come to pass, while wiping out our freedom to act. People can avoid becoming trapped in their own calculations only by opening themselves up to others and situating their own joy in the experience of another's happiness:

> En accueillant le visage nous célébrons le monde.
> En le repoussant, nous condamnons celui-ci.
>
> (109)

> (By welcoming a face we celebrate the world.
> By pushing it away, we are condemning the latter.)

Hence the experience of joy is predicated on the shared space of welcomed bodies, or, as Jabès puts it, "to exist is to open oneself progressively to sharing; it's sharing life with life" (134).

Although this impulse to share, and to reinvent oneself through care for another, is universal, Jabès does not believe that it exists as a descriptive truth, or as a statement given originally by God, which the course of humankind has then had to confirm. Indeed, the wars that have marked not only our century but also earlier ones prove just the opposite. In "L'Héritage, II" he writes:

> La vérité est sans partage.
> Elle est, à l'origine, déjà partagée.
> Reste à légitimer le partage
>
> (27)

> (Truth is without division.
> It is, originally, already divided.
> The sharing remains to be legitimized)

The apparent contradiction formed by the first two sentences in this extract underlines the basic ambiguity of ethical truths. In order for these to be truths they must be accepted under any circumstance, without any reserves, and yet, by definition, they are truths that demand to be shared with other people, since they bear directly on our connections with others.

In the lines that follow, a second speaker questions the validity of these claims:

> "Ce que tu nommes *Vérité*—disait-il—est vérité en lambeaux.
> (...)
> Une fois arraché au Tout, ce misérable lambeau n'a plus, pour réalité, que sa misère.
> Il est vérité du malheur." (28)

> ("What you are calling *Truth*—he said—is a tattered truth.
> [...]
> Once it has been torn away from All-ness, this sorry rag is, in fact, nothing but its own pitiful state.
> It is a truth of unhappiness.")

In the wake of the Holocaust and other genocides, it would indeed seem that a fundamental caring for others is a destroyed principle. Yet to this Jabès replies that such a principle should not be understood as a truth that human behavior either confirms or denies, but that the "truth of sharing" should instead be considered as a shorthand way of pointing to the onward movement of life:

> Nous sommes *pour* la vérité; mais si ce *pour*, afin de nous conforter dans nos pensées et nos actes, s'adressait moins à la vérité qu'à nous-mêmes, détenteurs présumés de cette vérité?
> Il vaudrait mieux, alors, dire: Nous sommes *aux côtés* de la vérité, comme on est tout près de ce à quoi l'on croit, sachant pertinemment que toute croyance n'est jamais que reconnaissance de soi, à travers ce qui donne un sens à la vie.
> Une vérité comme justification d'une vie, en somme. (28)

> (We are *for* truth; but what if this *for*, so as to comfort us in our thoughts and actions, was addressed less to truth than to ourselves, the presumed holders of this truth?
> It would then be better to say: We are *at the sides* of truth, as one is extremely close to things that one believes in, knowing all

too well that all belief is never anything but a recognition of one-
self, seen through whatever gives a meaning to life.
    In short, a truth in the form of the justification for a life.)

Consequently, the logical form of the word *truth* is not that of a noun
(naming a thing), but that of an adverb (which qualifies each individual's
path of self-making). Phrased in J. L. Austin's terms, this means that true
and false when used in Jabès's way are not values ascribable to constative
statements, but instead qualify the relative success or failure of the perfor-
matives (linguistic and otherwise) that make up a person's life. When a
person acts truly then the actions will justify his or her life, and when he
or she does not then living as sharing comes to a stop and the person's
speech acts and other public interventions can no longer be joyous.
    Here Jabès touches on a central property of all the poems examined
in this chapter. Poetry that lends voice to the human body and to its
connections with life does not aim at discovering truths about people,
since such truths always take the form of ideas, or constative propositions
that the mind inspects and that human behavior either endorses or invali-
dates. Instead such poetry teaches its readers (and writers) how to better
open up to patterns of living that ground their everyday actions. Know-
ing better how to live (which is a performative know-how conveyed by
poetry's co-opting of language[13]) takes precedence over any knowledge
that life is x or y. Noël puts it this way:

> autrefois nous mâchions le savoir
> pour donner un nom à chaque chose
> et la domestiquer
> mais la route a détissé la trame

(112)

> (in earlier times we used to chew over knowledge
> in order to give a name to each thing

---

13. See Jabès's comment that "Avec les mots de la langue, l'écrivain (...) fonde une
seconde langue (...) qui, dorénavant, lui appartient en propre, ô paradoxe, et n'appartient
plus à personne" (With the words of a language, the writer [...] founds a second language
[...] which henceforth belongs truly to him, and yet paradoxically, no longer belongs to
anybody) (51–52). Performative language is precisely the type of discourse that is part of
the speaker's particular makeup (since its speech acts help give that speaker an identity, by
changing his or her actions), while at the same time being a force of words that belongs to
nobody in particular. It is a type of discourse that beckons anyone (or any reader) to use it.

and domesticate it
but the road [followed by our lives] has pulled the fabric apart)

The forward movement of life, metaphorized in the above lines by a road each person takes, undoes the patterns of explanation that we set up, and puts knowledge secondary to present and future action (rather than the other way around).

Andrée Chedid makes a similar criticism of investigations into personal pasts (such as a psychoanalytic study of the supposed causes of a person's behavior), since these too ignore the fact that action oriented toward the future constantly transforms our past and redefines our present. In a poem titled "Pour savoir" (In order to know) she writes:

> A quels gouffres descendre?
> A quelle folie consentir?
> A quelle porte guetter?
> (...)
> Parvenus enfin au soleil des racines,
> N'aurons-nous pas perdu la lucarne
> Qui donne sur nos souvenirs?[14]

> (To what chasms should we descend?
> To what madness should we consent?
> At what door should we stand lookout?
> [...]
> When we finally will have reached the sunshine of roots
> Won't we have lost the skylight
> That looks out onto our memories?)

The "sunshine of roots" forms an oxymoron that ironically undermines the supposed clarity coming from the discovery of a source of pain. In addition, the entire descent into hell that is sketched out in the opening stanza is done in vain once the narrator realizes that one's remembrances bring joy only if they are used to this effect. In themselves they are neither joyous nor sad, but how we weave them into our projected future (metaphorized by a skylight) is what counts.

Returning to our point of departure in this chapter, Jacqueline Ris-

---

14. Andrée Chedid, *Seul, le visage*, in *Textes pour un poème* (Paris: Flammarion, 1987), 184.

set's transformation of physics exemplifies the antiknowledge claims made by body-poetry. For in *Petits éléments de physique amoureuse* physics stops being a science, and "all mental activity is suspended, postponed," while "another, more interior, activity has taken its place" (18). What this is, writes Risset, is "le corps vif, le corps qui sent, comme on dit, par chaque pore" (the living body, the body that feels, as we say, through all its pores; 10). Although one might be tempted to interpret Risset's characterization of this "strange body" in terms of Ponge's poetic materialism, discussed in Chapter 5, what we have demonstrated above is that this new language of the body acquires meaning only by upending the discourses of thought, self, and knowledge. For whereas these three are constative uses of language, the poeticized and upended versions given by the poets in the present chapter are models for a powerfully performative type of speech and gesturing.

eight

READING, MOUNTING, SPACING

(GARNIER,

ROUBAUD,

LEIRIS,

ET AL.)

What is reading? It's letting your eyes roam over a graphical ensemble.

—*Louis Marin,* Etudes sémiologiques

With this remark, Louis Marin has given the concept of reading its broadest possible definition. As such, it corresponds perfectly to the idea of a poem as montage, which is commonly defined as "an artistic composition made up of different kinds of items (such as strips of newspaper, pictures, bits of wood) arranged together."[1]

First of all, there is the question of knowing how to look at things. The spatial architecture mounted on a page, which gives the text's verbality the appearance of an object, has taken on an ever-increasing importance in contemporary French poetry. As in Dada aesthetics, the fusion of the construction produced with the written signs that compose it gives a tangible aspect to the figure while at the same time leaving readers perplexed, forcing them to discover new rules of reading for themselves.

1. *The Merriam-Webster Dictionary* (New York: Pocket, 1976), 456.

Their eyes must learn to roam over a new graphic system, to use Marin's terms.

Yet this type of montage is, in itself, not a recent invention. Long before calligrams (or lyrical ideograms, as Apollinaire first thought of calling them), figurative verse or *figurata* had always been an important part of poetry. Sometimes these works were called rhopalic verse, using the Greek word *rhopalon* (or club), which named the most common shape given to this kind of poem, with a wing, an egg, and Pan's flute. In the writings of Samosate, Fortunat, or Alcuin,[2] and later on with the Grands Rhétoriqueurs in the last quarter of the fifteenth century, readers had to discern an enigmatic image embedded and concealed within the text.[3] Any poem written in figurative verse may indeed be considered, first and foremost, a cryptogram.

With Apollinaire the visual poem compels the reader to undertake a meticulous reconstruction of the visual image and its associated message. Reading his calligrams demands that we combine the effects of sound, meaning, and spatial arrangement. Furthermore, the deciphering does not stop with the discovery of a hidden icon, whether it be an image, a word, a name, or a maxim. Several paths and relationships are arranged in the text for the reader to follow, and it is the slow recovery of this system of interdependent levels, which is itself the artful montage of tightly fitted components, that constitutes the main focus of our reading, rather than the discovery of a particular hidden element in the poem.

One must, nevertheless, realize that the reading principles that are called for by such systems of verbal patterning differ markedly according to the type of montage-poem in question. To illustrate this wide variety of reading principles, we give three examples. The first is a poem by Paul Eluard, which opens his collection *Mourir de ne pas mourir* published in 1924:

L'Egalité des sexes

Tes yeux sont revenus d'un pays arbitraire
Où nul n'a jamais su ce que c'est qu'un regard

2. See André Massin, *La Lettre et l'image* (Paris: Gallimard, 1973); and Roselyne Dupont-Roc and Jean Lablot, "La Syrinx," *Poétique* 18 (1974): 176 ff.

3. See Paul Zumthor's *Langue, texte, énigme* (Paris: Seuil, 1975) and his *Le Masque et la lumière: La Poétique des Grands Rhétoriqueurs* (Paris: Seuil, 1978).

Ni connu la beauté des yeux, beauté des pierres
Celle des gouttes d'eau, des perles en placards,

Des pierres nues et sans squelette, ô ma statue,   5
Le soleil aveuglant te tient lieu de miroir
Et s'il semble obéir aux puissances du soir
C'est que ta tête est close, ô statue abattue

Par mon amour et par mes ruses de sauvage.
Mon désir immobile est ton dernier soutien   10
Et je t'emporte sans bataille, ô mon image,
Rompue à ma faiblesse et prise dans mes liens.[4]

(The Equality of the Sexes

Your eyes have come back from an arbitrary land
Where no one has ever known what a look really is
Nor known the beauty of eyes, beauty of stones
That of water drops, of pearls in cupboards,

Stones naked and without a skeleton, o my statue,   5
The blinding sun serves as your mirror
And if it seems to obey the forces of evening
It's because your head is closed, o fallen statue

Knocked down by my love and by my wild man ruses.
My immovable desire is your last refuge   10
And I carry you off without a struggle, o my image,
Broken by my feebleness and trapped in my bond.)

Several critics have commented on Eluard's frequent use of sight as a
metaphor for love,[5] and this poem confirms the point—hence the expan-
sion of "the beauty of eyes" in line 3 into "the beauty of [precious]
stones / That of water drops, of pearls in cupboards," the latter phrase

4. Paul Eluard, *Oeuvres complètes,* ed. Lucien Scheler, 2 vols. (Paris: Gallimard,
Pléiade, 1968), 1:137.
5. See, for instance, Raymond Jean, *La Poétique du désir* (Paris: Seuil, 1974): "The
act of love always coincides for [Eluard] with the act of seeing, because it implies the
existence of a translucent medium in which the two gazes can meet and where the poem is
transcribed" (390). See also Gabrielle Polin, *Les Miroirs d'un poète: Images et reflets de Paul
Eluard* (Brussels: Desclée de Brouwer, 1969).

being an analogical metaphor whereby cupboards are to pearls what eye-lids are to eyes. There is, however, no exchange of looks between lover and beloved in the poem, since from line 2 onward the gaze of the latter is gradually erased, with the earlier expansion of "the beauty of eyes" taking on the attributes of sadness and death: tear "drops," inanimate "stones," a petrified "statue" that is then knocked down by the force of the lover's desire. The desired person has gradually become objectified into a lifeless image (line 11). Consequently, the "last refuge" offered to the beloved in line 10, which is the embrace described in the poem's last line, is but another of the "wild man ruses" or a trap set by the narrator.

The definition of seeing put forward in the poem's narrative there-fore consists of receiving a reflection of one's own desire, which has re-placed the person seen with a fictitious copy. Put in another way, there does not appear to be any *equality* of the sexes in the text (contrary to what its title claims), but solely a fictional equation established between the desirer and his desired image. This turning of sexual equality into a purely visual equation is borne out in the poem's typographic form, which makes visible a phonetic and typographic symmetry arranged around its central rhyme of *miroir/soir* (lines 6 and 7), with the *rimes croisées* (crossed rhymes) of the first and last quatrains held in balance by the *rimes embrassées* (embraced rhymes) of the middle stanza: ABAB DC/CD EFEF. The rhythm of the poem reinforces this symmetry with the regular alexandrines (divided into balanced six-syllable hemistiches) offset by two hemistiches on each side of the center line between lines 6 and 7 that do not have a hemistich division (lines 3 and 5, 9 and 11). This prosodic symmetry around the word *miroir* then leads the reader to the other mirror structure embedded in the poem: that of the word *sexes* in the title. For *sexes* can be read just as well from left to right as from right to left. More and more it seems that the equality of the sexes pro-posed optimistically in the title, then replaced by a mere economy of desire, is actually a typographic pattern that structures the poem's fabric.

One might wonder at this point if the text's typographic pattern is just a secondary reinforcement for its linguistic meaning—the frustrated gaze of a lover who finds his own image. If this were so, no special importance could be attached to the visual mounting of the poem since such a mounting would be simply the effect of conventional prosody, or the "icing on the cake" of poetic meaning, just an extra luxury that readers could take or leave without impairing their understanding of the text. What Eluard's poem proves, however, is that certain poems cannot be fully understood until one recognizes their particular mounting. For only then will one be able to see, in this particular case, that the opening lines are also a metalinguistic signpost for the reader, telling one how to read the montage-poem: "Your eyes [dear reader] have come back from an arbitrary land [one of rules of reading and seeing] / Where no one has ever known what a look really is"—namely, the type of looking that poetry teaches us, which does not merely follow the direction of prosaic reading, from left to right, but which also moves from right to left and from bottom to top. Eluard leads his reader to a new appreciation of language, a poeticized language, that supersedes the impoverished tool of communication with which it is usually identified.[6]

Our second example of a montage-poem with its own reading principle is taken from the Surrealist game of *cadavre exquis* (exquisite corpse), borrowed by Michel Leiris in his book *Mots sans mémoire* (Fig. 17). The term *cadavre*, which appears in the middle line of the text, makes this borrowing quite plain.

On a superficial level, each sequence is presented in a typographic form that accentuates the differences and discrete quality of each one. Furthermore, the graphic structure of the text that privileges the horizontal plane—or, in other words, the normal direction of reading from left to right—does not disrupt the standard order of reading, so that the readers will tend to follow their normal habits when facing the text and jump from line to line, thus following the linear development of the phrases.

6. From the aesthetic standpoint put forward by Eluard in the early 1920s, poeticizing language's visual properties is of prime importance since the dominant thesis in his Dadaist works, such as *Les Animaux et leurs hommes, les hommes et leurs animaux* (Animals and their men, men and their animals; 1920), and in his review *Proverbe* (Proverb; begun in February 1920) is that the arbitrary language of everyday communication must be destroyed and replaced by a purer tongue that would ensure a "common exchange" among all people (*Oeuvres complètes* 1:37). (See Chapter 2 for a discussion of this aesthetics and the poems that support it.) Eluard visually indicated this type of direct exchange in his poems' typography—not only in such mirror-titles as *Les Animaux et leurs hommes, les hommmes et leurs animaux*, but also in his earliest published verse poems, from *Le Devoir* (Duty; 1916) up to *Répétitions* (Rote learning; 1922), which almost always follow a symmetrical pattern arranged around an invisible vertical axis. Indeed, "L'Egalité des sexes" is the last in a long series of poems that Eluard constructed around a typographic mirror pattern. Although he abandoned this technique for the most part after 1924, he continued to be fascinated by the ideal of a purely visual form of communication that would dispense with verbal signs. Consequently, we read in *Les Frères voyants* (The brother-seers; 1952) that "from the depth of the ages comes the irrepressible necessity of seeing [and] also the necessity of speaking a universal language that goes beyond frontiers and epochs" (*Oeuvres complètes* 2:512).

LE PASSÉ   LE PRÉSENT

une peau douce
des joues roses

UN CADAVRE TOUT NU

POUR FAIRE PONDRE
LES POULES

Vous en trouverez partout

Figure 17

    The word association in the text is based first and foremost on elementary accumulation. Just like the model sequence "exquisite corpse," this poem associates two verbal elements that usually exclude each other: "cadaver" versus "rosy cheeks" and "soft skin," which produces an oxymoron. It is this basic opposition that produces the "scandal," emphasized by the fact that the term employed (*cadavre*) has a taboo status within the French sociolect. The reading could stop here, with our eyes caught by the oxymoron, but quite clearly a reader could continue to work on the text and handle it as a montage. In other words, once the provocative nature of the verbal ensemble has been spotted and defused, it is no longer of any great importance since what counts is the reader's reconstructing the system of verbal relationships that makes the text into a discrete semiotic unit.

    In our third example of a montage (Fig. 18) the singularity of the graphic elements is not emphasized, since they are all neutralized through use of the same typography. Instead, it is the new arrangement of the linguistic elements building up the text that produces a strange effect. The words' horizontal dimension is replaced by a spatial distribution that

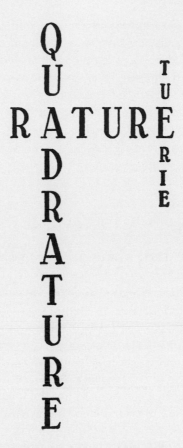

Figure 18

is limited to the surface of the page. Besides its semantically unifying function, the title "La Hache" (The axe)[7] clearly serves as a model for the visual representation it labels, and the size of the words is linked to the particular part of the axe depicted: for instance, the word *quadrature,* which is in the place of the handle, is the longest one. The main purpose of the reading is to refigure the semiotic bonds that explain the combination of these three words and their relation to the formal model. The reader's approach to such a text can be nothing but heuristic, since, unlike the previous example, this poem does not produce a shock effect but instead calls for some sustained exegesis.

As a first step toward a taxonomy of montage-poems, we would like

7. In Michel Leiris, *Mots sans mémoire* (Paris: Gallimard, 1969), 92.

to suggest that there are four types of montage in contemporary French poetry. The four types all bear out what Apollinaire wrote about *simul-taneisme*—that the reader of a poem recognizes all of its elements simultaneously—since the traditional linear chain of words is broken down in various ways (by blank spaces, side groupings, quincuncial ordering, and so on). The four types are: the form-onomatopoeia, the cipher, the re-fraction, and the scrap-poem. We will demonstrate how each of these types calls for a different reading strategy, while all entail the same general consequences for an understanding of poetry.

FORM-ONOMATOPOEIA

In his polemical and proselytizing book *Spatialisme et poésie concrète*, Pierre Garnier asserts that "le poème visuel ne se 'lit' pas. On se laisse 'impressionner' par la figure générale du poème" (one does not "read" a visual poem. One has to be "impressed" by the poem's general appearance).[8] This type of poem, which follows to the letter the literary tradition of the *carmina figurata*, imposes a representation of its the-matic content on the reader that is perceived through its most immediate effects. There is a game of echoes played between the text as image-sign and the verbal material as symbolic medium (be it a gloss or a definition). The surface of the page is taken as the framework for the image's ar-rangement and, by necessity, any reading implies a visualization of the poem. It is a poetry that cannot be read out loud, because, in the wake of the main principles of futurism and constructivism, words are reduced to a merely graphic substance out of which the poem as object is built.

Pondering the specific nature of this type of poem, which breaks away from the expected norms of poetic form, Garnier forecasts the ap-pearance of a new species of reader:

> Visual poetry changes the "reader's" destination. Up until now he was a passive contributor. The poem would close in on him. The new poetry requires his collaboration. [...] Visual poetry stimulates his psychic energy: starting with the proposed words and their ar-chitecture, he has to exercise both his body and his mind; he him-self takes the place of the poem's content. In so doing every person

8. Pierre Garnier, *Spatialisme et poésie concrète* (Paris: Gallimard, 1960), 202.

takes back a position for which he had been previously challenged. He washes away his self. In every reader there gradually appears an I, the active principle of creation. (136)

By way of illustration and analysis we propose two visual poems: "La Porte du soleil" (Sungate) by Pierre Garnier and "La Fronde" (Sling) by Michel Leiris. Both are based on the same principles of montage, but they do not exploit it in the same way.

Garnier's poem displays an obvious effort to destroy the linguistic material that makes up a linear sequence of writing (Fig. 19). The letters are reified, becoming an isolated mass on the page, and thus turned into the building blocks that are required for a montage. The predominant arrangement is vertical, contrary to normal written language in which the horizontal plane takes precedence. Furthermore, this poem does not have any syntax, but is instead built around the isolated lexical unit *soleil* (sun), which appears both in its complete state and in fragments cut off from the word. Such is the case with the repetition and expansion of the same letter, as in *sssss,* or with truncations of the word that produce a new meaning, as in *sol* (ground) and *soleils* (suns), or that produce none at all, as in *eil*. The title "La Porte du soleil" functions as a definition of the poem-as-object. At the same time, it justifies the connection between the text's shape and the verbal material (namely, the word *soleil*) that is used to establish it, for the shape is that of a Dutch door (or in French, *une porte à claire-voie*—that is, a door that lets the sunshine in even if the bottom half stays closed).

Leiris's mounted poem (Fig. 20) is very similar to "La Hache," which was discussed above, and it illustrates the same interaction between its shape and title as Garnier's text. For the title gives us the key to what is represented, and, again, the words are used as material for the montage. Nevertheless, the difference between this text and Garnier's is that its three words—*vent* (wind), *aiguillon* (goad), and *conjecture* (conjecture)—give a gloss for the word *fronde* (sling). At one semantic level or another, they all share some common motifs or semes with *fronde*. For instance, in French, the semantic connection between *fronde* and *conjecture* passes through a common etymology in their definitions: *fronde* is first of all an "arme de *jet*" (missile weapon) and *conjecture* has as its first meaning "*jeter* une idée" (to toss out an idea). Consequently, in this type of montage, the reader's task consists of retracing the network of conjunctions that support the privileged link between the verbal material and

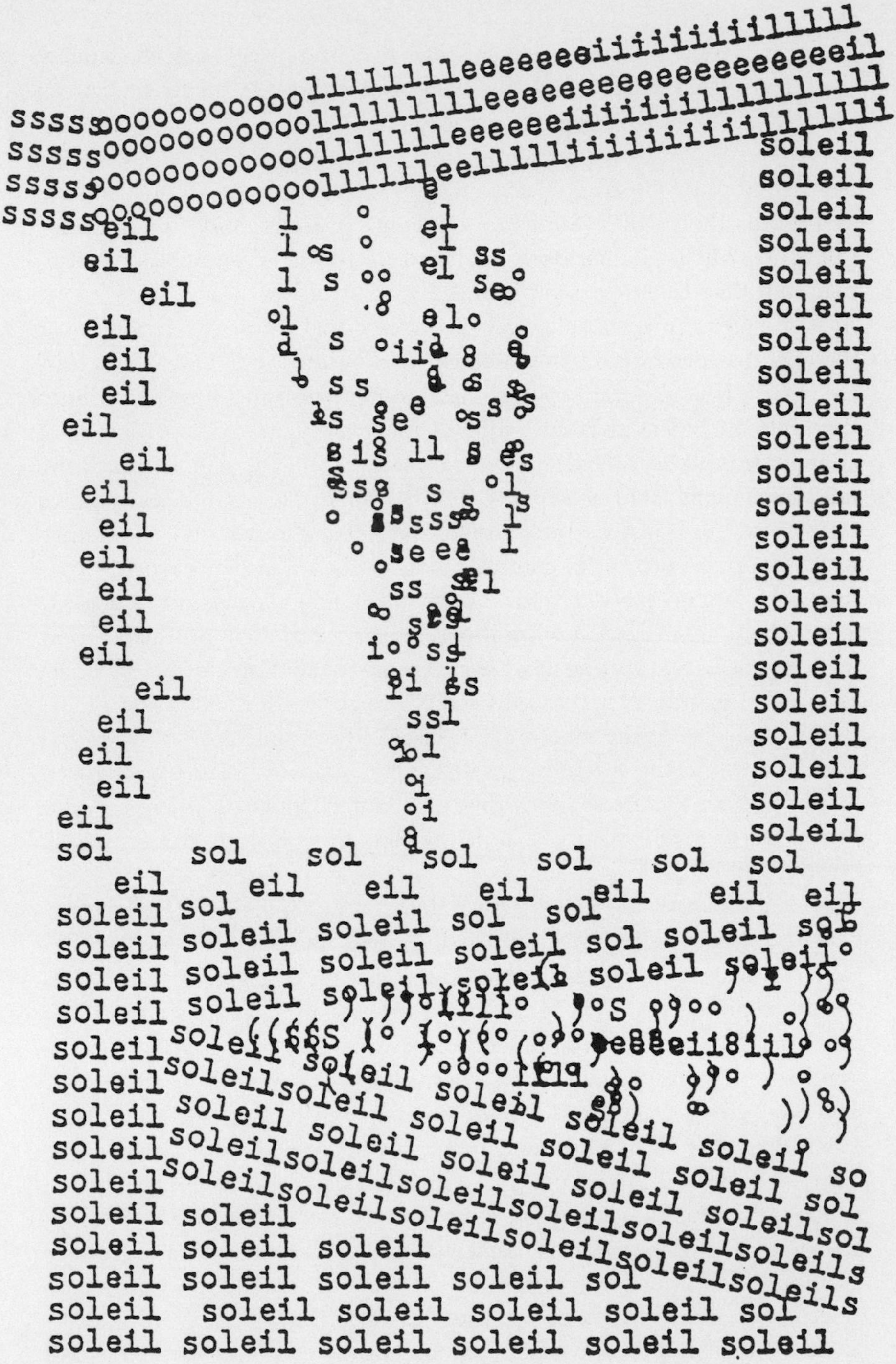

Figure 19

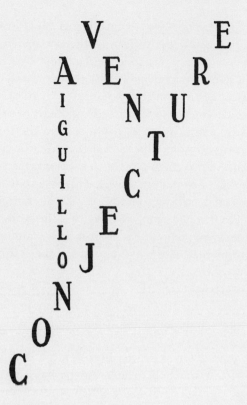

Figure 20

the given figure of the poem. In Garnier's poem, the shape took its origin from the meaning of the title, and it is this meaning that motivates and justifies the selective appearance of the words that are proposed as material for the montage.

CIPHER

> *And what if there were no cipher? We would be left with that endless call of things remaining secret, the expectation of discovery, and errant steps taken in the labyrinth of exegesis.*
>
> —*Jean Starobinski,* Les Mots sous les mots

Many people have read about Saussure's so-called madness, which consisted of studying classical Latin poems in order to recover what he labeled anagrams and later hypograms.[9] According to him, words, phrases, or names were hidden below the surface of the completed text, though it was possible to reconstruct this concealed subtext by identifying within the surface text some component words, syllables, or phonemes whose presence and distribution seemed to be dictated by rules other than those of grammar. Inside every poetic text, then, there is supposedly a palimpsest marked by a *locus princeps,* a sequence in the text's surface that provides the reader with some clues about the structure of the underlying secondary system. After recognizing this *locus princeps* and understanding its underlying mode of operation, the reader is able to reconstruct a set of numerical rules based on scansion and/or the alteration of vowels and consonants. Once the numerical pattern of distribution has been unfolded, the reader may pinpoint the appropriate scattered elements and reassemble them in such a way as to produce the normal arrangement given in the hypogram.

Unlike the cabala's exegetes, however, Saussure does not ascribe a mythological value to the hypogram. Its discovery is void of any sacred implication, since, as Jean Starobinski points out,

> The hypogram is for Saussure nothing more than a piece of material data, whose function, which was perhaps initially sacred, was limited very early on to that of a mnemonic aid for the improvising poet and then to a regulating process that is intrinsic to the *écriture* itself—at least in Latin. Saussure never stated that the final text preexists in the theme-word; the text builds itself *around* the theme-word, and this is quite different. (64)

It is probably just such a technical conception of the hypogram that led Saussure to see in it the prototype of every poetic system that is based on rhythmic rules. The phonic repetition of the hypogram's constituents foreshadows rhyme and the rule-governed distribution of the component parts that make up metrical prosody.

This theory has the merit of strongly supporting the hypothesis that every classical fixed form in a poem is simply, so to speak, a genetic mutation of the cipher-type montage. However, we are reserving the label of cipher for those poems that do not conform to traditional fixed forms but which generate a specific organization based on a metrical ordering. In

---

9. On Saussure and hypograms, see Jean Starobinski's *Les Mots sous les mots: Les Anagrammes de Saussure* (Paris: Gallimard, 1971), 160. The term *hypogram* appears in his studies on Homer (Ms. f. 3963) and Lucretius (Ms. f. 3964).

this case, the numerical definitions are not given, but are part of the hidden network that the reader has to uncover. At the same time, the numerical cryptogram organizes the elements in the poem and, indeed, *is* the text.

In contemporary French poetry, the works of Jacques Roubaud are a perfect example of this cipher-type montage. The collections of poetry written by this author, who is a member of the *Change* group of literary theorists, are all based on a mathematical ordering: ∈ (the mathematical symbol indicating "is a member of" in set theory), *Mono No Aware*, and *Trente et un au cube* (Thirty-one cubed).[10] This is hardly surprising since Roubaud introduces himself as a "poet and mathematician." The book ∈ offers a relevant example of reading guided by a set of numerical rules. It is only by understanding the strict distributional rules of the Japanese game Go—an exercise in strategic skills in which the pieces are moved progressively on a square plane—that the reader can gain access to the text's significance, since these rules are the ones that govern its overall arrangement.

Roubaud takes the trouble of providing the uninitiated reader with a "Mode d'emploi de ce livre" (Book's operating manual). This foreword is nothing less than an exhaustive code of the book's reading procedures, and a firm warning that the possible strategies involved are limited to the ones inscribed in the abstract system that has been laid out as the book's formal model:

Ce livre se compose, en principe, de 361 textes, qui sont les 180 pions blancs et les 181 pions noirs d'un jeu de GO. (...) Les textes ou pions appartiennent aux variétés suivantes: sonnets, sonnets courts, sonnets interrompus. (...) Les pions entretiennent entre eux différents rapports de signification, de succession ou de position. Ce sont certains de ces rapports (ou absence de rapports) que nous proposons au lecteur selon quatre modes de lecture explicitée aux numéros suivants:

1. Selon le premier mode de lecture, des groupements de pions, d'importance inégales peuvent être aidés. (...)
2. La deuxième "lecture" est celle qui détermine la répartition en paragraphes du présent livre. (...)
3. Le troisième mode de lecture suit le déroulement d'une partie de GO, reproduite à l'Appendice. (...)

10. Jacques Roubaud, ∈ (Paris: Gallimard, 1967), *Mono No Aware* (Paris: Gallimard, 1970), and *Trente et un au cube* (Paris: Gallimard, 1973).

4. On peut enfin, sans tenir compte de ce qui précède, se contenter
de lire ou d'observer isolément chaque texte. (7–9)

(This book is composed, in principle, of 361 texts, which are the
180 white pieces and the 181 black pieces of a Go game. [...] The
texts or pieces belong to the following categories: sonnets, short
sonnets, interrupted sonnets. [...] The pieces are interconnected
through different relations of meaning, succession and position (or
their absence) that we are offering to the reader under the four
modes of reading explained below:
1. According to the first mode of reading, one can isolate group-
ings of pieces of disparate size. [...]
2. The second "reading" determines the distribution of the present
book into paragraphs. [...]
3. The third mode of reading follows an actual Go game presented
in the Appendix. [...]
4. One may also follow none of the above and be satisfied with
reading or looking at each text taken separately.)

A square surface as shown in Figure 21 corresponds to the third
type of reading and is a representation of one particular Go game. It is
also the abstract numerical diagram of the organization of the text's ele-
ments.

This very abstract grid must be filled out by the multiple compo-
nents of the text-as-set. In the appendix this mapping is reinforced by the
play-by-play unfolding of the distributional strategy. As Diagram 3 indi-
cates, for each move and within the framework of an ordered reading one
can find the corresponding page number of the poems to "play."

The first and second types of reading cover an empirical reading
during which each component is evaluated in its own right. It is the
text's *nature*—in the mathematical sense—that is retained, which leads
to puzzling conclusions. In his "operating manual" Roubaud directs the
prospective reader to "chart 1, page 132," but the reader looks in vain
for the chart on this page. Only by a lonely, empirical, page-by-page close
reading can the reader reconstruct these two subsets composed either of
white or black pieces (i.e., poems), since there is a black or white dot
preceding each poem. This deceitful ruse strengthens the constraining
effect of the book's overall patterning. Moreover, at the semantic level,
there is a confirmation that all our attention should be concentrated on

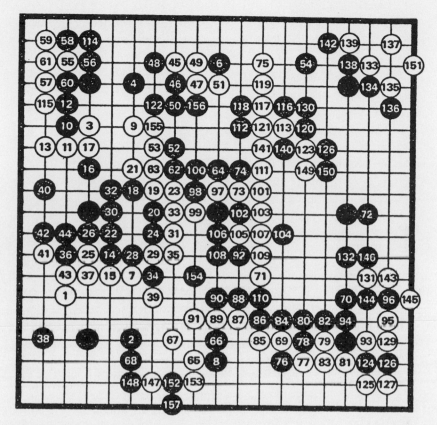

Figure 21

the pattern that is governed by the plays of the actual Go game given as a program. Any attempt to connect some components forms only paragraphs ("The second 'reading' determines the distribution of the present book into paragraphs"), which, it must be admitted, presupposes the existence of a whole at a higher level. In one of his theoretical works, Roubaud considers ∈ to be a "sonnet of sonnets," which underlines the fact that the constitution of subsets is less essential than the understanding of the set as a whole. The global system of the text prevails over the addition, piece by piece, of equivalent minimal units.

The fourth type of reading, which invites readers to do as they wish, could be labeled the stochastic drift. As such this reading poses many problems since it reintroduces chance by allowing indetermination to enter the general economy of the numerical network. How can Roubaud

Number of each move in game	Page	Number of each move in game	Page
1	116	29	85
2	109	30	66
3	133	31	61
4	110	32	77
5	58	33	61
6	116	34	43
7	58	35	52
8	76	36	53
9	46	37	53

Diagram 3

attempt to bring chance into his prearranged and closed system? Does this mean that there is a particular instance in which the systematic concatenation does not encompass all the aspects of the text, and that consequently there is a hitch in the combinatory texture? Could it be that the interweaving of the text is not tight enough to redirect the reader back onto the preordained tracks?

If such were the case, this notion of the text as an incomplete system would be similar to the one formulated by Kristeva in *Séméiotiké:*

> If all [language] is linear, that is to say a concatenated system that can be formalized by means of propositional logic, and if, as such, it puts forth a rhetorical law that is already a limit that cannot be broken, the text needs this line in order to move *away* from it; and also to slide over it, to follow its movement, absorbing it then suddenly opting for a "vertical line" that it follows for a while then opens out onto another space with multiple possibilities.[11]

A close study of $\in$ has convinced us that there is certainly some wavering, or at least some ambiguity, in Roubaud's position. As a result, this undetermined aspect of the text leads us to believe that a formal setting is only a superficial structure that cannot account for all of a text's combinatory features.

Without pursuing all the implications of this question (which would

11. Julia Kristeva, *Séméiotiké* (Paris: Seuil, 1969), 343.

lead to the canceling out of the book's ritualized patterns), let us simply suggest that the systematic model of the Go game may itself be at fault. As a game it favors the establishment of a waste product, or irretrievable residue, which is at odds with the project of wholeness and completion. On page 76 the notion of *KO* appears and is defined as "the door through which all the pieces are rushing out." If there is a situation in which all pieces (or poems) may disappear at once, without any planning and order, then there is no room for numerical constraints. The finite and closed aspect of the system would appear to be a fallacy. The finite game, which is artificially limited by its rules and enclosed in its neatly designed square board (termed "the walls"), is undermined by the actual language-piece, which can always sneak away, led by unforeseen principles: "mais elle qui soudain fuyait d'un mot," "La bouche retrouva les mots enfreints" (but she who suddenly fled from a word, The mouth rediscovered the infringed words; 78, 137).

According to Roubaud's appendix, the poem appearing on the last page is also the last piece to be played. This symmetrical ending does not, however, seem to encompass language. The text is finite whereas its material is free—a literal interpretation of the poem "O glib o liebe . . ." confirms this (79). For beyond the obvious homophonic pun, what is asserted here is that language in its infinite flight cannot be bent in order to conform to a predetermined systematic grid. If the text takes no chances, its material will. It is interesting to notice, in this respect, that the last sentence of the last poem ("nous sommes seuls nous sommes plus loin nul ne passe nul ne devient" [we are alone we are farther on nothing passes by nothing is comnig about]) does not have a period and that Roubaud proclaims, "Cette partie n'est pas achevée" (This game is not over).

Moreover, if we look closely at the spatial representation of the actual Go game (between Masami Shinohara and Mitsuo Takei, in the April 1965 issue of *Go Review*) that should provide the distribution program, it is fairly obvious that a certain number of black pieces have been placed on the board prior to any move (they do not carry any numbers). The places where they appear seem to be dictated by a spatial arrangement (a square), which means that these pieces are not, therefore, part of the arrangement generated by the moves in the game.

Finally, if the text's system is based on a sonnet-type arrangement, as Roubaud himself suggests, the canonical number is 12 (the measure of the alexandrine line) or its main constituents 4 and/or 3 (since $4 \times 3 =$

12, and since the sonnet can be divided into quatrains and tercets). Now the numerical reference that Roubaud starts with, 361, cannot be divided either by 12, 4, or 3, but both 180 or 360 can. Obviously, then, the book's numerical system leaves one remaining. It is this supplementary unit, necessary to the process of the game in order to ensure that one player can surround the other in the last move, that impedes the terminal unity of the system. Consequently, the merging of the programming model and the material of the text is endlessly deferred.

This tacit acceptance of a waste product existing at one level of a text that is supposed to be finite has given rise to a criticism of Roubaud's poetry by Henri Meschonnic. In "Fragments d'une critique du rythme," Meschonnic asserts that,

> To treat forms as if they were numbers is to get rid of meaning. Semantic aspects are ignored, and meaning is left up to the inclination of each individual reader, by remaining outside all concerns with structure. [...] The theoretical thrust to the project and its mathematical style are nevertheless covering up a characteristic confusion. [...] A certain vagueness follows from this and a new type of empiricism lurks behind the theoretical façade.[12]

Ten years separate Roubaud's ∈ and *La Vieillesse d'Alexandre* (Alexander's longevity), and once one reads the latter work, along with *Trente et un au cube,* it is clear that Meschonnic's criticism must be revised. In *La Vieillesse d'Alexandre* Roubaud admits that an overformalized conception of criticism might seem empty, but he goes on to caution against a simple abandoning of our awareness of form. "A rather extreme form of criticism," he writes,

> considers that the whole edifice of traditional poetry is merely a garment of convention. All one needed to do was remove it, a task that could be accomplished without danger, and after being relieved of its burden poetry could attain a state of freedom. [...] It was thought that language, like a dancer, could evolve without any constraints, and would reveal its innermost rhythms. Such is the point of view that Julia Kristeva proposes with her usual enthusiasm and naiveté. It is the viewpoint of *limited formalism* since it rests

12. Henri Meschonnic, "Fragment d'une critique du rythme," *Langue française* 23 (September 1974): 17.

upon a refusal or even a repression of formal qualities. (12, our emphasis)

Henceforth there is no longer any place for Kristeva's notion of "a 'vertical line'" at the end of which the text "opens out onto another space with multiple possibilities." This is simply denounced as a scientific imposture. Roubaud places a lid on language so that it is no longer a means by which a text can escape its own predetermined necessity.

Trente et un au cube differs in many ways from ∈. In ∈ the text was not said to be either prose or verse, and only a lexical association—with the preface mentioning sonnets and verses—allows it to be considered poetry. In contrast, *Trente et un au cube* has the subtitle *Poésie* (Poetry). In *Trente et un au cube* there is also no prescriptive preface. The title itself can be viewed as the sole regulating formula in the book, since it is the principle that opens and closes a text whose combinatory numerical features are clearly marked. The title acts as both the numerical apparatus and abstract theoretical principle for the text as a whole, whose writing gets its quality and its value—both in their mathematical sense—from it. The title in this way triggers off the production of meaning in the book. This is possible because within the text the numerical principle does not work solely at a superficial level, but is embedded deeper in the abstract process that intervenes between the primary and secondary systems. How is this put into effect? The title of the preceding book, ∈, is a mathematical symbol. *Trente et un au cube* could also have been written numerically as 31^3, but because it was not, it illustrates the conversion from a numerical to an alphabetical order, or the shift from one symbolic system to another without any leftover elements. There may also be, as a fringe benefit, a play on the signifier "thirty-one cubed," which is a quantified volume, so that the title means, by metonymy, "This is a volume (book)."

What basic theoretical principles warrant the text's quality as an imminent set, self-generated and also finite? How does the formula 31^3 establish itself as the numerical force coercing the book and its "innermost rhythms" into its unavoidable combinatory process? In *La Vieillesse d'Alexandre* Roubaud states very clearly what the role of numbers in a text should be: "The role of numbers is to establish an abstract system of rules to overcome chance and memory, to help us find, within a structure that is both very constrictive and very rich in formal relations, a deeper understanding of the poem's grammar" (16). In our introductory remarks we indicated that Roubaud's theoretic-poetic work was indebted to the latest linguistic theories (as the word "grammar" in the quotation above indicates), and especially to the model provided by generative grammar. As a matter of principle, the generative theory requires deductive reasoning. The main idea is that there is a finite set of rules that is able to generate—or enumerate, to use the proper word—the complete set of all the grammatical sentences that can be uttered in a given language. It postulates "the creativity of the language within the framework of the rules," so that aleatory factors such as chance and personal motivations are excluded. These rules saturate the language under scrutiny, so that every utterance that falls outside their control is not part of the grammar of the given language system (or *langue*).

In this theory two pairs of concepts have operative value. The first pair opposes competence and performance—the former being the formalized and finite set of the transformational rules of grammar as accepted by an ideal speaker-hearer, and the latter being the actual application of these rules. The second pair opposes the deep structure—or the artificial base of the sentence to which no transformation has been applied—and the surface structure, which is the actual occurrence of an uttered sentence, including its transformation. In principle generative theory cannot accept any leftover elements from a transformation. Since it is directly aimed at the language process, the implication is that a sentence will conform to the rules and thus is part of the language studied, or else will be deviant and therefore lie outside the scope of the grammar. Through deductive reasoning the facts must coincide with the rules within the finite theoretical framework. Linguistically speaking, phonology and semantics, which are designated as secondary components in orthodox generative theory, are also bound by the constraints placed at the syntactic level.

We have sketched out these basic hypotheses of generative theory not in order to give an exhaustive account of the theory but to provide some background for the ensuing discussion. Consequently, we have retained only those concepts that are relevant to the system at work in *Trente et un au cube*.

It is our assumption that in *Trente et un au cube* the number 31 plays the role of a user's competence. In other words, it generates in a very potent way the text's systematization. But why "cubed"? Mathematically broken down it gives $31 \times 31 \times 31$. It seems, therefore, that we could find at a macroquantitative level three instances in which 31 plays the role of an organizing matrix. Indeed there are 31 poems, each occupying one page, and every poem is composed of 31 lines, with each line capable of being decomposed into 31 metrical positions. We have used the latter term instead of syllables because in Roubaud's theory (as well as in the abstract polyrhythm theory put forward by Jean-Claude Milner[13]) syllables and feet are empirical data that may or may not conform to the deductive versification process that follows directly from a chosen meter. Moreover, were we to use the term *syllable* for an analysis of Roubaud's lines we would discover that some syllables would have to be left out of our calculations. However, each line has a fixed number of metrical positions, so that if a given line contains too many syllables it means that some have to be left out in order to fit the prearranged numerical count.

Within the text's systematization, then, 31 is the basic element of the logarithm. But where does this number come from? Thirty-one is a prime number—it cannot be divided. Nevertheless, it can be broken down into the addition of repetitive numerical subsets. In the specific case of *Trente et un au cube* the sequence is 5-7-5-7-7, and it is shown in the text's arrangement. Two independent but complementary procedures help uncover it: the work's intertext and the arrangement's internal numerical constraints. Jacqueline Guéron, another member of the *Change* group, believes that *Trente et un au cube* is a "tanka of tankas."[14] The tanka is a Japanese lyric form of 31 syllables in lines of 5, 7, 5, 7, and 7 syllables apiece, and it is considered to be the classic Japanese poetic form. Here again there is definitely an interpretant relation between the intertextual model (which is Japanese, as in the Go game) and Roubaud's actual text. Nevertheless, the numerical system of the latter is also established in its own right. First, each line has the form of a tanka poem since the sequence 5-7-5-7-7 is present in each one (not as syllables but as metrical positions); second, the 31 lines of each poem are divided into five paragraphs according to a pattern of 5, 7, 5, 7, and 7 lines. This produces a homography between the vertical and the horizontal plane that is not present in the original Japanese tanka (see Fig. 22).

Thus far we have presented the most notable features of the text's

---

13. For a discussion of these problems as they occur in English verse, see Joseph Beaver, "A Grammar of Prosody," *College English* 29 (1968): 310–21; "Current Metrical Issues," *College English* 33 (1971): 177–97; Samuel Keyser, "Old English Prosody," *College English* 30 (1969): 331–56; Samuel Keyser and Morris Halle, "Chaucer and the Study of Prosody," *College English* 28 (1966): 187–219; and *English Stress, Its Form, Its Growth and Its Role in Verse* (New York: Harper and Row, 1971).

14. Jacqueline Guéron, "Jacques Roubaud: Analyse d'un discours et d'un poème," *Critique* 310 (March 1973): 275.

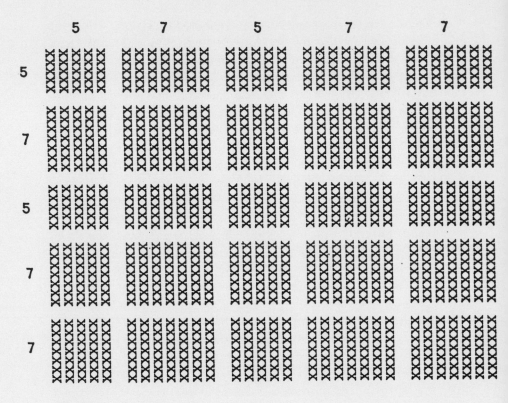

Figure 22

macroquantitative arrangement. It can be assumed that 31 determines the text's surface construction and that the formal simplicity of the grammatical construction encompasses all the superficial aspects. As far as we are concerned, 31 must be understood as the procedural ruling model of the text when viewed as a secondary system. To put it bluntly, the systematization built around 31 is a main part of this text's literariness.

One further point should be made. Thirty-one is also the basic rule involved in the transformation from the base component (language) into the literary text. It not only formalizes the external structure but generates it at the same time, assuring the wholeness of the text as an autonomous and integrated system, a hypothesis that can be verified by an analysis of the microquantitative aspect of the numerical constraints.

Meschonnic's main criticism of Roubaud's work stemmed from the fact that, for him, the "mathematical style" of the literary text failed to take into account the creation of meaning. *Trente et un au cube* is exempt from such a weakness if we consider the way meaning is generated in the light of André Martinet's work in semantics. In his theory, the appearance of meaning is closely related to precise segmentations in the continuum of linguistic material. For instance, in English, there is no meaning attached to the sequence o-d but there is meaning attached to o-d-d, and if we change only one component of this sequence, as in o-d-e, the meaning becomes quite different. So if we can think of 31 (or its subsets 5 and 7) as a machine, or a as transformational device (in the abstract sense explained earlier) that affects some elements on the line by regulating their movement, suppressing them, or adding them, then we can assume that it also produces the meaning of the new sequence. Of course, Martinet's demonstration points out the structural field of the unit (which is lexical meaning), whereas from Roubaud's generative perspective the field affected is the overall significance of the entire sequence.

To give an actual demonstration of this inner working of 31, we selected four lines that are repeated in *Trente et un au cube*. Since they appear at the beginning of poem 1 and at the end of poem 31, it must be stressed that the repetition reinforces the finite nature of the text, as if the book were framed by parentheses that directed the reader to the text's organizing principle.

Let us first consider the sequence *je détiens million* (I own million), which we have underlined (see Fig. 23).

The sequence is organized around a system based on 5 or 7 metrical positions:

		5
Poem 1	line 1	//JE/DE/TIENS/MIL/LION/de//
		7
	line 29	//je/dé/tiens/mil/lion de//
		5
Poem 31	line 18	//je/dé/tiens/mil/lion//
		7
	line 29	//je/dé/tiens/mil/lion/de/syl-//

The discrepancy between *je détiens million de* (poem 1) and *je détiens million* (poem 31), with both occurring in the setting of 5 metrical positions, is only empirical. The mute *e* in *je* (poem 1) should not be pro-

Poème 1

ligne 29   cela est vrai ma   réponse n'est qu'une fuite   je détiens million de
            [syllabes placées pour toi   qui dorment ou me répandent
ligne 30   fond de neige et nombres   je puise selon mes lignes   des chaînes
            [plausibles   qui vont leur chemin dans l'ordre   de mes contraintes pourtant
ligne 31   j'ai répondu la   répone est là prise dans le   mouvement contraire :
            [désordre sûr, véridique   à travers la voix battante

Poème 31

ligne 29   je ne vois pas la   moindre lueur démontrable   cela est ma vrai
            [réponse n'est qu'une fuite   je détiens million de syl-
ligne 30   labe placées pour   toi qui dorment ou me répandent je puise selon
            [mes lignes des chaînes plausibles sous mes contraintes
ligne 31   pourtant j'ai répondu la réponse est là prise   dans le mouvement
            [d'ensemble : désordre clair   derrière la voix battante

Figure 23

nounced (as in *j'*, poem 1, line 31). It is an empty metrical position and,
as a result, *JE/je* disappears.[15]

$$//(-)/\text{dé}/\text{tiens}/\text{mil}/\text{lion}/\text{de}//$$
$$\quad 0 \quad 1 \quad\ 2 \quad\ 3 \quad\ 4 \quad\ 5$$

15. Regarding the suppression of the mute *e* in Roubaud's poetry, although the
system of *Trente et un au cube* requires it, it may be necessary to explain that this is also a
confirmation of the argument that Roubaud has advanced in his theoretical works. In
"Mètre et vers. Deux applications de la métrique générative de Halle-Keyser," (*Poétique* 7
[1971]: 366–87), Jacques Roubaud indicates that in Chaucer's poetry the initial metrical
position of a verse can be left empty (the "headless line"; *Poésie, et cetera* 369). In the
conclusion of *La Vieillesse d'Alexandre* he singles out the specific properties of the mute *e*:
"If meter was more than just number and rhyme, it was in fact rhythm in language because
of one tiny yet essential element, upon which the entire scaffolding and tension of poetry
was grounded: the mute 'e'" (200). The result is that, more than any other case of syn-
aloepha (as in French with synaeresis and dieresis), the mute *e* is seen as the optimal ele-
ment par excellence in any verse situation. It can be pronounced or not, depending not on
phonological rules but on the abstract model of metrical positions: "the mute 'e' [...] bore
practically by itself the weight of the confusion between meter and rhythm in verse. Once it
is taken away from verse, the rhythmical monument that verse constitutes disappears. At
the same time, the rhythmical compass of writing, which no longer has verse as its absolute
pole, goes wild" (201).

By contrast, in poem 31 *je* occupies a full metrical position in both the 5 and 7 setting:

$$
\begin{array}{cc}
5 & 7 \\
//je/dé/tiens/mil/lion// & //je/dé/tiens/mil/lion/de/syl-// \\
\begin{matrix} 1 & 2 & 3 & 4 & 5 \end{matrix} & \begin{matrix} 1 & 2 & 3 & 4 & 5 & 6 & 7 \end{matrix}
\end{array}
$$

The implication is that if *je* disappears in the first poem before *toi* (*syllabes comptées pour TOI* [syllables counted for YOU]), then both will be present in the lines of the last poem.

The reinsertion of *je* is also programmed by the numerical order at the suprasegmental level, for in French the most important stress is always placed on the last pronounced syllable in a linguistic sequence. In this text, since syllables have been replaced by metrical positions, one has to assume that the stress appears on the last full metrical position within a metrical grouping. In the first poem this stress places emphasis on *toi:*

```
Poem 1        line 1  //syl/la/bes/comp/tées/pour/TOI//
                       1   2   3    4    5    6    7
              line 29 //syl/la/bes/pla/cées/pour/TOI//
                       1   2   3   4    5    6    7
```

In French there is also a secondary stress that is often placed on the first syllable of the first word in a sequence—so here it would be on the first metrical position. The effect in poem 1 is to add a slight emphasis to *dé*, which is a privative prefix that reinforces semantically the disappearance of *je*, whereas in poem 31 it equalizes *je* and *tu:*

```
Poem 31
line 18 //JE/dé/tiens/mil/lion//...//TOI/pas/et/tours/des//
         1   2    3    4    5       1   2   3   4    5
line 29 //JE/dé/tiens/mil/lion/de/syl-
         1   2    3    4    5   6  7
        //...//TOI/qui/dorment/ou/me/ré/pondent//
                1   2     3     4  5  6     7
```

These are not "let's pretend rules."[16] The same system of emphasis based on the numerical distribution produced by 31 (and its numerical

16. "Let's pretend rules" is an expression coined by P. M. Postal during a lecture at

subsets) leaves no part of the text untouched. And we can play the same games with the morphemes *dé-* (as in *DÉtiens, DÉsordre* [own, disorder]) taken as a metaphor of loss, and *ré* (*RÉponse, RÉpondre* [response, to reply]) as a metaphor of togetherness. Both take part in the basic relation between *je* and *toi* that runs thematically throughout the whole text and traces the path of its significance through the linguistic material rearranged by the rules of the 31 matrix ("la réponse et là prise dans le mouvement" [the response and there taken up in the movement]). This thematic isotropy is also present at the semantic level—for example, in the two sequences *mouvement CONTRAIRE/mouvement d'ENSEMBLE* (CONTRARY movement/COORDINATED movement).

Our final remarks concern the nonsegmented line 31 in poem 31 (see Fig. 23). For generative theory the sentence "An article is concluded by a conclusion" is the equivalent of "A conclusion concludes an article," since both have the same underlying structure. Thus, even if there is a superficial difference between line 31 in the first poem, where the continuum is broken up by the arrangement of numerical positions, and line 31 in the last poem, which is a continuum produced without any blanks, both are based on the same numerical division: 5-7-5-7-7. In both cases numerical competence has laid out the constituents according to the distributional model. Behind the apparent disorder of the lexical items, then, there is a tight structure that underlies their placement.

Traditional French poetry was loaded with conventional formal devices such as verse divisions, rhyme, and types of poems. Verse was the skeleton of this formal apparatus, and so when it disappeared the old system crumbled. Nevertheless, it should be understood that this taxonomic grid was just a conventional cover for two basic principles: number and rhythm. These were what gave poetry its particular traits of unity, compression, and systematic patterning. We would like to suggest that if the surface patterns of French poetry (such as rhyme and verse divisions) have disappeared, certain basic principles are still at work in a certain number of texts. What faded away was a universally accepted picture of what a poem's patterning should be, but in its place a more fundamental structure has become apparent. Poetry no longer resides in a text's external form; it is entrenched in its basic principles.

M.I.T. In generative theory it designates the made-up rules for a case that does not seem to fit the general competence that is required.

REFRACTION

> *Debris*
> > *Fragments*
> > > *Accidents*
> > > > *Horrendous*
> > > *—Friedrich Nietzsche*

Under this heading we retain the simultaneous meanings of fracture (or break) and refraction (or distorted reflection). Fracture is important since the type of poetry examined under this heading breaks into pieces the historical framework of classical poems that were organized according to a body of strict formal rules. Refraction names the new type of poetry that has replaced this old form, since it is a distorted image, or in some ways a parodic inversion, of such classical poems.

The category of refraction-poems includes texts that reject the massiveness of the complete page as being tantamount to prose. Instead they adopt a more imaginative spacing of words that brings with it supplementary meanings. Without being figurative in the pictorial sense (unlike the form-onomatopoeia), and without being numerically arranged (as opposed to the cipher), refraction-poems play mainly with spatial distribution in order to consolidate their individual significance. Contrary to classical poems, however, where a spatial arrangement is a by-product of formal encoding, in refraction-poems it is spatial arrangement that dictates its own form on the text. Since the organizational code is no longer linked to a universally applied formal system, this code functions merely as a variable that is internal to the combinatory process of each particular poem.

Motion, space, and sign prevail over the ordering of the refraction-poem's verbal elements. The syntactic line is broken up by the reader's scanning of the text and it ends up as a succession of inconsequential groupings that are endowed with temporary autonomy. The continuity that a reader detects in such a text does not entail the apparently natural or "organic" quality of standard verbal sequences. The refraction-poem's entire significance resides in a potential geometry that is made up of abrupt breaks, interrupted lines, and apparent continuity or contiguity. Several poems by Michel Deguy, Denis Roche, and Jean-Pierre Faye (among others) belong to this category. The example that we have chosen to analyze is "Change 21" by Jean-Pierre Faye (Fig. 24).[17]

17. Jean-Pierre Faye, "Change 21," *Change 1* (Paris: Seuil, 1968): 143.

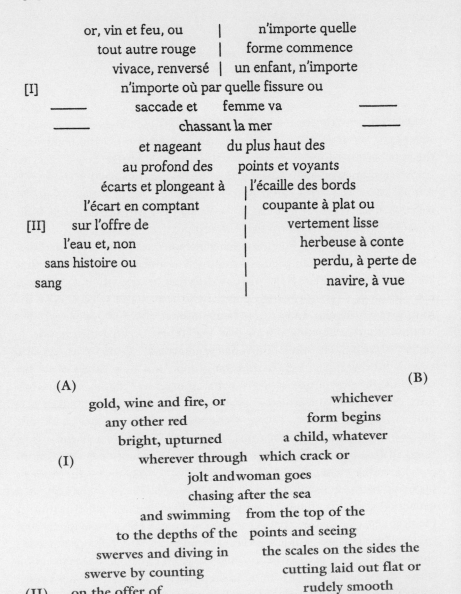

[A]   [B]

            or, vin et feu, ou | n'importe quelle
            tout autre rouge | forme commence
            vivace, renversé | un enfant, n'importe

[I]   n'importe où par quelle fissure ou
————   saccade et   femme va   ————
————   chassant la mer   ————
          et nageant   du plus haut des
         au profond des   points et voyants
       écarts et plongeant à l'écaille des bords
        l'écart en comptant   coupante à plat ou
[II]   sur l'offre de   vertement lisse
     l'eau et, non   herbeuse à conte
sans histoire ou   perdu, à perte de
sang   navire, à vue

(A)   (B)

         gold, wine and fire, or   whichever
          any other red   form begins
          bright, upturned   a child, whatever
(I)   wherever through which crack or
          jolt and woman goes
         chasing after the sea
       and swimming   from the top of the
      to the depths of the points and seeing
     swerves and diving in the scales on the sides the
     swerve by counting   cutting laid out flat or
(II)   on the offer of   rudely smooth
    the water and, not   grassy with a tale
without a story or   lost, as far as
blood   ship, in sight

Figure 24

As an icon, the text obviously takes the form of the letter *X*, or, in a more abstract manner, using de Brès's work on the form of letters, it is two vertical, obtuse, and symmetrical triangles joined at their apex. Here the shared point where they join is the sequence *chassant la mer* (chasing after the sea), which is not only the vertical meeting point but also the juncture of the two triangles when they are horizontally separated. The verticality of the textual triangle on the left is determined by the presence of a blank space following *ou, rouge, renversé,* and so on in the syntagmatic line. Since this space is left empty on the horizontal plane (which is the normal direction followed by reading), it reinforces the fact that we cannot read the text in our normal way. When our eye encounters the blank space, the other element in the act of reading (namely, the vertical succession of lines) forces it to jump to the beginning of the next line. Consequently one reads *or, vin et feu, ou / tout autre rouge / vivace, renversé,* and so on.

Little by little the open space in this crack is reduced in preparation for the apparent rejoining of the two upper legs of the *X* in the fourth line. In this line the illusion of spatial linkage is reinforced syntactically by the proximity of *n'importe où,* which leads the reader to pull together *n'importe où par quelle fissure ou.* This sequence is overdetermined by the work of a chiasmus involving *n'importe* and *quelle,* since this lexeme is already present in its unified form (*n'importe quelle*) in the first line of the right-hand triangle. A trace of this joining of the two vertical triangles is marked out in the phonetic repetition of *ou* and *où.*

By the same token, the *X* figure establishes two triangles arranged horizontally on their sides and joined, just like the two vertical ones, in the line *chassant la mer.* When reading the text closely, one cannot fail to notice that this montage, which divides the text into vertical triangles (A and B) and horizontal ones (I and II), actually triggers off a system of oppositions that activates the poetical qualities produced by the triangles' entangled codes. A thematic analysis would point out that in triangle I there is a group of terms marked by the semes [+ abstract] and [+ material] at a morphological level (determiners that would give a concrete value to the nouns that are missing), and also at a semantic one (since all the terms mentioned have a high archetypal value). This grouping is different from triangle II, which is based on the semes [+ concrete] and [+ form] that are also indicated morphologically (with the presence of determiners) and semantically. Yet there are connecting points that link IA to IB and IIA to IIB. In IA the nouns are indeterminate; in IB they are indefinite, with the lexeme *n'importe* belonging to both systems. By contrast, IIA and IIB display a mixture of definite and indefinite determination (IIA—*des écarts, à l'écart;* IIB—*des points, l'écaille*). Regarding the organization of the determiners that gives rise to a noun or not, we can see that an axis linking IA to IIB brings about a new configuration in the poem since both these parts of the text are characterized by a quantitative lack of determiners.

The montage sets up a similar network of oppositions and correlations in the text's phonic material since sound patterns begin to follow a pattern from the horizontal to the vertical planes. IA is characterized by the sounds /ʳR/ and /u/, but /ʳR/ also belongs to IB (*n'importe, forme*) and to IIB (*bords*). IB is characterized by the sounds /ʳR/, /ɛ/, and /ã/, but these reappear with a lesser and nonsystematic frequency in IIB: *coupante, vertement, voyant, point*. IIB is, in itself, characterized by /ã/ and /ʳR/, but there is one occurrence of /eka/ (*écaille*), which echoes the repetitive system of IIA (*écarts, écart*). The sound /ã/ dominates this section. If we consider what has been excluded, the phonological code maps out a structure of correlations that is organized around the diagonal rows of the X. The sequence *chassant la mer* brings together the two sounds /ã/ and /ɛR/ that give rise to the polarization (Fig. 25).

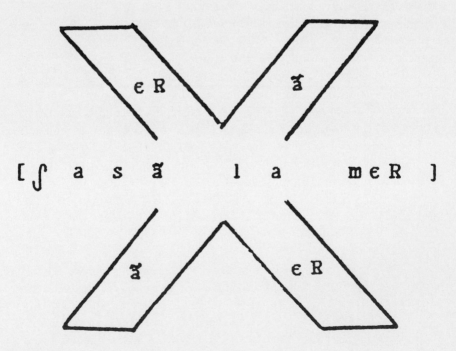

Figure 25

Likewise syntax plays an important role, being both the separator and the integrator of sequences. In the tenth line, for example, it is impossible to read the two parts together: *coupante* is in the feminine form and *écart* in the masculine. Consequently, *écaille* in line 9 (IIB) necessarily appears to be the noun to which *coupante* refers. Triangle A is marked by a structure that is centered around the conjunction *et* (*vin* et *feu,* et *chassant,* et *nageant, l'eau* et), whereas on the opposite side triangle B offers a repetition of the preposition *à* (à *plat,* à *conte perdu,* à *perte,* à *vue*). Since the two triangles are trying to counter their moving apart, it is necessary to note that each occurrence of the basic element in each triangle appears in the other.

It is difficult to dismiss these systems that a close reading uncovers as the mere product of chance. In fact, under the apparent guise of disintegrating fixed poetic forms, the refraction-poem accomplishes the very act of self-constitution. An internal type of formalism gives the text its poetic force.

SCRAP-POEM

This post-Mallarmé poetic technique of asyntactical verticality, which is certainly the most prevalent characteristic of contemporary French poetry, is already in evidence in certain refraction-poems. The only reason for proposing this final category is to accommodate Raymond Queneau's *Cent mille milliards de poèmes* (Hundred thousand million poems), which is rightfully considered to be something of a curio.[18]

A fragmented and parceled body of pages, the book is made up of thousands of cutouts, or tonguelike strips of paper, each of which contains one line of verse. By turning over different combinations of these cutouts, readers can piece together one line with another until they reach the bottom of their multilayered page, and thus construct the text that pleases them the most. Using ready-made sequences, readers consequently "write" their own poems, the only limitation being their inability to cut up the parts of each horizontal line, since the latter makes up the very materiality of Queneau's book.

From the standpoint of creative principles, this text is an extension of the *cadavre exquis* games mentioned at the start of this chapter. Nevertheless, it is still an example of a montage for two reasons. First, the

18. Raymond Queneau, *Cent mille milliards de poèmes* (Paris: Gallimard, 1961).

heterogeneous content of each cutout is counterbalanced by the book's overall unity (each cutout is the same size, and all the combinations form a standard page format). Second, from a technical standpoint the text is not presented as an immutable product but has to be built up by the reader.

The importance of the vertical succession of sequences in Queneau's book indicates the sort of attack on language that is going on in the text. For by giving prime importance to the reader's vertical substitutions, Queneau is admitting the subordination of linear syntax to a more fundamental ordering—and, by extension, he is admitting the derivative role of semantics, which is merely the result of combining lexical elements. As a montage *Cent mille milliards de poèmes* is located at the very borderline of poetry reading, or the limiting point where reading becomes writing, since the standard framework for literary discourse has been removed. The text-as-montage has become the reader's private space, and its organization no longer consists of an interplay of codes that are internal to the text itself. Instead it is merely a playful expedient that propels readers into taking on the role of author. In place of the apparent disorder of textual significance readers substitute the order of their own reading pattern and their own encoding of significance. This is a combinatory textual system that anticipates the principles found today in the most recent interactive electronic books with development "à la carte."

In "Figurations" Michel Deguy declares that language is much too important an issue to be left in the care of linguists.[19] Linguists could return the compliment and say that poetry is much too important a matter to be left in the care of poets. This point takes on importance once we consider that all four of the above types of montage are connected, in one way or another, to properties of language. The verbal component is always present, be it in the form of a truncated, fragmented, or even barely recognizable word, or as a seemingly ever-expanding phrase. Deguy himself is compelled to define poetry as a "pushing of language to its limits." He goes on, moreover, to situate poetry "in language itself." It is language as action, or a medium that is transforming itself in an impersonalized activity "occurring before [the appearance of] an I that is subservient to the spoken words that pass through it under the old name of

19. Michel Deguy, "Figurations," *Poèmes: 1960–1970* (Paris: Gallimard, Poésie, 1973), 105–34.

the Muse" (Deguy 48). Consequently, montage must be seen as an arti-
fact through which language transcends its instrumental role in commu-
nication and leaves behind its function as the transmitter of information.
The particular architecture of a poem-montage expels language from the
realm of concatenated meaning and places it in a world of seemingly odd,
fortuitous encounters and juxtapositions.

However, these poems in fact display guideposts that signal the for-
mal relationships and give readers access to their meaning. The spatial
distribution in each montage literally forces the reader to travel along
prearranged paths that lead to the poem's significance. These intrinsic
formal constraints take the place of the external ones to be found in
traditional poetry. A contemporary poem is first and foremost an exercise
in its own internal rhythmical properties. One can recognize a traditional
poem because it is organized according to criteria that come with a fixed
form; one can spot the poetic structure of any text when the latter gener-
ates its own form, be it figurative, numerical, or geometrical. We are not
saying that poetry is limited to its external features. On the contrary, it is
our contention that the most important element to consider is the pro-
cess whereby significance is produced, and that the external form of a
text is part of this process, not just an independent feature.

What motivates these spatial artifices is the need to restore language
to its primal semic quality by pulling it out of syntagmatic arrangements.
The new arrangement of letters mounted on the page then generates its
own pattern of encoding and provides readers with the necessary indica-
tions for understanding the montage-poem. When verse and other con-
ventional formal devices disappeared from French poetry the task of iden-
tifying poems became more difficult, and some critics even went so far as
to reject any distinction between prose and poetry.[20] The four types of
contemporary poetic "dialects" that we have outlined above are designed
to help in this identification, and also to prove that the four types of
poem discussed share some common features that must be considered
fundamental to the elusive concept of poetry.

In conclusion, the picture of a universally accepted pattern for
poems has faded away, and poetry is no longer determined by its external
form. Instead it is entrenched in principles that take on a topical pattern

20. Consider, for instance, the following statement by Michel Butor in *Obliques 2*
(1971): "Today there are no longer any genres. We now simply produce literature or writ-
ing, and it is no longer legitimate or useful to distinguish one mode from another within
this activity that absorbs all the old genres" (6).

specially tailored to the nature of the specific text they govern. Conse-
quently, Louis Marin's statement quoted in the epigraph to this chapter
now appears to have certain limitations. Because they cover such a broad
spectrum, montages that otherwise would have been relegated to the
realm of the plastic arts find a place in the framework of reading. Yet
Marin's definition fails to recognize that the primary function of the
graphic ensemble is to catch the eye. While disjointed collages allow the
eye to go on wandering, a montage will always force it to come to a halt.
From this it follows that there is no such thing as a poetry reduced solely
to its visual quality. Whenever there is poetry, the reader has to pass
through the incongruity and apparent disorder of the elements encoun-
tered in order to enter the labyrinth of exegesis and, as in the case of
montage, uncover the hidden regulating system that generates the text's
significance.

nine

COMPOSED SCORES

(OULIPO)

There is a marked critical silence that enshrouds the writings and theories of the OuLiPo group. For despite the public success of certain neo-Pere-quian writers, or the 1985 exhibit-cum-demonstration titled "Les Imma-tériaux" (Immaterials) at the Pompidou Center,[1] university-led literary critics in France have shied away from discussing this major literary movement. There is not a single line about OuLiPo, for instance, in Serge Brindeau's *La Poésie contemporaine de langue francaise depuis 1945,* nor is there any OuLiPian text in the special issue of the review *Europe* (February 1983) that was devoted to the latest French poetry. Yet to study contemporary French poetry one seems almost obliged to con-duct a detailed analysis of this movement, its ambitions, and its achieve-

1. "Les Immatériaux" (Immaterials) was mounted by the Centre National d'Art et de Culture Georges Pompidou in the center's main gallery from March 28 to July 15, 1985. The directors of the exhibit were Jean-François Lyotard and Thierry Chaput. Since 1995, the term designates in French all the elements of the virtual cyberworld.

ments. The very fact that its techno-ludic type of writing has been expelled from the field of poetry proper by the administrators of university-led literary study would suggest that it is well worth examining.

README.DOC

Anyone who has a rudimentary knowledge of computer technology knows that it takes many initial hours of practice before being able to master a software program. In many instances this period of apprenticeship is made easier by a special computer file, found outside the program itself, which is called README.DOC. It is a preliminary document that is supposed to be read before using the program itself. This file name has become generic and is found on introductory files on several software diskettes in France and the United States. The file itself is, in some ways, the computer equivalent of the earlier prefaces or editor's introductions that used to initiate us to book culture. The analogy with a user's manual is, however, a more useful bridge to understanding README.DOC.

It may be surprising to find the concept of a preface placed alongside that of a user's manual, since, after all, the former is used to introduce such artifacts as *La Comédie humaine* whereas the latter only accompanies the Cuisinart type of object. And what possible connection is there between Balzac and a food processor? In principle, there is none at all; and yet the most recent forms of experimental French literature are now adding to what has been called the paratext a new type of textual machine that is closer to manuals for mechanized machines than to highbrow literary forewords. Up until recently, any statement that preceded a text was considered, from a linguistic angle, to be a declaration designed to direct the attention of the reader, the writer, or her proxy, by marking the boundaries that were supposed to guide the subjective process of reading. In the case of such textual prolegomena, the author's intentions are given clearly, which sets up a back-and-forth movement between the preface and the pages that follow it. In their own preface to the *Anthologie des préfaces des romans français du XIXe siècle*, Gershman and Whitworth point out judiciously that "what a great novelist has to say about his craft [...] can spotlight more precisely his own work, as well as [...] developments in theories of the novel." It's on this basis that a research group at the Université de Paris-VII, headed by Claude Duchet, has been doing an exhaustive study of nineteenth-century prefaces to

novels. After fifteen years of work they are well advanced in their classi-
fication of types of prefaces, and of the ties between a preface and the
story it introduces.

For the sake of brevity, we mention only two of the generic distinc-
tions that the research group has formulated so far. According to these, a
preface can be either an exposition of the novel's aims—as is the case in
Manon Lescaut, where the preface states that "the entire work is a treatise
of morality, reduced to the pleasing form of an exercise"—or a manifesto
for a particular theory of writing—as in *Germinal,* where we read that
"the whole [writing] operation consists of taking facts from nature, then
studying their mechanisms by acting on them through changes of cir-
cumstance and environment, without, however, deviating from the laws
of nature." Yet from a linguistic standpoint, none of these prefaces in-
volves the pragmatic modality of an illocutionary utterance. In other
words, they might engage a form of *doing,* whether this be making the
reader read in a certain way, or else making the writer write in a specific
fashion. A user's manual, however, is by definition firmly rooted in this
pragmatic modality since its main function is to help us *make the machine
work.*

We could exploit recent metaphorical uses of the word *machine* (as
a name for literary texts) by arguing that the new type of preliminary *hors-
texte* invented by experimental literature allows its users to make the
reading-machine work, which leads eventually to making the writing-
machine work as well. This is precisely the viewpoint belonging to the
writers in OuLiPo: L'Ouvroir de littérature potentielle (The workroom
for potential literature). The original concept behind this group was put
forward by the College of Pataphysics in the following terms: "Can there
be any other canon (whether this word be used seriously in its profane or
pataphysical sense) than the project of treating the future as a bundle of
Imaginary Solutions—in other words as potentialities?"[2]

Since 1960 writers such as Raymond Queneau, François Le Lion-
nais, Jacques Roubaud, Paul Braffort, Jacques Bens, and others, have pro-
posed a wide variety of writings that are preceded by introductory texts of
the user's manual type. The most emblematic of these, and perhaps the
most famous, is Georges Perec's novel *La Vie mode d'emploi* (Life, a
user's manual). Before coming to the experimental user's manual type of

---

2. Dossier 17 of the Collège of Pataphysique; quoted in *OuLiPo: La littérature
potentielle* (Paris: Gallimard, 1973), 40.

textual machine, we will briefly survey the variety of OuLiPian prefaces from the traditional angles of the preface as a statement of goals and as a statement of theory. This will allow us to show the usefulness of our third category, the user's manual.

STATEMENTS OF GOALS

It is easy enough to argue that the OuLiPo group represents the current avant-garde in French writing and poetics. But once this is accepted, how can we explain the huge distance that separates previous avant-garde movements (for instance, Dada and Surrealism) from OuLiPo when it comes to artistic upheaval? In OuLiPo's case, there have been no battles between literary Titans, no scandals, no public denunciations, nor even any initial attacks that threatened to launch the movement into literary headlines. It is as if the group wanted nothing to do with influence, but instead engaged in quiet, confidential work reserved only for the expert eyes of a few connoisseurs.

The basic ambiguity in this approach, which combines both private labor and the avowed aim of opening up literature to new paths for the future, has been clarified in several theoretical works that have accompanied the group's more well-known writings. Some of these are grouped in collective works, such as *OuLiPo: La Littérature potentielle* or *OuLiPo: Atlas de littérature potentielle,* while others can be found among the hundreds of works that group members published individually.[3] One characteristic is immediately obvious. OuLiPo has no intention of repeating the exhibitionism and recruiting strategies made famous by innovative movements between World Wars I and II, but instead prefers the confidential developments that come from rigorously planned experimentation and research. For anyone who revels in the apparently infinite possibilities of verbal free play, or for writers and critics who subscribe to the small joys afforded by chance combinations of words, and who are always eager to wander aimlessly through the magical wonderland of *écriture,* the forced

---

3. The three most important works for statements of the group's theory are *OuLiPo: La Littérature potentielle* (Paris: Gallimard, 1973), *OuLiPo: Atlas de littérature potentielle* (Paris: Gallimard, 1981), and *La Bibliothèque oulipienne* (Geneva: Slatkine, 1981). A more extensive bibliography can be found in the appendix to *OuLiPo: Atlas,* 409–26.

explorations and imposed figures that OuLiPians develop are synony-
mous with deathly boredom.

However, if OuLiPo were to be any different it would be in contra-
diction with its founding principles. As Jacques Bens writes,

> And if we now consider the fact that *potentiality,* more than simply
> a technique of composition, is also a way of defining the literary
> phenomenon, then one will perhaps admit that it opens on to a
> perfectly authentic and modern form of realism. For reality only
> ever reveals a part of its face at a time, giving rise to hundreds of
> interpretations, meanings and solutions, each one as probable as the
> next. In this respect, studying potentialities will save writers both
> from the hermetic games of literary cliques and from the emptiness
> of mass populism—two tendencies that spoil much of the writing
> of today. (*OuLiPo: Atlas* 33)

This concern for the writer's "health" is one of the most modern and
forward-looking aspects of OuLiPo. In contrast to the vaudevillian per-
formances of the self-proclaimed vanguard movements of the sixties and
seventies, with their dilettante proclamations, such a defense of the
writer's craft and of his daily obligations guarantees OuLiPo a firm fol-
lowing, a well-informed readership, and an increasing number of disci-
ples. Whoever is unfamiliar with a text's hardships will never be a true
writer. "It's by writing that one becomes a writer," prophesized Ray-
mond Queneau, and more recently we find the following comment by
Georges Perec: "Literary history seems ignorant of the practice of writ-
ing, of its craft," he wrote in *OuLiPo: La Littérature potentielle* (79).

The desire to rehabilitate the writer's craft nevertheless leads to a
reevaluation of the social status enjoyed by a "person of letters." Hence
these remarks by Jacques Roubaud:

> The OuLiPian project is considered to be radically innovative, or at
> the cutting edge of literature. It cannot count on support coming
> from any so-called "serious" aims, or from any of the criteria that
> are nowadays used in scientific areas to eliminate research that alters
> the standard perspectives too much. Such elimination is done in the
> name of existing machines that have been well run-in, and for
> which the criteria are: What's it used for? Who guarantees that it
> will work? What problem does it solve? All this means that OuLi-

Pian work is inevitably classified under the rubric of "game."
(*OuLiPo: Atlas* 52)

It follows from this, as Jacques Bens pointed out in the 1981 special issue
of *Action Poétique* devoted to OuLiPo, that the group refuses to accept
the distinction between playful and serious as a valid one when applied to
writing. Following on from this refusal, the group also erases the line that
separates fiction from theoretical work, since OuLiPian work conjoins
both concepts in a unified activity. The presupposed joining of the se-
rious to the playful deliberately goes back to the unity of *ludus* that was
extolled by the Great Rhetoricians of the Middle Ages. Etymologically,
ludus designates the realm of active leisure, and, in its literal sense, the
latin verb *ludere* has nothing to do with frivolous and irrational amuse-
ment, but instead designates an intellectual endeavor that, although dis-
tinct from day-to-day obligations, is not less rigorous or demanding than
any other intelligent activity.

Another, rather neglected, aspect of OuLiPo's modernity comes
from the fact that, despite all appearances, the group has the avowed goal
of breaking the historical chain that links recent French poetry to the
direct descendants of Surrealism. This has the effect of placing OuLiPo
among the literary movements that people have called, for want of a
better name, post-Freudian. In opposition to Breton, who attacked logic
and placed the future of poetry on the risky trail laid out by uncontrolled
psychic associations, which were supposed to produce texts via the dic-
tates of the unconscious, OuLiPo proposes a literature of formal con-
straint, totally mastered and controlled. The opening text in *OuLiPo: La
Littérature potentielle* declares that "OULIPO is not a literature of
chance," and later on Jacques Roubaud would insist that "OULIPO's
work is anti-accidental" (*OuLiPo: Atlas* 56). In addition, the unconscious
aspects of the act of writing are harshly criticized, as in Queneau's claim
that literature can only be produced from an understanding of what liter-
ature is.

The radical tone with which this position is adopted is generally
ignored, but it is in fact essential for an understanding of some of the
firm oppositions that exist in French literature and criticism today. For
instance, it explains why Jacques Roubaud finds himself forced to take
issue with Julia Kristeva's poetic theories, and why, in his *Vieillesse d'Alex-
andre*, he criticizes the latter for believing that in order to escape from
literary and linguistic rules all one needs to do is act as if they did not
exist. For during the last fifteen years, many theorists such as Kristeva

have assumed that the subject and the writing subject are one and the same through the upheaval that the writing process creates. In Kristeva's *Révolution du langage poétique* it is assumed as an a priori principle that the subject of an utterance and the subject *in* an utterance are the same thing. Consequently the medium of writing is assumed to be transparent. In contrast, what OuLiPo reestablishes in both its theoretical and fictional works is a clear distinction between the subject and *the subject of language*. To make an utterance therefore involves adopting a specific ordering system—that of language. The issue of writing and the problems posed by any use of discourse are consequently situated at the threshold of consciousness, once an understanding and mastery of this imposed external order have been accomplished. As Queneau has pointed out, "The powers of poetry are always at [the poet's] disposal, always within the range of his wishes, always dependent on his activity."[4]

STATEMENTS OF THEORY

To OuLiPo's avowed goals (a rehabilitation of the literary craft and the elimination of chance and approximation in writing) there corresponds a particular theory based on an order, a method, and rules, and the theory appears in several of the group's prefaces. Writing, we are told, means first of all submitting oneself to the constraints of formal logic, and knowing how to ignore or cancel out the unstable influence of inspiration. Rimbaud had committed poetic suicide at age twenty-one by crossing out this visionary inspiration with his pen. As everyone knows, Mallarmé laboriously held out as a writer and refused to hide his disgust for an inspiration that he called "spiritual anarchy." "A writer is never inspired, since he always is," decreed Queneau, and he went on:

> Another false notion that is also quite prevalent today is the presumed identity between inspiration, the exploration of the subconscious, and liberation—or, in other words, between chance, free associations, and freedom.
>
> Yet such an inspiration, which means blindly following any impulse, is actually a form of slavery. The classical writer who wrote his tragedy by observing a certain number of known rules is more free than the poet who writes whatever goes through his head, and

4. Quoted in Jacques Roubaud, "La mathématique dans la méthode de Raymond Queneau," *OuLiPo: Atlas de littérature potentielle* (Paris: Gallimard, 1981), 57.

who is a slave to other rules about which he knows nothing. (*OuLiPo: Atlas* 56)

OuLiPo's activities can be described as a rigorous and exhaustive exploration and exploitation of the constraining rules that govern the language in which literature is produced. The concept of a potential literature, which is OuLiPo's working hypothesis, is put forward immediately as an attempt to exhaust, through a series of formal transformations, the stock of creative capital that is allocated by the finite rules of a concrete language. In a moment of premonition, the inaugural text that founded the movement also puts its finger on OuLiPo's theoretical uniqueness: "To replace the era of CREATED CREATIONS, which is that of the literary works known to us all, we should begin an era of CREATING CREATIONS, or works that are capable of developing out of themselves, and even beyond themselves, in a perfectly predictable manner" (*OuLiPo: Littérature* 42).

OuLiPian literature can therefore be defined as a system of combinations and exchanges that tries to identify and enumerate a number of *scores* that make up the finite body of language. In addition, the latter is viewed as the material for certain formal processes that are designed to reveal a broad range of potential texts and readings. In his introductory essay, "The Matrix-Analysis of Language," Jacques Roubaud is led to make the following recommendations:

> One should approach language as if it could be mathematically organized, which it can be, moreover, if it is directed toward a very specific goal.
>
> If language can be manipulated by a mathematician, it is because it can be translated into an arithmetical form. This means that it is made up of discrete (or fragmentary) units, that it is not a merely accidental accumulation of these units (but has a disguised order), that it is not affected by topological properties, and is therefore controllable piece by piece.
>
> As for the relations [...] between mathematics and language [we are led to think that there is] some truth in the following propositions:
>
> 1. That when arithmetic acts on language it gives rise to texts.
> 2. That when language produces texts it gives rise to arithmetical patterns. (*OuLiPo: Atlas* 47)

An exploration of literary potential is thus initially grounded in an appraisal of the linguistic domains that are open to experimentation. This metaphorical transposition of language into a geographical universe that is open to discovery gives partial justification to the subtitle *Atlas of Potential Literature* that is given at the outset of OuLiPo's program.

The paired model of linguistics and mathematics that is used by OuLiPo to set up its theoretical framework owes a lot to the terminology of generative and transformational grammar. In the concluding section of this chapter we examine the linguistic limitations that come along with this choice of vocabulary, but already it is clear why the combinatory logic that underpins the OuLiPian enterprise is not static in nature (as it would have been if a structuralist model had been adopted), but instead follows a transformational dynamic. It does not classify specific *states* of the language, but rather certain *operations* that are implicated in the production of a given text.

In his *Second Manifesto* for OuLiPo that appeared in 1973, François Le Lionnais is consequently justified in claiming that "[OuLiPo's] creative work bears principally on all the formal aspects of literature: its constraints, its programs, or structures that set an arrangement of letters, of consonants, vowels, syllables, phonemes, graphemes, or of versification, rhyme, rhythm and number" (*Bibliothèque* 362). The important term in this extract is the word *programs* since OuLiPian theory leads to the view that any literary text is first and foremost a program-text that has to be rediscovered or elaborated upon. Hence Jacques Bens's mechanistic description of a text:

> The definition I am proposing implies that there is a statement, a formal generation, an algorithm [...].
>
> I will therefore classify under the heading "recurrent" any text that contains, explicitly or implicitly, generative rules that invite its reader [...] to follow out the textual production *ad infinitum*. (*OuLiPo: Atlas* 81)

THE USER'S MANUAL

Since every OuLiPian text is a linguistic machine that can be reduced to an algorithmic program, it is clearly necessary to give its potential users a preliminary set of instructions, or a user's manual, that would

allow the user to operate this textual machine, and eventually to take
over the responsibility for production. This is even more obvious when
we consider that the basic mechanism in each work has been deliberately
encoded in the work by the author, and can be rediscovered only by a
reader who takes on the dual role of mechanic and linguist. This is why,
as Jacques Bens points out, OuLiPian works are not easy to get into:

> We must remember that the first axiom of potentiality is the notion
> of a secret, which is what lies underneath all appearances and en-
> courages people to make discoveries.
>
> Nothing prevents us from assuming that there will be poten-
> tial literature as soon as a work offers resistance and an explorer is
> there to overcome it [...].
>
> Potential literature is the type that is waiting for a reader, that
> is hoping for one, and that needs one in order to realize itself fully.
> (*OuLiPo: Atlas* 24)

Given the particular nature of OuLiPian texts, then, the experimen-
tal literature produced by the group is obliged to help its readers in the
task of decoding. Hence the new type of literary preface that serves this
function. However, given the fact that the prefaces' commands vary ac-
cording to the type of use that is envisaged, one is confronted by a whole
range of user manual models. In what follows we give a quick overview
of these different forms of how-to prefaces.

The most important type of user's manual is the one that helps the
reader understand the work that follows it. A clear example of such a
manual is the preparatory text that opens Jacques Roubaud's collection
of poems, $\in$, which was examined in detail in Chapter 8. This inaugural
text, which is titled "How to Use This Book," recommends four princi-
ples for reading that give each of the apparently scattered poems in the
volume a set place within the general structure of the book, which is
modeled on a match of Go, and in which every poem would be a pawn.
The lists and groups of interrelated meanings are determined by the nu-
merical system on which the text is built, and only by referring to this
initial algorithm can the reader find his or her way through the collec-
tion.

In a similar vein, although in narrative form, is Jacques Duchateau's
Les Sept Coups du tireur à la ligne en apocalypse lent... (The seven shots

by the rifleman in a slow apocalypse...).[5] As one might expect, the introduction to the numerical pattern underlying the work is called "The User's Manual":

IA. 1) First of all read the first and last paragraphs labeled A.
2) Then read the first paragraph A, followed by B, and finally the second paragraph A. Continue this operation by inserting a new letter each time that will appear between the preceding letters. So by introducing C one gets:
3) A, C, B, C, A. By introducing D one gets:
4) A, D, C, D, B, D, C, D, A. By introducing E one gets:
5) A, E, D, E, C, E, C, E, D, E, B, E, D, E, C, E, D, E, A. [...]

IB. Each of these seven readings begins with the letter A.

At the end of each paragraph there is a reference mark that should help the reader find the following paragraph, according to the choice that is made. For instance, at the end of paragraph A there is the code number 2:B 14, which means that if you chose the second of the possible readings then after reading the first A you should look for paragraph B, which is on p. 14. Or else 3 (third reading), C (paragraph C), 10 (on page 10), etc.

The seventh reading will, of course, entail reading all the paragraphs one after the other.

Another type of preface that is designed to help the reader's understanding is the kind that precedes Perec's *La Vie mode d'emploi* (Fig. 26).

5. Jacques Duchateau, "Les Sept Coups du tireur à la ligne en apocalypse lent, occupé à lire 'Monnaie de Singe' de William Faulkner" (The seven shots by the rifleman in a slow apocalypse, busy reading William Faulkner's "Payment in Kind"), in *La Bibliothèque oulipienne*, 299–322. One can also contrast the instruction format of the user's manual with the open-ended command to "do as one pleases" that is common to several nineteenth-century prefaces. An obvious example of the latter is Baudelaire's dedication letter addressed to Arsène Houssaye at the start of *Le Spleen de Paris*:

I invite you to consider for a moment the advantages afforded by this combination [of poems] to all of us—you, me, and the reader. We may cut wherever we like—me my flow of thoughts, you the manuscript, and the readers their reading pattern. For I am not unaware of the reluctant effort that the reader has to put in after following the interminable twists of a superfluous plot. Take away one of my collection's vertebrae and the two pieces of this meandering fantasy will easily join together again. Or else cut it up into several pieces and you'll see that each of them can exist independently.

FIGURE 1

FIGURE 2

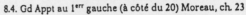

8.4. Gd Appt au 1ᵉʳʳ gauche (à côté du 20) Moreau, ch. 23

FIGURE 3

Figure 26

Monter
Classement
Verne　(I.M. p. 224, V.M.L. p. 75)
Joyce　(p. 637)
2 personnes
Occupants
Agendas
Faire un rêve
Boiseries
Faux ⎰ Tapis de laine
⎱ Après-guerre　Antiquité 19ᵉ ⎱ Canal de Suez
Moyen-Orient　? ⎰
Style chinois Manque
Manque ⎰ Bibliothèque
⎱ ~ 10 pages
Physiologie en 1860
Nouveau-né
Chat
Manteau

FIGURE 4

Under the title "Four Figures" it enumerates and describes the four verbal and figurative elements in the combinatory logic that underpins the novel. The first one (figure 1) is that of the architecture of the apartment building in which the novel's events take place. The second one (figure 2), which retraces the movement of a knight in a chess game, gives an order to the sequence of apartments in which the different episodes are placed. The third diagram (figure 3), which is mathematical (the bi-quadratic Latin orthogonal to the base of 10), governs the sequencing of characters and their particularities. The fourth diagram (figure 4), called "The Specification Booklet," lists the different themes and intertextual references that are to be found in a given chapter.

It might be argued that, in principle, a precise knowledge of the combinative sequence that governs these four figures is unnecessary for an understanding of Perec's novel. For readers can quite easily read the book at a simple level in complete ignorance of these underlying structures. In this case the user's manual in fact functions as a catalogue of initial constraints that the author imposed on himself, in the same way as when we read a sonnet we know which rules preceded its composition, and can therefore judge the degree to which the sonnet has perfected these rules. Consequently, it is his combinative virtuosity that the author is underscoring in his user's manual—his ability to follow a rigorously preset order.[6] The only difference between Perec's rules and a sonnet's versification is that in the former case the textual constraints are made up by the author himself.

This type of explanatory document is extremely common in OuLiPo's writings, whether the authors are reactivating old-fashioned constraints and bringing them up to date, or else producing new constraints that are based on a better understanding of the linguistic workings of a literary text. This is especially so in the collective work *La Bibliothèque ouli-pienne,* where each work is accompanied by an explanation that gives the implicit principle and constraint that lies at its foundation. "L'Hôtel de Sens" (The hotel of meaning) by Paul Fournel and Jacques Roubaud is defined, for example, as a syllabic cylinder:

> *Definition:* The cylinder is a text that bites its own tail so perfectly that one can no longer tell where the mouth or tail are.
> *Example:* "The pilot closes the empty cockpit" [*Le pilote ferme la carlingue vide*] can also be read in a more sinister way as "The cockpit empties the firm pilot" [*La carlingue vide le pilote ferme*]. (*OuLiPo: Atlas* 183)

Harry Matthews's text "Le Savoir des rois" (Kings' know-how) is based on the generative principle of the *perverb:*

> *Definition:* A perverb joins the first half of a proverb to the second half of another one.
> *Example:* "A rolling stone leads to Rome." (293)

---

6. On OuLiPo's "combinatorics," see Warren F. Motte Jr., *OuLiPo: A Primer of Potential Literature* (Lincoln: University of Nebraska Press, 1985).

Jacques Bens's "irrational sonnets" are built on the number pi, and therefore run contrary to the standard rules for the layout of verses in a sonnet:

> An *irrational sonnet* is what we call a poem with a fixed form, of fourteen verses (in accordance with the sonnet's length), but whose structure is based on the number pi (hence the adjective irrational). Consequently, the poem is grouped into five stanzas, made up respectively of 3, 1, 4, 1, and 5 verses each—these numbers being the first five digits of pi. (*OuLiPo: Littérature* 254)

Such explanatory notes lie at the outer limit of those user manuals that are designed to facilitate the reading of a text. Not content with giving their own user instructions, they also introduce their reader to a code that lays down a certain principle of textual production. In this way they mark a transition from the user manuals that do not accompany completed texts but give a list of isolated principles or rules that allow the reader-as-author to create his or her own texts. In such cases the user's manual is an open invitation to creativity, or a stockpile of generative principles—which explains some of the success that these documents have had in free-expression workshops.

It is hard to give detailed examples of such cases, other than just copy word-for-word the user manuals that have already been published in OuLiPo's wide variety of writings. One can, however, get a rough idea of such invitational user manuals by consulting the second part of *OuLiPo: La Littérature potentielle,* which is devoted to certain "Synthoulipisms" such as Boolean poems, S + 7 sequences, dash-poems, or the *phane-armé* (Sté*phane* Mallar*mé*).

Controls, systems, algorithms, and programs all coexist en masse in OuLiPian writings. The explorations that they conduct are all guided by a desire to exhaust the verbal potential and combinative rules that certain contemporary linguists have listed in the form of a generative core for the French language. Up until now, this desire has generally been satisfied by means of empirical and craftsmanlike approaches. And yet it calls out for the ultimate machine, which would be systematic, untiring, and comprehensive in its approach. It is the sort of machine that was invented precisely to undertake millions of discrete and repeatable operations, and that has led Paul Fournel to make the following comment: "Potential literature is, by definition, full of all possible forms. Among the forms that await us, there is obviously the realm that has been opened up by computer science" (*OuLiPo: Atlas* 297).

And so after cybermusic, and cyberimages, the time has come for cyberwriting. OuLiPo has made itself a pioneer movement in this area, since it quickly spotted the vast exploratory powers of a machine that can untiringly retrace all the implied developments in a work, whose basic axioms have been supplied to the computer in advance by the author who is keen to work out several imaginary solutions to his text. In this vein François Le Lionnais, Paul Fournel, and Paul Braffort have related some of their exploits in computer composition in a chapter from the above work titled "The Computer and the Writer."[7] By wholeheartedly embracing the combinative potential of their machines they have set the stage for a revolution that will change the very character of writing itself. Yet strangely enough, they seem to be unaware of the fundamental transformation that their enterprise inaugurates, and of the new sorts of questions that it provokes in our understanding of literature.

The "literary" text that is produced via computer is a nonrandom result springing from a systematic program of anticipated results that contains in a most explicit way the constraints, laws, and initial data that bring about the text's creation. The preliminary program that lies outside the text itself thus functions as a sort of pre-text (to use a term from geneticist criticism) for the one the reader receives. Nevertheless, such a pre-text should not be turned into an object of critical reverence, or a fetish of the kind that traditional criticism likes to dig up. For it is the generative potential of the pre-text that deserves attention and is a type of "creating creation" that grounds the work the reader confronts. This is why Paul Fournel can claim that

> the computer works as a rough sketch and can be used to "compose" the text. For example, the author might draw up a list of characters and situations, then ask the computer to combine them in a progressive sequence according to their affinities.
>
> Consequently, the author is able to work on material whose quantity far exceeds his understanding, and yet he is able to master it with the help of the machine. (*OuLiPo: Atlas* 300)

Pushed to its extreme, this model for literary composition allows us to imagine each canonical work of literature as being only one variant of a possible set of works that could be produced from a generating program

---

7. See the section "OuLiPo et informatique" (The computer and the writer) in *OuLiPo: Atlas*, 298–331.

(the pre-text). Once all the combinative components of the realized "masterwork" are discovered, it is thus possible to imagine the establishment of an initial pre-text. This generating program, in turn, would generate a potentially infinite number of variations on the "original" realized literary text. The hypothetical existence of such a lost pre-text would explain the similar patterns of theme, characterization, and so forth, that appear in the field of intertextuality. Italo Calvino points implicitly to this fact in the following remarks:

> Paul Braffort, who is responsible for the development of computer programs that have helped my writing, has also written a series of selection-programs which increasingly respect the *constraints* that the story must follow in order to appear "logically" and "psychologically" acceptable.
>
> This proves clearly, I think, that the help of computers in no way *substitutes* for the artist's creative work, but instead frees the latter from the forced labor of researching all the possible plot combinations, thus giving the author a better chance to concentrate on the unique "swerve" that alone turns a text into a true work of art. (*OuLiPo: Atlas* 331)

From this standpoint, all the systematized structures that one finds, for example, in Mallarmé's poetry (such as condensation, abstraction, or asyntactic groupings) would merely be elements in the layout of the initial program from which they were generated. Such an interpretation would be in complete agreement with the axioms of impersonal creation and control exerted over chance—axioms that form the foundation of OuLiPian literary theory. In fact, in some of the programs that have been envisaged by OuLiPo, all the practical potentialities can already be found in the pre-text program, so that the reader does not have to discover them but simply chooses and verifies the ones he or she wants:[8]

---

8. All these computerized writing and reading procedures that were developed by OuLiPo were on full display at "The Immaterials" exhibition at the Georges Pompidou Center in 1985. Apart from the *Épreuves d'écriture* (Writing proofs) that were included in this exhibit—and that owe a lot to OuLiPian principles of composition since they too require a user's manual (or menu), which was stored in the machines that visitors to the exhibit had to use in order to consult certain texts—there were also computer-assisted combinatory stories that gave a perfect illustration of OuLiPo's notion of menu writing.

Even though the pattern for each of the book-format user manuals that we have quoted so far is closely linked to the particular form of communication that books allow, if

In [a] small text the reader is constantly invited to choose the continuation of the story, through a play of double questions. First the computer conducts a "dialogue" with the reader by proposing a series of choices, and then the computer edits a "correct" version of the chosen text, according to these choices, with the earlier questions for the reader edited out. In this way the pleasure of reading and playing are combined. (*OuLiPo: Atlas* 299)

François Le Lionnais has remarked that "it is *first of all necessary* to give computers a large amount of complex information" and his comment reveals an important fact about the completed texts that are produced via such procedures. It is this type of experimental writing that requires the author to initially elaborate a pre-text that lies outside the work itself. This pre-text occupies a central position in the act of writing, since it becomes the key text for us to read, with the effect that the finished work becomes one of many possible creations to be sparked off by the computerized muse.

COMPUTERIZED PRODUCTIONS

Computer technology along with developments in word processing seem to hold a lot of promise for OuLiPo since they allow writers in the movement to achieve their goal of exhausting all the possible derivations

---

one passes to the realm of electronic communication the user manual principle not only remains valid but is actually reinforced, despite the complete change in format. In his "Post-scriptum" to *Les Immatériaux: Epreuves d'écriture* (Paris: Editions du Centre Georges Pompidou, 1985), Lyotard correctly points out that computerized composition entails a fundamental distinction between writing and its schematized framework, or machination (Lyotard's term). There are, then, two time frames and two domains in the writing process and they lead up to the user's manual and the completed text. As Lyotard remarks:

> The writer-artist, who is but a dignified craftsman, used to fill his texts with traces of his labor (his corrections, erasings, additions, and insertions), which helped both him and his decipherers to reconstruct the arduous path that he had cut in order to arrive at the final text. Ultimately, these traces offered a better understanding of this text. Seated in front of his word processor, however, the craftsman senses, for right or for wrong, that such markings and neglected resources have been taken away from him and that he must propose his text in its finished state, so that it becomes readable to others the moment that it is set down. Once it has been revealed, the craftsman's inner space of composition is no longer there for him to use. (281)

from a given pre-text. In this way they can finally achieve Apollinaire's dream, mentioned in Chapter 1, which was to "mass-produce poetry in the same way that the world has been mass-produced." Nevertheless, one could argue that such computer-generated texts are still invented in accordance with an initial program, for which the writers themselves are completely responsible. It is they, after all, who choose the organizational framework for the linguistic data. Yet for most of the writers in the group (and especially for Jacques Roubaud) the criteria on which this framework is based come directly from generative linguistics.

In *OuLiPo: Atlas de littérature potentielle* Raymond Queneau offers an initial attempt at classifying the group's work (74–77). The classification attributes to each linguistic domain a specific type of operation that gives rise to an OuLiPian text. More recently the so-called TOLLÉ table (or Table of Elementary Linguistic and Literary Operations) has been substituted for this list by Marcel Bénabou (Fig. 27). This table gives a clear overview of the field of linguistic potentialities exploited by the group's members.

Despite the fact that expressions used in the table such as "operation table" bring together the group's "clinical" approach and a fascination for numbers, it is clear that the terms designating the effect of each operation have exact counterparts in the field of linguistic analysis. The operational terms proposed by OuLiPo (namely, "displacement," "substitution," "addition," and so on) all originate in models that have been identified and enumerated within the domain of transformational grammar.[9] It is therefore no surprise that the only category in the table that has a full set of operational potentialities is that of the phrase—the preferred object of all generative studies. The influence of this linguistic the-

---

9. Generative grammarians have formally defined the following syntactic operations found in the TOLLÉ table: displacement—"Où vous allez?"/"Où allez-vous?" (Where are you going?); substitution—"Ce texte, je le lis"/"Cette page, je la lis" (This text/page is what I'm reading); addition—"Je lis le *Nouveau Discours du Récit*"/"J'ai lu le *Traité du Tout-Monde*" (I am reading the *Nouveau Discours du Récit*/I have read the *Traité du Tout-Monde*); subtraction—"Moi, je n'aime pas ça"/"Je n'aime pas ça" ([As for me,] I don't like that); division—"Je n'ai pas écrit *Le Parleur beau* puisque je ne suis pas Joël Gail"/"Je n'ai pas écrit *Le Parleur beau*, je ne suis pas Joël Gail" (I didn't write *The Fancy Talker* [since] I'm not Joël Gail); withdrawal—"Il est temps de déclarer que ce n'est qu'un début, nous continuons nos ébats"/"Il est temps de déclarer: 'Ce n'est qu'un début, continuons nos ébats'" (It's time to declare that it is only a beginning and that we are carrying on frolicking/It's time to declare: "It is only a beginning, let's carry on frolicking"); contraction—"Une pierre qui roule n'amasse pas de mousse"/"Pierre qui roule n'amasse pas mousse" ([A] rolling stone gathers no moss).

OPÉRATIONS OBJET LINGUISTIQUE	DÉPLACEMENT	SUBSTITUTION	ADDITION	SOUSTRACTION	MULTIPLICATION (répétition)
Lettre	anagramme palindrome loucherbem métathèse	paragramme (coquille) cryptographie	prothèse apenthése paragoge	aphérèse syncope élision lipogramme belle absente contrainte du prisonnier abréviation	tautogramme
Phonème	palindrome phonétique contrepétrie Rose sélavy (Desnos) glossaire (Leiris)	à-peu-prés drame alphabétique	bégaiement	lipophonème	allitération rime homeoteleute
Syllabe	palindrome syllabique contrepètrie		bégaiement javanais gémination echolalie	haplographie liposyllable (=(con)trainte des Précieuses) abrégement	bégaiement allitération rime
Mot	algorithme de Mathews permutations (Lescure) pelindrome de mots inversion	métonymie S + 7 homosyn- taxisme L.S.D. traduction trad. antony- mique	redondance pléonasme	liponyme La Rien que la Toute la (FLL)	épanalpse pléonasme anaphore rime défec- tueuse

Figure 27

ory is so strong that when Jacques Roubaud, in another study, offers a synopsis of the operations that affect poetry's rhythmical component, he feels obliged yet again to use terminology borrowed from generative grammarians—"embeddings," "complementizer," "subjacency," "permutations," and so on.

As for the division into vertical columns in the TOLLÉ table, the algorithm that is used is not a homogeneous one, and the selection criteria that it proposes are much more eclectic. It seems to allow a high degree of objectivity and scientific precision, but once one goes beyond this initial impression one discovers a certain degree of vagueness and incoherence. This is largely because the categories that are used to name the various linguistic units are approximate and not indicative of the most rigorous distinctions made by contemporary linguists. Despite its careful elaboration, the mapping proposed by the TOLLÉ table is consequently not much more advanced than the *difficiles nugae* diagrams produced by the *Grands Rhétoriqueurs* of the Middle Ages, or the terrae incognitae that have been handed down from the darkest corners of literary history. It would seem as though beyond the most obvious conceptual markers there lies a vast unexplored territory that no OuLiPian map has yet been able to demarcate.

We are convinced that the existence of such indecisiveness is not due to artistic reasons but can instead be attributed to OuLiPo's dependence on the methodological tools of linguistics. In principle there is no problem with using such tools as the basis for a literary enterprise that places the various functions of language at the heart of its aesthetics. Instead, it is from the OuLiPians' specific selection of linguistic objects for study and their related operational models that uncertainties arise. With such uncertainties come tentative explanations that tend to lose their effectiveness as taxonomies.

In his *Second Manifesto,* François Le Lionnais openly avows the inherent limits of the OuLiPian enterprise and its dependence on linguistic theories that have come to dominate the movement. "The great majority of OuLiPian works that have appeared up until now," he writes, "are part of a SYNTACTIC structurElist approach (and I would ask the reader not to confuse the penultimate word used here, and coined for the express purpose of this Manifesto, with the term 'structurAlist,' which many of us view with great caution)" (*OuLiPo: Littérature* 23). In this remark the importance of the term "syntactic" is underlined by the use of capitals, and if one looks at the TOLLÉ table one notices that the linguistic units listed on the left-hand side are all derived from a linguistic model that is based on syntactic divisions. Le Lionnais's neologism "structurElist" is therefore both a mark of his refusal to be assimilated with a fashionable intellectual trend, and a statement about basic linguistic principles. In the TOLLÉ table we find that the linguistic units listed, from the smallest up to the largest, are indicative of a phenomenological approach to language whereby the linear form of a sentence takes precedence over all the other underlying relations that are established between words. These relations are totally independent of the linear order that our everyday reading habits impose on language.

In actual fact, linguistics has moved quite far ahead of this phenomenological approach, and has begun to investigate new domains in its attempt to answer questions that do not always give preeminence to syntax. This again lends credence to the view that when it comes to poetry one cannot always trust the poets' intuitions. In addition to this outmoded insistence on syntax, one can also criticize the fact that the scores proposed by OuLiPian diagrams reveal a certain historical and methodological confusion that points to the vast differences between the levels of linguistic sophistication that are shared by the group's members. To use a geographical metaphor, OuLiPo's way of identifying linguistic structures is akin to mixing up, in the same study, certain data that has been calculated from the Greenwich meridian with data derived from the Paris meridian.

It is, of course, true that such notions as letter, phoneme or sound, syllable, and word have been able to coexist, at least since the sixteenth century, in a unified analytical model of language. This explains why OuLiPo was able to immediately assimilate certain fixed formal practices that had already been used by the *Grands Rhétoriqueurs* (palindromes, anagrams, acrostics, and so on). Nevertheless there is no serious linguist alive today who still speaks of *words*, since although this term designates a reading unit, and is dear to a certain neophenomenological trend in philosophy (words versus things), it is not a functional linguistic unit. At the dawn of the structuralist movement in 1960, which was the same time that OuLiPo was being set up, André Martinet wrote that "it would be pointless to search for a more precise definition of the notion of 'word' within the field of general linguistics. One may try [...] but [...] by applying rigorous criteria to this notion one often ends up with analyses that hardly bear any resemblance to the common usage of the notion."[10] The notion that is awkwardly designated by the term *word* was subsequently divided into more precise units that Martinet called "morphemes," "lexemes," "monemes," and even "autonomous phrase." Other linguists from the structuralist era would substitute the terms "lexie" and "synapsie."

Moreover, if the vertical axis in the TOLLÉ table were to be in accord with its horizontal axis, the former would have to use terms from the componential analysis of generative lexicology, and apply these to a set of "pertinent semantic features" that would function as basic units

10. André Martinet, *Eléments de linguistique générale* (Paris: Armand Collin, 1967), 115.

within the confines of what one usually calls a word. However, this
change in approach would necessitate a more basic understanding of se-
mantics which, as we will now demonstrate, is the missing link, or rather
the blind spot, in the OuLiPian project.

The notion of a phrase (*syntagme* in French) had a completely sepa-
rate development from that of a word. From the seventeenth to the
twentieth centuries the term *syntagme* had a purely military usage, desig-
nating the organization of an army corps, as for example in the expres-
sion *un syntagme d'infanterie*. It was only toward the end of the 1950s
that the term came to have a specifically linguistic meaning. It was pre-
cisely at this time, however, that the notion of syllable became paired
with that of morpheme. As far as the last item in the TOLLÉ list is
concerned—namely, the concept of paragraph—it is obvious just how
shaky this concept is from an analytical standpoint. The term was intro-
duced into the TOLLÉ table as a reflection of the interest that linguists
took during the 1970s in studies that went beyond the restrictive bound-
aries of the sentence. Nevertheless no linguistic school ever adopted such
a phenomenologically descriptive, and methodologically impoverished,
term.

It might be argued that these comments would be more at home in
a treatise on linguistics than in a study of a contemporary school of po-
etry. Since what difference does it make for a poet if she can tell a mor-
pheme apart from a small phrase? It would be inappropriate to dwell on
the linguistic resources used by OuLiPo unless these resources revealed,
as indeed they do, basic contradictions in the presuppositions that are
shared by the members of the group. A poet can certainly be forgiven for
not having a technical understanding of the tools and materials that he
uses. Yet it is precisely such "professionalism" that is loudly proclaimed in
OuLiPo's manifestos. In addition, we should not forget that OuLiPian
literature tries to put itself in a position of total control over, and com-
plete awareness of, its materials. Since the group's project was conceived
from a set of scrupulously examined parameters, how can we justify the
fact that the objects used to mark out the different stages in the project
have been chosen so blindly from a hodgepodge of pre-Saussurian and
pregenerative linguistic theory?

This methodological problem has obvious effects for the group's
poetics. For instance, in the collective work *La Cantatrice sauve* (The
prima donna is safe),[11] which is based on a metathetical transposition of

11. Paul Fournel et al., "La Cantatrice sauve," in *OuLiPo: La bibliothéque Ouli-*

the phonetic elements in the name of the opera singer Montserrat Caballé, 27 out of 101 derivations are based on the possessive adjective *mon* (which is phonetically present in the singer's first name), and these 27 in turn lead to 9 derivations based on the feminine form *ma*. Nevertheless none of the 36 versions has any direct phonetic relation to the names Montserrat or Caballé. By contrast, only 5 derivations are generated by the word *mont* (mountain), which is actually an autonomous semantic unit that is included in the name Montserrat. In this instance, it is clear that the written sequence *m-o-n-t* was immediately identified with the minimal phonetic unit [mõ], which in turn gave rise to the morpheme *mon*. Such a morpheme is clearly richer in potentialities than *mont* since it allows for certain variations on the morphological paradigm of possessive adjectives (*ma* being one of the examples). As a result, a loosely organized and parasitical type of derivation takes over, with the phonemic algorithm no longer controlling the morphemic one. The transformation from *mont* to *mon* to *ma* and so on undermines the entire effect of constraint, on which the rules of the text are based, since it opens up an infinite possibility of variants. The generative matrix (Montserrat Caballé) thus loses its function as a coercive model and hands over the production of subsequent verbal chains to the effect of chance.

In practical terms there is nothing to condemn in this sort of literary enterprise—the verbal threads that run throughout Michel Leiris's book *La Règle du jeu* (The rules of the game) operate in exactly the same manner, with an emblematic name triggering off a sequence of free verbal association. Yet Leiris himself is forced to admit the failure of his enterprise, and to concede that the verbal chain is worthless since it is based on no underlying necessity. In OuLiPo's case the situation is reversed, for such necessity and its allied constraints are stated explicitly from the outset. If the purpose of OuLiPo's deliberately introduced scores is to show that they have been quite literally composed according to a fixed pattern, then it can be legitimately argued that the scores not generated (through some oversight) by the fixed pattern are the downfall of the pattern itself. The composed scores that make up the text then appear to be the mere product of chance, so that their apparent rigor begins to *de*compose.

Similarly, the first part of Jacques Roubaud's collection, *Jo est le loup* (Jo is the wolf), is defined as a derivation from the prefix *ante*. The notion of the prefix is, however, never given a specific function in the

---

pienne I (Geneva: Slatkine, 1981), 337–57. This is a paronomastic pun of the "minimal pair" type based on the title of Eugène Ionesco's play *La Cantatrice chauve* (The bald soprano): *chauve/sauve*.

work, so that there is an ensuing confusion between morphemes and phonemes in the derivations that are produced. For instance, one of the poems in this work is called "Chêne, chien, chiendent" (Oak, dog, couch grass), which would lead us to expect a series of original morphemic derivations. Yet another poem in the book is called "Hum hum," where we find sound derivations based on a simple repetition of homophones. Italo Calvino's poem "Piccolo Sillabario Illustrato," with its strings of consonantal substitutions, exemplifies the generative power of phonemes (to the exclusion of morphemes) since a simple equation gives rise to the sequence *ba-be-bi-bo-bu, ca-ce-ci-co-cu, da-de-di-do-du, fa-fe-fi-fo-fu,* and so on all the way up to *za-ze-zi-zo-zu.*

This misunderstanding of the basic constituents of language is not, however, shared by all of OuLiPo's members. For instance, one finds among the writings of Daniel Grojnowski, who is a member of the Bled-OuLiPo writers' workshop, a text composed exclusively of morphemic derivations akin to the ones that make up irregular French verbs (*savoir—sachant, sais, su, saura,* or *faire—faisant, fais, fis, ferais,* and so on):

> Les uns l'appellent
> le corps en*seignant*
> Parce qu'il *saigne* sang et eau
> à son corps défendant
> —C'est en *saignant* que l'on devient en*seignant*
> D'autres à voix de Rumeur Publique
> l'appellent le corps en*feignant*
> parce qu'en *feignant* d'en*seigner*
> il se prélasse à l'ombre des copies.
> Tel un roi *fainéant* il est *fait de néant*
> *feignant* à longueur de journées
> —C'est en *feignant* qu'on devient *fainéant.* (our emphasis)

> (Some people call it
> the teaching body
> Because it bleeds with blood and water
> under coercion
> —It's by bleeding that one becomes a teaching body
> Other people, spreading common rumors,
> call it the faking body

since while pretending to teach
this body struts about imitating others.
Like a do-nothing king, he is faking
pretending for days on end
—It's by faking that one becomes a do-nothing.)[12]

Here the derivations are morpho-phonetic in nature, generating the possibility of a new verb in French, *seigner,* composed on the basis of false derivatives (*enseignant* leading to *seignant*), which in turn gives rise to another hypothetical verb, *feigner*—a replacement for the verb *feindre* (to fake, pretend). One can also detect in these shifts a trace of the fundamental linguistic mechanism that allowed Rimbaud to write in his poem "L'Éclair" from *Une Saison en enfer:* "Allons! feignons, fainéantons, ô pitié!" (Come on! Let's pretend, let's be lazy, o pity!). Quite obviously, this type of textual generation that is a direct result of linguistic mechanisms leads one to reconsider the overly narrow view of intertextuality as a set of borrowings from a *literary* tradition.

It would be pointless to continue the list of examples showing how a more up-to-date classification of linguistic units would allow OuLiPo to use more rigorous (and hence productive) constraints. In conclusion, we would simply like to suggest that the lack of semantic formalization (as evidenced in the TOLLÉ table by the absence of such terms as *seme, classeme,* or *ideologeme*) lies at the basis of the critical neglect for OuLiPo's work. This lack is even more troubling when one considers that over the last fifteen years linguists have paid more and more attention to the meanings of utterances. Already in 1973 François Le Lionnais urged the group to devote more attention to these matters:

> It would seem worthwhile to move beyond [an interest in syntax] and examine the field of semantics, by trying to gain mastery over concepts, ideas, images, feelings, and emotions. It is a bold and difficult enterprise, but for that very reason one worth considering. [...] It is such an ambition that shows OuLiPo for what it should be. (*La Bibliothèque oulipienne* 362)

Queneau's 1974 "Classification of OuLiPo's Labors" is distinctly lacking in examples for its category "Semantic Constraints" (*OuLiPo:*

12. Daniel Grojnowski, *Aux commencements du rire moderne* (Paris: José Corti, 1997), 167.

Atlas 76–77). From this standpoint it is significant that a work such as *L'Hôtel de Sens* (The meaning hotel), which would appear, at least from its title, to offer an examination of the semantic realm, in fact understands the word *sens* only in its secondary meaning as "direction." The work is based exclusively on the representation of a moving clock hand that gives rise to a set of narrative sequences repeated three times according to the hand's movement—its initial direction, the contrary direction, and the proper direction. Such "directions" affect only the rotation of a predetermined group of syllables. Other projects that are more explicitly linked to semantics are based on developments from logical propositions. For instance, Queneau generates a text from the formula "The relationship x puts y in the place of z." Braffort borrows a so-called Scheffer symbol in order to construct a poem on the model "is is-not." Nevertheless such textual production on the basis of logical propositions does not belong only to OuLiPo. The popular poet Claude Roy, for example, uses such a resource in his collection *Enfantasques* and is able to produce some surprising pieces as a result. The proposition "If c, then q" (in which c is a condition, and q a consequence) produces the following text:

> Si les escargots savaient téléphoner
> Ils resteraient toujours au chaud dans leur coquille

> (If snails could telephone
> They would always stay warm inside their shells)

In short, when OuLiPo's derivations are applied to units that are larger than simple letters they run the risk of unintentionally breaking sets of linguistic constraints that were never defined or recognized. The rules produced by OuLiPo consequently appear arbitrary and unduly limiting, while the literary exercises themselves, once their flaw is perceived, tend to lose their virtuosity, and hence their value. A "sad" spectacle (to use Gérard Genette's term for such exercises[13]) is not only one that plunges us into tears of despair. It is also a boring spectacle that, apart from its weak premises and low stakes, tires us with the laxity of its own enterprise. If there is a sadness in OuLiPo it is probably because of such

13. A remark made by Gérard Genette in response to Jean-Jacques Thomas's paper on OuLiPo ("Arcature numérique"), delivered at Columbia University on 15 November 1978. On this question, see also Nöel Arnaud's article, "Gérard Genette et l'Oulipo," *Sureau* 1 (1984), p. 7.

weaknesses. As a result, the all-important form that the group is pursuing cannot be found in the group's writing principles (since the foundations on which these principles are built remain unclear), but instead at a higher level. In particular the linguistic nature of such form becomes apparent once we apply a method of formal analysis to OuLiPo's texts, a method that has been derived from the most recent research in linguistics. For then we realize that OuLiPo's scores do not only have to be composed, they also have to be orchestrated—that is, built on the basis of language's own generative and memorial power.

ten

THE ENDS OF LYRIC?

(ROCHE,

HÉBERT)

In the formal explorations undertaken by the OuLiPo group, and even in poems by Garnier and Roubaud that are derived from visual or numerical patterns, there is clearly little room for a lyrical expression of the poet's self. Indeed the very notion of expression, which implies the putting into language of experiences that lie outside the realm of words, is suspect for reasons that were examined in part in Chapter 5. If expression has any meaning at all for the poets examined so far it is this: contemporary poems develop, expand, or express formal patterns (of meaning, syntax, or rhythm) that are inherent to the modern French language. The contours of a poetic persona, or self, that occasionally emerge from these expressions of form are secondary, and not prior, to the particular structuring that makes up each poem. Apollinaire's composite persona that gives body to an ever-expanding set of intertextual derivations is a case in point. Another is the figures of body that emerge from (rather than precede) the rewritings of self that we examined in Chapter 7.

Is there, consequently, any room left for the concept of lyric in the sort of linguistic experimentation that characterizes contemporary French poetry? Is it not possible to define lyric more precisely on the basis of poetic structures rather than a putative autobiographical content? The following two chapters will answer these questions in the affirmative.

We begin this chapter with the work of two very different poets to whom the label lyrical is still attached, and who draw together many of the experiments that have been discussed in the pages above: Denis Roche and Anne Hébert. To appreciate the wide divergence in the styles of these two writers one has only to consider the surface appearance of their poems. Grouped in stanzas and carrying such titles as "La Voix de l'oiseau" or "Mystère de la parole" (The bird's voice, Word's mystery), Hébert's poems have an apparently traditional form, whereas Roche's typographical experimentations, which incorporate, among other things, solid lines and hieroglyphics, and have such titles as *Trois pourrissements poétiques* (Three poetic putrefactions), are quite the opposite. Born on two different continents, their first collections of poems appeared more than twenty years apart. Anne Hébert's *Les Songes en équilibre* (Dreams in balance) was published in her native Quebec in 1942 and was followed by "Le Tombeau des Rois" (The kings' tomb) in 1953, whereas Denis Roche's first poems, provocatively titled *Récits complets* (Complete stories), came out in 1963, followed by *Les Idées centésimales de Miss Elanize* (The percentage ideas of Miss Elanize) in 1964. While the former became well-known for her prize-winning novels *Kamouraska* and *Les Fous de Bassan* (The Bassan gannets), the latter continued to produce avant-garde works within the Tel Quel group, such as the poems in *Le Mécrit* (The miswritten) or the novel *Louve basse* (She-wolf bringing forth), and then recently abandoned writing after becoming increasingly involved as an editor at the Seuil publishing house in Paris. On first glance, then, their literary output would seem to be of two very different orders. Yet by questioning the validity of lyric expression, albeit for different reasons, these two poets draw attention to certain limits that are inherent to poetic writing today.

When the lyrical aspect of Denis Roche's writing is underscored, as Jean-Marie Gleize does when he claims that Roche "is still navigating, in his own way, between the borders of [Lamartine's poem] 'The Lake,'"[1] several problems arise. For instance, there is the obvious contradiction

1. Jean-Marie Gleize, *Poésie et figuration* (Paris: Seuil, 1983), 303.

between Romanticism's definition of lyricism as self-expression, which is the one our century has inherited, and a famous slogan put forward by Roche in the Tel Quel manifesto *Théorie d'ensemble* (Group theory): "La poésie est inadmissible, d'ailleurs elle n'existe pas" (Poetry is inadmissible, moreover it doesn't exist).[2] In other words, poetry is a "puerile expression of an aestheticizing personal activity" and doesn't exist since such an aestheticizing activity is purely illusory (223). In these attacks against the metaphysics of a speaking subject that is supposed to speak through poetic conventions, Denis Roche appears to be a staunch adversary of Romantic lyricism. There seems to be nothing at all in common between him and what he terms the "horrible exemplary bard."[3] "We will no longer believe in the village soothsayer, in the bard who brings forth mysteries or good words," writes Roche (*Théorie* 227). How then are we to understand Gleize's bringing together of Lamartine and Roche, or else the following declaration made by Michael Bishop: "Roche [...] endeavors to render in his [writings] the 'general song' of humankind, [...] the extraordinary 'music' we, and the things of the world each make and gather within ourselves yet which is never otherwise really heard."[4]

It is clear that current theories of the lyric genre are ill-equipped to answer this question, since the lyrical tends to be a catch-all category that is extended to any text containing first-person pronouns and not fitting into a standard definition of narrative. This broad definition matches Jean-Marie Gleize's characterization of modern poetry as "writing experiences [...] that articulate a subject in history, as well as in his or her history" (307). More precise criteria are put forward by Northrop Frye in his essay "Approaching the Lyric" that appeared in 1985.[5] According to Frye, a lyric poem does not develop in a continuous way any particular story or argument. Instead it offers its readers a fragmented meditation that repeatedly returns to a particular emotion felt by the poet and which

2. Denis Roche, *Tel Quel: Théorie d'ensemble* (Paris: Seuil, 1968), 221.
3. Roche quoted in an interview with Jean Ristat in *La Gazette de Lausanne,* 28 August 1970.
4. Michael Bishop, *The Contemporary Poetry of France: Eight Studies* (Amsterdam: Rodopi, 1985), 82–83.
5. Northrop Frye, "Approaching the Lyric," in *Lyric Poetry: Beyond the New Criticism,* ed. Chaviva Hošek and Patricia Parker (Ithaca: Cornell University Press, 1985), 31–37. See the recent collection of essays, *Figures du sujet lyrique,* edited by Dominique Rabaté (Paris: Presses Universitaires de France, 1996), which explores the connections between Romanticism, the lyric subject, and figures of utterance. See also our discussion of the lyric in the first part of Chapter 11.

poses a problem for the latter. Frye calls this emotion a "blocking point" and says that because of it most lyric poems deal with "a specific, usually ritual, occasion [...] like drinking and lovemaking" (32). In such cases the blocking point "seems to be the entrance to another world of experience [which] is one of magic and mystery" (36).

The vagueness of the terms used here, such as "magic" and "mystery," alerts one to the weakness of Frye's definition, as does his contrast between narrative continuity and discontinuous verse—don't stories also lead their readers back to events, or "blocking points," that they have already recounted, and is there not poetic continuity in the gradual accumulation of meaning within each poem? There is a central weakness in any account of lyric, such as Frye's, that focuses on a poem's themes rather than its structure, since such an account is tangential to lyric's main features. Consequently, although many lyric poems are celebrations of love or drinking, just as many are not. It may be true that the lineage of French lyric poets often coincides with that of famous love poets (from Ronsard through Eluard), yet how can a thematic definition of lyricism help one understand such an exemplary lyric as Verlaine's "Dans l'interminable ennui de la plaine..." (In the interminable boredom of the plain...), in which no blocking point seems to figure? Even in a poem where drinking is foregrounded, such as in the liminary poem "Salut" (Good health [greetings]) in Mallarmé's *Poésies* (Poems), where the action of lifting a glass in a toast forms the crux of the poem, the "beautiful drunkenness" of which the narrator speaks goes well beyond a banquet celebration, whether it be ritualized or not. For Mallarmé, the action of lifting a glass (or in French, *un verre*) is more closely tied to that of elevating its homonym—*un vers* (verse)—to a new and forceful level of language in which banquet and text, narrator and reader, are carried along by the performative good health that effective speech acts (such as the utterance "Greetings!") bestow on those who enact and receive them.[6]

---

6. Mallarmé mentions the elevation of verse in the following extract from his lecture "La Musique et les lettres" (Music and letters). In the paragraph from which the extract is taken, Mallarmé is discussing an underlying rhythm in the French language that appears intermittently, thus signaling the poeticity of certain texts—in either prose or verse: "Surtout la métrique française, délicate, serait d'emploi intermittent: maintenant (...) voici que de nouveau peut *s'élever* (...) Le *vers* de toujours" (The metrics of French, in all their delicacy, would seem to have an especially intermittent use: now [...] here once again *the verse* of all times can *rise up*; in *Oeuvres complètes*, eds. H. Mondor and G. Jean-Aubry [Paris: Gallimard, Pléiade, 1945], 644, our emphasis).

Put in this context, lyric poetry should no longer be defined by its subject, but by its pragmatic ends—the production of intense effects on those who use it. Reading Denis Roche's 1980 book, *Dépôts de savoir et de technique* (Deposits of know-how and technique), one rediscovers this performative good health that is central to lyric's way of poeticizing language. In the book's preface Roche describes his pages as "des machines capteuses" (captivating machines) that are to catch not so much those events or emotions that preceded the act of writing as the reader who is gradually drawn into their hold.[7] These "états excités de langue et d'énergie" (excited states of language and energy; 65) get their force not from what they describe, but from the effects that they accomplish, and in this respect they are a perfect illustration of what J. L. Austin called performative utterances.[8]

The most famous example of these given by Austin is the statement "I do" pronounced by both partners in a wedding ceremony as a response to the question "Do you take this man/woman to be your lawfully wedded husband/wife?" In this context, the utterance "I do" does not describe the act of marrying one's partner; it *is* the act. Language becomes deed and buoys up its participants (spouses and witnesses) in its effectiveness as action and event, just as Mallarmé's toast carries along with it its reader-participants.

Not only in weddings are lovers' utterances effective, for when one person says to another "I love you" the statement functions for the interlocutor as some form of engagement by the speaker to act in certain tender ways toward this same interlocutor. It is, in short, a type of promise to do certain things and not do others. Such a performative is misunderstood with amusing effects in many romantic comedies where lovers argue back and forth in an attempt to put to rest the question "Do you really love me or are you just pretending?" It is, of course, a false debate insofar as it tries to unearth a sincere expression of feeling (rather than a set of public actions) that would supposedly guarantee

---

7. Denis Roche, *Dépôts de savoir et de technique* (Paris: Seuil, 1980), 12.

8. J. L. Austin, *How to Do Things with Words,* 2d ed. (Cambridge: Harvard University Press, 1975), 6. Philosophers of language such as H. P. Grice who further developed Austin's theory have coined the term *pragmatics* to name the field of study concerned with meanings determined not by an utterance's semantic properties but by the context and effects of its reception. See Peter Cole, ed., *Radical Pragmatics* (New York: Academic Press, 1981). For an application of certain pragmatic principles to poetry by Mallarmé, see Steven Winspur's "The Pragmatic Force of Lyric," *Yearbook of Comparative and General Literature* 42 (1994): 142–47.

the veracity of the love professed. Because "I love you" is a performative it cannot be judged true, false, or any degree in between, but is instead either an accomplished utterance or else what Austin calls a "misfire" (16). Like the wedding vow "I do," an avowal of love simply either works or doesn't: the utterer's future actions toward the addressee either endorse the performative or else empty it of its initial, and subsequent, force.

Much of the confusion surrounding lyric poetry hinges on this important point, since as long as one attaches words such as *truth* or *sincerity* to poems, one is obliged to try and explain their performative force in terms of a prior event—a lovers' spite, for instance, or some other blocking point, to use Frye's term. Rather than a linguistic act, the poem is thus turned into the putative expression of a preceding event whose own supposed force is meant to ground the text's power. Roche's *dépôts* not only resist this reduction of lyric to description, they also parody it. "Je vous dois la vérité en littérature et je vous la dirai" (I owe it to you to give you the truth in literature, and I'll tell you it) announces the title of the last "deposit" (209), but at no point in this final text, nor anywhere else in the book, do we find any truth that is supposedly contained within literature. Instead, famous models for such truth are upturned: for example, Freud, in the title to deposit 5—"Au-delà du principe d'écriture" (Beyond the writing [rather than "pleasure"] principle; 57), Descartes— "'Tu écris, donc tu penses; tu penses, donc tu techniques'" (You write, therefore you think; you think, therefore you technique; 63), or Mallarmé—"'Je t'apporte l'enfant d'une nuit de Corbeaux'" (I bring you the child of a night of Ravens [rather than "Idumaean"]; 181). Once one realizes that the capital letter in "Corbeaux" has turned this common noun into a title—specifically, a version of Edgar Allan Poe's "The Raven," which, under its French title "Le Corbeau," influenced a whole line of poetic formalists from Valéry onward—then one understands that Roche's transformation of the opening line to Mallarmé's "Don du poème" (Gift of the poem) is not gratuitous. Roche is telling his readers, in effect, that his own text is produced by the sorts of formal patterns and constraints that Poe, in "The Philosophy of Composition," had claimed lie at the source of lyric poetry. We examine some of Roche's formal patterns shortly, but to appreciate the extent to which the title "I owe it to you to give you the truth in literature . . ." is parodic, we only have to consider that it too is a slightly altered quotation from Cézanne: "Je vous

dois la vérité en peinture, et je vous la dirai" (I owe it to you to give you
the truth in painting, and I'll tell you it).[9]

It might appear from all this that the only place for truth in poetry
resides in a writer's style—that is, in the transformations that a poet
brings to the literary extracts that he or she has borrowed from others.
Yet to believe this would be to miss the point of Roche's undermining of
standard truth-claims. Insofar as his *Dépôts de savoir et de technique* are
amalgamations of performative excerpts, with each of the fifteen deposits
made up of fragmented conversations, reports, and quotations, their illo-
cutionary and perlocutionary effects on the reader constitute the particu-
lar goal of these pages. Exciting the reader with "energized language"
(65) is all that matters, since, in doing so, Roche takes his reader back to
a fundamental constituent of language—namely, its power to accomplish
actions. Like so many of the other texts encountered in earlier chapters,
Dépôts de savoir et de technique achieves its poetic purpose by returning to
its roots in language and poeticizing them.

The book's preface, titled "The Copán Stairway" and named after a
stone pyramid in Honduras, is both a user's manual for the subsequent
dépôts and an explanation of how "the transfer of energy from poet to
writer" works.[10] The sixty-three steps leading up to a small sanctuary at
the top of the pyramid are engraved with numerous hieroglyphs in which
specialists have deciphered dates, maps, and human faces seen in profile.
Roche describes a visit he made to the pyramid in the following terms:

Une volée de 63 marches, qui en ne rien changeant du tout, faisait
que tout *prenait:* immense "dépôt" où les lettres ont pu être sculp-
tées, qui monte en biais et s'intègre au paysage (...) un signifiant de

---

9. Paul Cézanne in a letter to Emile Bernard (23 October 1905), quoted by
Jacques Derrida in *La Vérité en peinture* (Paris: Flammarion, 1978), 6. Derrida's extended
discussion of Cézanne's statement explores the basic ambiguity of the phrase "the truth in
painting," which designates both the truth as it happens to appear and an inherent truth
about paintings. The latter, as Derrida points out, is a question of painterly style, and hence
of surface technique as used by a particular artist (7 ff.). As Roche mentions in his *Dépôts,*
composing texts simply as typographical surfaces, with no illusion of referential "depth" to
them, is one of his goals in the book (102 ff.). However, such surface writings should not
be compared with the style of paintings, but with a time frame that makes all talk about
style irrelevant ("Surlendemains du style" [Days following the day after style], *Dépôts* 185).

10. "La lecture du poème opère le transfert d'énergie du poète au lecteur" (Reading
poems effects a transfer of energy from the poet to the reader), in Roche, *Récits complets*
(Paris: Seuil, 1963), 12.

la beauté qui ne serait fait que de temps et sur lequel même on peut marcher. Je pensais à tout cela en revenant vers l'entrée du site, à cette "volée" à laquelle tout homme devrait avoir droit au moins une fois dans sa vie. (19–20)

(A flight of 63 steps, which by not changing a single thing, made everything *take on importance:* an immense "deposit" where the letters could be sculpted, and which climbs up on a slant and blends into the countryside [...] a signifier of beauty that would be made only by time and upon which one could walk. I was thinking about all this when coming back from the entrance to the monument: about that "flight" to which any person should have a right, at least once in their life.)

By shifting from the imperfect and perfect tenses in the opening phrases to the present and then conditional tenses in the phrases that follow, Roche moves from an account of what he actually saw in Honduras to an ambiguous description of both the pyramid and another artifact that *would* have the same effect if it were constructed. In fact, the Copán pyramid has precisely those attributes of an artwork that Roche has created in *Dépôts de savoir et de technique:* "Un texte entier dont le langage, assez perdu pour qu'on ne le déchiffre jamais complètement, ne cessera de s'agiter sous les yeux de ceux qui seront venus jusque-là" (A complete text whose language, hidden just enough so that no one will ever decipher it completely, will not stop shimmering under the eyes of those who will have come up to it; 19–20). Both are monuments whose materials (stone steps in one, pages of paper in the other) frame sets of words and cultural know-how ("dépôt de savoir"), in which people's outlines can be found.

Roche designates these human pictures with the technical term *antéfixe:* a sculpted human form that is often used as an ornament on the roofs of old buildings. Climbing the pyramid gives the traveler an impression of lyrical rapture or "flight." Similarly, reading Roche's published deposits in the pages that follow this preface, one realizes that their layout and progression invites readers to reach a state of dizzying joy. With every line in each *dépôt* containing the same number of typographical marks and ending abruptly before another cut-up phrase begins in the next line, the *dépôts* are built out of carefully measured steps whose rhythm forms a stairway of literary readings, classical music, notes from foreign travels and sexual adventures, and even hieroglyphs and drawings (142–43, 214–15). As their eyes move along this stairway, readers not only encounter monuments to past events and to the narrator's friends, they also become intoxicated with the *dépôt*'s accumulated performative know-how—musical, sexual, or cultural.

Consider, for instance, the following extract:

Ah!...non morrai!...in quegli accenti,...Nè ciel, nè terra... La voici en effet, fracassant les arbres, foudroyont les murs ans succès des mangosteens et on achète 1 pet. maison en arge et ton ventre, mais c'est bob, continue mais fais-le bien cri ar le mur du Sud. D. TOUR DE GALATA. Appelée autrefois "tour que ce sont les + vivants portraits que la littérature ait ja

(115)

(Oh!...you won't die!...in these words,...Neither sky, nor earth... In fact here she is, shattering the trees, cracking the walls thout success some mangosteens and we buy 1 sm. house in mone and your belly, but it's swollen up, continue but make it sho rough the South wall. D. GALATA TOWER. Bygone times called "tower that they're the most living portraits that literature has ev)

Beginning with part of the libretto for Bellini's *Beatrice of Tende*, this opening to deposit 9 sets the frame for the lines that follow. The five lines that come after (as well as the entire deposit, which is titled "Our *antéfixe*" and commemorates the tenth anniversary of the poet's love affair with Françoise Peyrot) report different types of climax. A quotation in line 2 from Marguerite Duras's novel *Détruire, dit-elle* describes the sudden appearance of the book's protagonist, Elisabeth Alione, who has just returned from a walk in the woods, and who is eagerly awaited by Max Thor and Alissa, two other characters who desire her. The third and fifth lines, Roche tells his reader in the notes to deposit 9, come from travel notes and a guide to Turkey that he and Françoise used while journeying. Line 4 recounts a moment of sexual excitement and line 6 gives a comment on what commemorative texts can achieve. It is not the things described in these lines that give meaning or force to this particular "deposit of know-how and technique," but rather the strong emotions that each line encapsulates and invites its readers to retrace. Singing with passion an extract from an opera score (line 1) thus becomes a model for each reader's reenactment of the scenes that follow—scenes from love, literature, or exotic travel. Consequently, lyrical fever in Roche's text (and there is indeed plenty of it) resides not in what the book is about (its themes, recurring events, and so on) but in the seemingly endless flow of performative language that its readers must enact. Like Apollinaire's *poèmes-conversations* (for example, "Les Fenêtres" or "Lundi rue Christine" in *Calligrammes*), poetry lies in the "transposition of the general song" that is recorded in the public world of events and conversations (13). The transposition is central here since it is only through readers' transposing the quoted fragments of songs, travels, or events into their own acts of reading that these fragments can take on life.

In his preface Roche makes an interesting remark. Composing the book assured him that

> these sets of writings in action [*ces ensembles d'écriture en action*] that I was calling everywhere pages of deposits, *Deposits of know-how and technique,* had brought me to the point where what I was writing was neither prose nor poetry, nor what too many people today are calling "texts," "fictions," "narratives," and other "etc." (11)

Not only is Roche claiming that his writings are not poetry, but he is also denying that they belong to any other literary genre (or mode of representation). For rather than copy actions, their peculiarity is to *become* actions whenever they are read. Nevertheless, this redefinition leads Roche to compare the texts to a medium that maintains a curious connection to lyric: photography. Calling his deposits "photographic plates" on which he captures "the world's moltings" (65), and comparing the framing of each of the lines in a deposit to the manual gesture of clicking the shutter button on an instamatic camera, which is an experience of "raw material that is more precise than any theory of literature ever was" (102), Roche underscores the instantaneous capturing of meaning that is produced by his cut-up lines of typed text. Is there not a trace here of Lamartine's famous project in "Le Lac" to capture in writing the elusive passing moment of emotion? Jean-Marie Gleize certainly thinks so, as we noted earlier. Commercial slogans that advertise cameras and film moreover exploit this lyrical topos indefinitely.

What is more important, however, than any vestigial thematic link between photography and lyric is the *use* to which photos and lyric poems are put. As Roche states in the phrases just quoted, collecting and looking at photos means multiplying the variety of surfaces that the earth has to offer, and by the same token celebrating these innumerable "moltings" that give us infinitely more pleasure than our attempts to grasp the hidden truth, or essence, of things:

> It's a well-known fact: there is no human activity, artistic or otherwise, and especially literary, that is not a question of surfaces. So there are millions of people attached by the soles of their feet to the huge lawn that makes up our earth, and that don't know what to do with whatever is underneath its surface. Similarly, there are façades of houses and buildings that are suspended perpendicularly [...], as is our own skin which is the tiny amount of what we know about our bodies, even if a finger or a tongue or a genital occasionally sets off to explore a hole in its partner.
>
> Is it possible to detect [...] in this obvious fact, *through the very absence of all interiority,* an explanation of language [...] or of its substitute, which is to say, art? (99)

What the proliferation of surfaces in photographs, or in Roche's deposits, allows its users to do is precisely to situate themselves in relation to the pleasurable rediscovery of surfaces that these works allow. Roche uses his particular composition techniques, he claims, "in order to give the deposit as big a chance as possible to appear" and "before that, to give the [...] people who will pass in front of the text's frame their biggest chance to find themselves in it, both 'in charge' and 'deposited in it'" (53). Readers acquire their own know-how, then, by looking at the performative enactment of beautiful bodies, songs, sculptures, or pictures. What is important is not *what* these surfaces tell them, but *how* the surfaces initiate them to self-sufficient bodily pleasure, so that, just as much as the poet, each reader "seem[s] to have in his or her hand a gigantic magnetized horseshoe, a magnetic harp that vibrates along the very skin of their torso," with the result that they "completely become that fascinating swarm of signs, with its protruding bundles of syllables" (12). This pleasure, which Roche compares here to the vibrating harp of Orpheus, and which is nothing other than our bodies in action, simply *is* lyrical force. Consequently, photography is one more figure (alongside operatic arias, references to music, or invocations of the muse) for this force, and for the performative structure inherent in poetry itself.

Roche's texts demonstrate that lyric is still the privileged place for performative language (or language in action), and that lyric's force resides in the transfer of this performativity to its readers. Anne Hébert also situates lyric in a language of gestures and actions, as we can tell from her poem "Nos Mains au jardin" (Our hands in the garden), which begins with the following project:

> Nous avons eu cette idée
> De planter nos mains au jardin
>
> Branches des dix doigts
> Petits arbres d'ossements
> Chère plate-bande.[11]
>
> (We had this idea
> Of planting our hands in the garden
>
> Branches of the ten fingers
> Little trees of bones
> Dear flower bed.)

The wish that the planted hands (and their metonymy of poetic writing) would grow and flower into a new language of gestures is, however, thwarted. As we read two stanzas later,

> Nul oiseau
> Nul printemps
> Ne se sont pris au piège de nos mains coupées
>
> (No bird
> No springtime
> Fell into the trap of our severed hands)

Indeed, the majority of Hébert's poems are concerned with the inability to create lyric force, or a renewed language of action. What thwarts the narrator in these poems is the ossified discourse of patriarchy.

11. Anne Hébert, *Poèmes* (Paris: Seuil, 1960), 49. Subsequent references to Hébert's poems are to this edition.

In one of Hébert's best known texts, the long poem "Le Tombeau des Rois" (The tomb of kings) that was first published in 1953, the longed-for language of action has as its figure a bird accompanying the female narrator on her descent into the tomb of the seven dead Egyptian kings named in the poem's title.

> Et cet oiseau que j'ai
> Respire
> Et se plaint étrangement.
>
> (61)

> (And this bird that I have
> Breathes
> And moans strangely.)

The bird, a traditional metaphor for poetic flight and creativity, is ill at ease in the land of the dead, and at the end of the poem we discover its longing to return to the land of living people (designated metaphorically by a new dawn):

> Et les morts hors de moi, assassinés,
> Quel reflet d'aube s'égare ici?
>
> D'où vient donc que cet oiseau frémit
> Et tourne vers le matin
> Ses prunelles crevées?
>
> (61)

> (And the dead ones outside me, assassinated,
> What flash of dawn has wandered in here?
>
> For what reason is this bird shaking
> And turning toward the morning
> Its hollow eyeballs?)

An explanation for the bird's blindness (imposed, like that of a falcon, so that it will not desert its trainer) can be found in the violence that the female narrator too has suffered:

La fumée d'encens, le gâteau de riz seché
Et ma chair qui tremble:
Offrande rituelle et soumise.
(...)
Un frisson long (...)
Agite sept pharaons d'ébène
(...)
Avides de la source fraternelle du mal en moi
Ils me couchent et me boivent;
Sept fois, je connais l'étau des os
Et la main sèche qui cherche le coeur pour le rompre.

(60–61)

(The smoke of incense, the cake of dried rice
And my flesh that is trembling:
A ritual and obedient offering.
(...)
A long shiver [...]
Stirs up seven ebony pharaohs
(...)
Hungry for the fraternal source of evil in me
They pull me down and drink me;
Seven times, I experience the vice-grip of bones
And the dried hand that searches for my heart in order to break it.)

The dried rice cake mentioned here alerts us to the intertext that Hébert's entire poem is reworking. The kings presented by the poet are not merely representatives of a lost political power; they embody the literary power held by male canonical writers—a power that poets from Virgil onward bestowed on themselves by incorporating into their works the topos of the descent into the underworld. The goal of such a descent is to allow the new poet's representative (Aeneas, for Virgil, or the character Dante in *The Inferno*) to converse with the great poetic heroes of the past (Achilles, Ulysses, and company), then bring back to the world of the contemporary reader the *living* voice of authority that has become lost in the burial of such canonical texts. The notion of *translatio imperii,* which critics such as Frank Kermode have used to explain this transfer of political power through the translation of literary intertexts, rests on the contrast we find in Hébert's poem between the dead texts of an alien culture and the living voice of a contemporary poet.[12]

The dried rice cake and the entire episode of visiting the dead in "Le Tombeau des Rois" are thus explained by the search for a fresh, new voice of authority—just as they are in the following extract from Saint-John Perse's poem *Vents:*

> Il a mangé le riz des morts; dans leurs suaires de coton il s'est taillé droit d'usager. Mais sa parole est aux vivants: ses mains aux vasques du futur. Et sa parole nous est plus fraîche que l'eau neuve.[13]

> (He [the contemporary, living poet] has eaten the rice of the dead; in their cotton shrouds he has cut out a user's rights. But his word is for the living, his hands are in the basins of the future. And his speech is fresher to us than new water.)

Yet why are Anne Hébert's narrator and the bird she carries constrained by the dead instead of being rejuvenated by them? The specific context of Hébert's use of the *translatio* topos gives one answer. "Le Tombeau des Rois" is not written against a dead literary tradition (as the Greek tradition was for Virgil's audience, or the Latin one for Dante), but against a living one: the French literary canon. As a Quebecois writer, Hébert uses the same language as her French literary forebears and, consequently, the forging of a new poetry of action that would both carry the authority of past masters and yet be unique to Quebec is all the more difficult to accomplish. The French language and its literary canon suppress all attempts to recast them as words used to create a non-French identity. "Seven times, I experience the vice-grip of bones," we read in the passage quoted above.

Poetry gives Hébert one way out of this impasse. For just as Virgil presented himself as the writer who captured better than Homer the transcultural "spirit" lying behind all civilizations, or just as Dante, in turn, translated this spirit into the one he knew best (namely, Christianity), so "Le Tombeau des Rois" recounts a journey back to a poem's ideal origins in the dream (or *songe*) of creation that precedes all composition:

12. See Frank Kermode, *The Classic* (New York: Viking, 1975), 30–39.
13. Saint-John Perse, *Oeuvres complètes* (Paris: Gallimard, Pléiade, 1972), 181.

Quel fil d'Ariane me mène
Au long des dédales sourds?
(...)
(En quel songe
Cette enfant fut-elle liée par la cheville
Pareille à une esclave insensée?)
L'auteur du songe
Presse le fil,
Et viennent les pas nus
Un à un
Comme les premières gouttes de pluie
Au fond du puits.

(59–60)

(What Ariadne thread leads me
Along the deaf passageways of the maze?
(...)
[In what dream
Was this child attached by her ankle
Like a deranged slave?]
The author of the dream
Pulls on the thread,
And bare steps arrive
One by one
Like the first drops of rain
At the bottom of the well.)

Visiting the dead Egyptian kings is therefore but one metaphor alongside another, Ariadne and the Minotaur, for a backward journey to the real power of lyric as postulated by the *translatio* myth: an inner voice that grounds the authority of poetry.[14] Returning to search for an earlier voice that would give meaning to the words uttered in a text is also a recurrent structure in Hébert's prose narratives. Protagonists such as Soeur Julie in

14. The choice of Egypt and Crete as metaphors in the poem is not accidental. Again, following the logic of *translatio,* Hébert postulates origins to civilization that predate (and hence escape) the dominant culture against which she is writing—the world of French letters and the time frame of Romance languages. In a similar fashion Virgil undoes the authority of Greek letters by tracing the original spirit of Rome back to an empire whose power predated that of the Greek city-states: Troy.

Les Enfants du sabbat, Elisabeth Rolland in *Kamouraska,* or Flora Fontanges in *Le premier jardin* all embark on a reconstruction of their past through disconnected phrases that they remember from their youth. The fact that some pages in these novels are saturated with lines from nineteenth-century French poems suggests that the backward journey into each character's past life goes hand in hand with another type of search: the movement toward an underlying poetic form of language.[15] The forcefulness of the poetic speech dreamt by Hébert's characters is consequently identified as both a power residing in the history of French and a property unique to poetry.

Anne Hébert discusses the authority of poetry's inner voice in a series of notes written in collaboration with Frank Scott (who translated her poem into English). These notes were published under the title *Dialogue sur la traduction* (Dialogue on translation). As might be expected, this dialogue is, by its very nature, also about the transfer of poetic authority from one language to another through the act of translation. Consequently, poet and translator turn out to be engaged in exactly the same sort of activity since the former, just as much as the latter, attempts through her writing to give new form to the original voice that speaks at lyric's birth:

> Even before the translator has thought out in his own language the words of the poem, already within him an agreement has been made. A sort of inner voice from before the coming of words translates the poem in the bottom of one's heart, by experiencing it gradually as an additional form of life. [...] The poet too is involved in this powerful and lucid adventure which is to grasp in the full light of day, without any weakness, the kind of poetry that is often received and given in the breaking apart of the most obscure and innocent being. The trails of innocence and night are followed back toward the source of the gift.[16]

15. Hébert's *Les Enfants du sabbat* (The children of the sabbath; Paris: Seuil, 1975) weaves into its narrative quotations from Pascal and the Bible (147, 51, 82), while *Kamouraska* (Paris: Seuil, 1970) offers a series of variations on Rimbaud's sentence "La vraie vie est ailleurs" (True life lies elsewhere; 104, 133, 146). However, the most sustained use of poetry as a vehicle for past truths of language and life occurs in *Le Premier Jardin* (The first garden; Paris: Seuil, 1988), where lines from Verlaine (57, 187), Baudelaire (13, 45), and Saint-John Perse (130) are adapted to fit Flora Fontanges's gradual rediscovery of her childhood as an orphan, and of an accident that traumatized her.

16. Anne Hébert and Frank Scott, *Dialogue sur la traduction: À propos du "Tombeau des Rois"* (Montreal: Editions HMH, 1970), 48–50.

In Hébert's novel *Les Fous de Bassan* it is through discovering "the source of their gift [of lyric]" that the tragic women in the town of Griffin Creek at last triumph over a history of male domination.[17] Literary authority is finally theirs once they start to speak through poetry. One of them, Nora Atkins, eventually drowns at sea, but when she is buried it is not into forgetfulness but rather into "le petit cimetière marin" (the small graveyard by the sea) that lies on the outskirts of town (224). Small though it may be, this graveyard is far from insignificant, since from Paul Valéry onward, the words "cimetière marin" have been synonymous with the power of lyric to go on inventing its own history.

17. "Ma mère (...) me parle en secret ma douce langue natale" (My mother [...] speaks to me in secret my gentle native tongue), says the novel's protagonist, Olivia (*Les Fous de Bassan* [Paris: Seuil, 1982], 217). By co-opting three lines from Baudelaire's "L'Invitation au voyage" ("Tout y parlerait / A l'âme en secret / Sa douce langue natale"), this sentence situates the ideal communication between mother and daughter squarely within the realm of poetry.

eleven

BOUDICA . . . AND

OTHER MONSTERS

(CÉSAIRE,

KEINEG,

GLISSANT)

In the preceding chapter we asked ourselves if, at the end of the twentieth century, there was still space for lyric poems after such a long tradition of linguistic experimentation in French poetry. Since the publication of Jean-Claude Pinson's book *Habiter en poète,* no one can ignore that French contemporary poetry is now "officially" divided into two skillfully delineated polar opposites. On one side there are the poets that he calls *logolâtres* and on the other the *lyrics.* The *logolâtres* (from *logos* [language] and *latrein* [to worship]) are the poets who, under the twin banners of Francis Ponge and the *Tel Quel* group of yore, created a language-oriented poetic neovanguard that "was led by an iconoclastic hype against any type of ideology that would turn the word of the poet into something 'sacred.'" It also "was convinced of the ridiculous vanity of trying to establish an 'enchanted' *locus amoenus* for poetry." Thus this neovanguard undertook a systematic undermining of all easy poetic language proficiency, a total destruction of all the bases of poetical metaphysics. For a while it [...] devoted all its attention to the "work of the signifier," even if the risk was the production of apparently autistic poetic pieces. In the end the fetishization of the "text," which nipped in the bud any attempt to produce meaning, led the reader to a seemingly mortal boredom and not, as attempted, to the language feast found in Ponge's poetry.[1]

At the opposite end of this depressing textualism, lyricism is now coming back supposedly to restore the personal jubilation found in the metaphysical union of the book and lived experience, in the reconciliation of the self and the real world found beyond textual representation. Thus Pinson can write:

We are now using the label "neo-lyricism" to define the surge, in this last ten years of the century, of a group of poets who, beyond their diversity, share the same longing for a poetry which would be less a "thinking" than a "singing" one; in addition they were eager not to be confined within the coercive limits of a monomaniac's attention to language. They were after a poetry that would be perceived in the tradition of Verlaine or Apollinaire more than Mallarmé. [...] This movement is such that lyrical subjectivity, even gushing poetic confession, has found, if not a new legitimacy, at least a new and growing acceptance in contemporary French poetry. (57–58)

A counter to this proselytism for lyricism can be found in Jean-Marie Gleize's *A noir: Poésie et littéralité*. The author refuses to "theorize himself," to "publish a manifesto," or to try to "entice followers."[2] Nevertheless, he recognizes that his poetry belongs to and is representative of something that can be defined as "negative textual supermodernity." Offering a defense for a possible "supermodern" poetry movement, he writes:

Why not admit that there exists, if not a negative "modernity," at least something that belongs to the apophyseal domain of poetry

1. Jean-Claude Pinson, *Habiter en poète* (Seyssel, France: Champ Vallon, 1994), 12–13.
2. Jean-Marie Gleize, *A noir: Poésie et littéralité* (Paris: Seuil, 1992), 14.

production? [...] The most important gesture is to recognize that this movement, against all accepted definitions of poetry, does not embrace the "poetic image," or "images" as its core component, and even manifests a great intellectual suspicion about its poetic value. (15)

Pinson's *Habiter en poète* is a response to *A noir,* published two years earlier. Pinson wants to escape from the order of negative textual supermodernity, to free himself from the confining coercion of the text, and to destroy the "formalist abstract sentence of pure textual poetics," wishing instead to rehabilitate reality, and a poetic contact with the world. To do so, he recommends only one means: the poetic image, which is the very element that Gleize says should have no part in a possible supermodern poetry. Similarly, another aficionado of contemporary lyrical poetry, Jean-Michel Maulpoix, is an advocate of the poetic image in his recent book *La Poésie malgré tout* (Poetry nevertheless). The title responds, in fact, to several slogans invented by current or proto supermodernists. As we have already seen in Chapter 10, Denis Roche wrote that "poetry is inadmissible," Raymond Queneau claimed that "one should make poetry without poetry," and Jude Stéfan pontificated that "from now on, poetry should have nothing to do with poetry." In all these logolatric formulas, the word *poetry* is taken in its more romantic sense: a very subjective text, declamatory in its form and effusive in its content. About such a poetic image that should be found at the core of a contemporary lyrical poem Jean-Michel Maulpoix writes:

Can we truly say that poetry is obsolete, inadmissible, condemned to aphasia or to a cold textuality without images, without colors and without pleasure? Probably not [...]. As a parody of the famous saying by Diderot, the poet could say: "My figures are my prostitutes." For poetry, truly, is the place for figures, that is to say the locus where the real world presented as severed and distant finds itself linked and intertwined with other things in a very unexpected manner. Thus the universe that could have seemed closed and already fully discovered suddenly opens and continues growing.[3]

As we indicated in Chapter 6, the sacralization or not of the poetic image as the principal component of poetry constitutes in the nineties the

3. Jean-Michel Maulpoix, *La Poésie malgré tout* (Paris: Mercure de France, 1996), 25.

litmus test between logolatric and lyric poets in France. In a poetic text, particular attention given to picturesque images is immediately perceived as a sign of allegiance to neolyricism; conversely, a text that functions on the basis of formulas, verbal concretions, and so on, can be said to be part of negative supermodernity. Obviously, like any litmus test, the distinction may appear extremely reductive. Yet an insurmountable void seems to currently exist between the two groups in contemporary French poetry. A heroic and explicit Manichaeanism divides *logolâtres* and *lyrics*. They confront each other with the proverbial mighty pen and a defiant gaze. In the late hours of this century they are ready to do battle. On each side one can hear the staccato beat not of words, but of phrases, names, and apostrophes. Meanwhile the crowd of poetry watchers and practitioners is awaiting the push that will finish once and for all Mallarmé's legacy of giving primacy to the Word. To end this waiting game and have the two groups finally engage in battle, some white knight probably needs to enter the fray by proposing yet another style of poetry.

Unfortunately, no such event has appeared on the horizon and the lingering vigil continues. Meanwhile, short of trouncing each other in the heroic manner of the ancients and moderns, both extremes seem to have found a ground on which they can agree: epic poetry is a thing of the past. Epic poetry is neither part of logolatric nor lyric poetry. Both groups reject it as opposed to what they would like poetry to be. Neither group's canon of contemporary poems seems capable of absorbing fully a text that could be recognized as epic according to past definitions of the genre. Since no one acknowledges this type of text as its own, epic poetry is simply excluded from the field of contemporary writing. Thus Pinson declares, "After all, why should the genre of lyric poetry (if it is a genre) last forever? It would have to be a Platonic ideal to be eternal; since it isn't one, it is condemned to obsolescence as was epic poetry" (42). In an article titled "Costumes," Gleize proclaims the same historical demise:

> In order for a costume to be called a "poet's costume," first you have to recognize someone as a "poet." There is not always a poet, sometimes there is more or less a poet, more a poet or less a poet. One may even say that poetry can go on without a poet. [...] Following our original line of thought: there are in fact (although only a few people are willing to admit it) a very *limited* number of poet's suits. [...] Vanished are the suits of armor (the heroic, the epic),

vanished are the *petit marquis* costumes (and the ribbons for literary salons, poets of epigrams and sonnets).[4]

As a matter of fact, when one asks an educated French person the title of an epic poem, the most commonly mentioned is invariably *La Franciade* written by Ronsard in 1574. Very few remember that, two centuries later, Voltaire wrote *La Henriade* (1723). Granted, these texts are already ancient and thus one can understand why Henri Meschonnic, in "Pour une poétique négative," declares:

> One knows what one is saying when it is said that [...] epic poetry [and] lyric poetry are poetic genres. Even if one cannot fully explain what lyricism is. And, as far as epic poetry is concerned, it is quite ancient and not that clear either. But, in the end, one can say that there are "genres" in poetry.[5]

It is as if, today, active French poetry were only where a few well-known figures decide to place it on the public stage. This is particularly paradoxical because poetry is very much in demand and shows signs of good health alongside the other literary genres in France. In fact, there is great diversity in the types of poetry offered to the public and it is extremely reductive to approach poetry with only two reading modes (not to say genres, following Meschonnic's misgivings about the actual status of logolatric poetry). Intellectual Parisianism has its rites, its obligations, its cartels. In order to read contemporary French poetry, we can take advantage of our faraway status to escape what may appear to be a case of local reductionism. In order to understand certain texts that are not immediately designated as archetypes of the dichotomy established by the current debate (for example, Ponge [textual] vs. Bonnefoy [lyric]) but are nevertheless texts that offer a poetic universe that engages the contemporary world, nothing prevents us from summoning interpretative tools that are not part of the current faddish panoply.

Following this principle, let us take three recent texts that would seem unreadable if one were merely to apply the current recommended reading grid. If, *in fine,* we conclude that they are neither logos centered nor lyric but endowed both with images *and* formulas, this will not qual-

---

4. Jean-Marie Gleize, "Costumes," *Le Français aujourd'hui* 114 (June 1996): 64–68.

5. In *Le Français aujourd'hui* 114 (June 1996): 31–40.

ify as a very rewarding reading. In addition, alas, it will lead us to miss the very reason why their being marginalized in current debates is precisely what makes them worthy of inclusion in an examination of contemporary French poetry.

In order to read these texts and to understand why they do have actual literary and social value, there is no other way than to consider them as part of what has to be called epic poetry—even if everyone seems to agree that such a thing does not exist anymore. Certainly, as today's critics are busy debating the value of notions such as language-centered poetry, negative poetry, negative supermodernity, and so on, very little time has been spent on elaborating a definition of what would be epic poetry at the end of the twentieth century. To orient ourselves, we then must retrieve recurrent pertinent features that characterize texts generally recognized as belonging to this genre.

In the three works we have chosen, the chronicling of the emergence of a collective identity is at the center of the poetic project, exactly as in *La Franciade* or *La Henriade*. Here, however, the community that comes into being is not also part of an emerging unifying nationalism; it responds to other criteria for group associations. It is also worth noting at the onset that the texts do not construct a fictional determinism leading to historical triumph. In *Boudica* by Paol Keineg, the community can be superficially perceived as the Breton people (or its Celtic ancestors), but since the identification takes the form of "Once upon a time there was...," past, present, and future are inextricably intertwined and the ideal community is all the communities that may have existed and now exist only as an imagined community, as individual people try to attach the idealized soil of an original culture to their wandering souls.[6] In Edouard Glissant's *Les Indes,* there is an attempt (supported elsewhere in his essays) to invent a new geographic domain by carving away pieces of territories that are already officially recognized.[7] It may help that somehow a false geographic hypothesis has given validity to the term Indies (*Les Indes*) by engendering the term West Indies. It is also worth noting that if the term is fairly banal when used in English, it is indeed not the case in French. The usual term is *Les Antilles* (or more recently, for political reasons, *La Caraïbe*) thus Glissant's term *Antillanité*. The mere fact that the term *Les Indes* is an archaism designating a land that never

---

6. Paol Keineg [Paol Quéinnec], *Boudica, Taliesin et autres poèmes* (Rennes: Editions UBACS, 1990).

7. Edouard Glissant, *Les Indes* (Paris: Seuil, 1965).

existed, except in the dreams of the conquistadores, thus adds, in French, a dimension of mystery and exoticism to the title of Glissant's work. Finally, the third text, *Cahier d'un retour au pays natal* by Aimé Césaire, is not a geographic entity that takes shape in the text; the community is of an ethnic nature.[8] Looking at his own origin on the island of Martinique, Césaire recognizes a specific type of human nature that he defines as "negritude" (ethnic blackness) and makes it universal while asserting that its roots are in Africa. Yet the text is not simply descriptive; it has a performative value. At the same time that Césaire calls for the recognition of the existence of negritude, he calls on his brothers to enact this new definition of identity and he invites others to notice the new world order that this emerging community will clearly produce.

Martinique, Guadeloupe, Finistère, Morbilhan, and Ile-et-Vilaine are French departments. We do not have to leave the domain of the French republic and look at the poetic production of the many countries included in the Francophone domain to find texts that do not conform to the current proposed division within French poetry. However, we believe that, notwithstanding their lack of presence in the debate, these texts are an integral part of current poetry writing in French. Because they all rely on both images and formulas to express many facets of current attitudes on important questions of identity, community, literacy, and so on, which may not be central to Parisian writers, the chronicle of their announced demise is probably premature. Undeniably, however, they can only appear as monstrous poetic hybrids likely to introduce chaos and confusion into the oversimplified dualisms that characterize current debates on French poetry.

What is striking about these three texts is that they conform in every aspect (except one to which we return below) to the established principles of epic poetry, at least to the ones that may be found in the definition given by Voltaire in his *Essai sur la poésie épique* (1733) and other references of the same type. First, it should be understood that an epic poem is a long poem often divided into *chants* (songs). All three texts respect this fundamental principle. *Boudica,* published for the first time in 1980 then reprinted in 1990, is composed of forty songs without titles, each one occupying one page. *Les Indes,* published in 1955, is divided into six songs, each with a title: "L'Appel" (The call), "Le Voy-

---

8. Aimé Césaire, *Cahier d'un retour au pays natal* (Paris: Présence Africaine, 1983).

age" (The journey), "La Conquête" (The conquest), "La Traite" (Slave-trading), "Les Héros" (Heroes), and "La Relation" (The relation). Each song, following the Homeric tradition, is composed of a varied number of stanzas: "La Relation" contains only one stanza while there are twelve in the song "Les Héros." *Les Indes* is the longest of the three texts. The original version of *Cahier d'un retour au pays natal* (1939) contained three parts without any obvious divisions; the "official" version of 1947 contains six parts, still without any physical separation.

Second, the epic poem is written in verse, but prose texts can be interpolated in it. *Boudica* reproduces graphically what appears to be the disposition of a sonnet or other fixed forms that have historically characterized French classical poetry. This effect is realized by the succession of short paragraphs in prose similar in shape to a distich. They are short formulas cut like dense, elliptical maxims. *Les Indes* is built on five songs as a succession of long verses (twelve to sixteen syllables). Yet the song entitled "La Traite" (Slave-trading), which names the trading mechanism whereby the West Indies became populated by native African slaves, is composed of long narrative passages in prose. Glissant, in stanza 44 at the beginning of this song, seems to explain why he is switching to prose in this particularly charged part of the book:

> Choses horribles, prose dure . . . Ce furent, au matin, Indes ouvertes d'épopée, d'un corps venteux d'ambition. Ce furent, saviez-vous, Indes en solitude, où le rêve tourna vers le passé tranquille son fuseau: or, sur la mer, l'homme recule. (104)

> (Horrendous events, cutting prose . . . It was, in the morning, Indies opening their body full of breezy ambition to epic posterity. It was, you know, lonely Indies, where the dream spun backwards to its peaceful past: indeed, on the sea, it is man who regresses.)

It is as if the "horrendous events" and the time of regression were not worthy of (epic) poetry, as if only prosaic prose were flat enough to narrate the mortifying events that accompanied the trade. This is also consistent with a certain purity of the epic genre, according to which only uplifting and exemplary moments constitute the core material of the text.

Césaire's *Cahier* also relies on prose passages to create a dramatic effect in the poetic text, in particular, to inscribe formulas that have a strong value as a slogan or motto. Such is the case of the main passage in which one can see unfolding at the same time an awareness of the black people's disgrace and the birth of the concept of negritude as a way to reassert the value and, ultimately, the triumph of the black community. In this passage a "narrator" who speaks in the first person encounters, in the Paris subway, another black person. In this somewhat theatrical scene (with indirect dialogue) the black narrator is dressed like a white, bourgeois French intellectual, while the other character is presented as a somewhat clichéd poor black: "pauvre nègre comique et laid" (poor, comical and ugly Negro). The representation of the fallen black people through the description of this poor and old man is simple prose without any concern for poetic formalism:

> Et l'ensemble faisait parfaitement un nègre hideux, un nègre grognon, un nègre mélancolique, un nègre affalé, ses mains réunies en prière sur un bâton noueux. Un nègre enseveli dans une vieille veste élimée. Un nègre comique et laid et des femmes derrière moi ricanaient en le regardant. (40)

> (The whole picture was that of a perfectly hideous Negro, a grumbling Negro, a melancholic Negro, a slumping Negro holding his hands together on an old wooden stick as for a prayer. A Negro disappearing in an old jacket far too big for him. A poor, comical, and ugly Negro and some women seated behind me were sneering at him.)

After this deplorable description, however, the text reintroduces in four lines the external formalism associated with poetry:

> Il était COMIQUE ET LAID,
> COMIQUE ET LAID pour sûr,
>
> J'arborai un grand sourire complice . . .
> Ma lâcheté retrouvée!
> Je salue les trois siècles qui soutiennent mes droits
> civiques et mon sang minimisé.
> Mon héroïsme, quelle farce! (41)

> (He was COMIC AND UGLY,
> COMIC AND UGLY for sure,

I flashed my most complicitous smile . . .
Bringing back to the fore my usual cowardice!
I salute the three centuries which gave me my
civil rights and my whitened blood.
Me, a hero? What a joke!)

This return, for a while, to an appearance of poetic formalism (or fixed form) signals here the potent appeal of poetic intertextuality. No reader well versed in late nineteenth-century French poetry can ignore that the expression "comic and ugly" appears in Baudelaire's famous poem "L'Albatros" (The albatross).[9] This poem, briefly summarized, represents the suffering of the poet who can graciously and flawlessly float in the sky, but when on the ground is simply an awkward and ridiculous bird that people abuse. Baudelaire indicates clearly that his sympathy does not go to the tormentors but to the poor "comic and ugly" bird.

Ce voyageur ailé, comme il est gauche et veule!
Lui, naguère si beau, qu'il est comique et laid!
L'un agace son bec avec un brûle-gueule,
L'autre mime, en boitant, l'infirme qui volait![10]

(This winged traveler, how awkward and feeble he is!
Not long ago he was handsome, and now he is comic and ugly!
One man harasses his beak with a clay-pipe,
Another, limping, mimics the cripple that used to fly!)

Under the "comic and ugly [Negro]" lies an undisclosed valorization (which will come at the end of the text) exactly as in Baudelaire's model. Thus the dichotomy found in Glissant's text seems to hold for Césaire as well. When the events presented are lofty and noble, poetry (as textual formalism) takes over; yet when the text has to describe unsavory events

9. We should remember that as a teacher of French literature and former student of the Ecole Normale Supérieure, Césaire taught the poetry of Rimbaud, Baudelaire, and Mallarmé, as well as the usual texts of the late nineteenth-century period, including Ducasse's *Les Chants de Maldoror.*

10. Charles Baudelaire, "L'Albatros," in *Les Fleurs du mal,* vol. 1, *Oeuvres complètes,* ed. Y.-G. Le Dantec (Paris: Gallimard, Pléiade, 1975), 10. For a detailed examination of this and other intertextual links between *Les Fleurs du mal* and Césaire's *Cahier,* see Stephen Walton's "Baudelaire and the Roots of Negritude," *Dalhousie French Studies* 39–40 (winter–fall 1997): 77–88. Walton takes issue with an earlier interpretation of these intertextual links proposed by Mireille Rosello.

that will bring forth an awareness leading to emancipation, liberation, and discovery of identity, then the despicable events are presented through interpolated passages in prose. In Baudelaire's poem, under the meek "winged traveler" the genial poet is hidden; similarly, the interpolation of a passage in verse in the prose part devoted to the "comic and ugly" black character encountered in the subway presents, as a palimpsest, the free "up and standing [Negro]" that will triumph in the last part of the poem.

> La négraille aux senteurs d'oignon frit retrouve
> dans son sang répandu le goût amer de la liberté
>
> Et elle est debout la négraille
>
> la négraille assise
> inattendument debout
> debout dans la cale
> debout dans les cabines
> debout sur le pont
> debout dans le vent
> debout dans le soleil
> debout dans le sang
> debout
>   et
>   libre.   (61–62)

> (The onion-smelling Negroes recover
> the bitter taste of freedom in the blood that is oozing
>
> They are up and standing the Negroes
>
> It was a seated bunch of Negroes
> that was expected, they are standing
> standing in the hull
> standing in the officers' quarters
> standing on the bridge
> standing in the wind
> standing in the sunshine
> standing amidst the blood
> up
>   and
>   free.)

The third and most important aspect of epic poetry is the fact that the poem is seemingly constructed like the apology of a hero to whom one community owes its identity: the source, as it is often said, of the "soul of the people." From this point of view, the titles of traditional French epic poems are significant: for example, *La Chanson de Roland* (The song of Roland) or *La Henriade* (Henri's story). The case of *La Franciade* offers a perverted example of this genre's requirement; Ronsard had to invent a putative son of Hector, Francus, to justify the title of his epic poem. Thus it is less France's story than Francus's story. Although at the time Du Bellay could present France as the "mother of all art," obviously it was not yet possible to write about France as the "mother of the people."

One can thus see that French literature has come a long way with Keineg's *Boudica*. Here, it is the Celtic queen who embodies the resistance to the Roman invaders. The first hurdle for the conquerors is how to translate the language of the vanquished. Will it be "Boudica," "Boudicca," "Boadicea," or "Boadicée"?[11] The floating signifier is established in the chronicle of the winning side so as to prevent ecumenical worship of the martyrs. In any case, it is a woman's story, even the Romans agree. Keineg provides us with a quotation excerpted from Tacitus's *Annals* (chapter 14), which presents the historical fact as follows:

> Boudica, with her daughters before her in a chariot, went up to tribe after tribe, protesting that it was indeed usual for Britons to fight under the leadership of women. "But now," she said, "it is not as a woman descended from noble ancestry, but as one of the people that I am avenging lost freedom, my scourged body, the outraged chastity of my daughters." (ii)[12]

Keineg's text thus retraces, in a nonchronological manner, Boudica's fight against Roman imperialism; indirectly, of course, the text is an at-

11. France—one and indivisible, Jacobean and centrally governed—has not kept alive the memory of this regional heroine. By contrast, Great Britain has transformed Boudicca into the first heroine of "splendid isolation" and resistance to all forms of invasion from the continent. Thus one can find, in London, a very Victorian statue of Boudicca and her daughters in their war carriage. It is also amusing to note that, even if her historical role is not well known, her name (Boadicea) is given on a par with that of Alexander, Napoleon, and Julius Caesar as the patronymic (matronymic?) name of one of the players in the vastly popular electronic game *Civilization II* (Sid Meier [Hunt Valley: MicroProse, 1996]).

12. All English translations of *Boudica* are from the American edition of the text translated by Keith Waldrop (Providence: Burning Deck, 1994).

tack against modern French cultural imperialism and centralism, which has never allowed Bretons to fully develop and celebrate their cultural specificity. Thus the text freely interlaces historical events taken from the chronicles of the conquest of Brittany and (often amusing) notations and comments on the contemporary life of the Breton people under French cultural, administrative, and political rule.

It is worth noting that because of this very fluid compositional system, the text escapes what could be the pitfall of politically committed poetry, which is to take on the appearance of military theatricality and the wooden language of militant leaflets. Instead Keineg's text offers a mixture of very powerful poetic formulas and verbal arrangements.

> La reine aux cent coups frappe juste. Les femmes fortes et les guerriers pare-balle font bloc. Nul n'accepte l'inacceptable.
>
> Ici la ferraille, les ficelles du destin. Le terrain vague. Là, le combat pied à pied, le cocktail Molotov, la douleur qui mange le sein gauche. (15)

> (The queen lands her hundred blows on target. Stout women and warriors form a bullet-proof block. Nobody accepts the unacceptable.
>
> Scrap-iron here, threads of destiny. Empty lots. Over here, foot-to-foot fighting, the Molotov cocktail, pain eating at the left breast.)

> Entourée des chefs et des grands reporters. La folle du logis, visage tourné vers les flammes de l'âtre. Elle se déprend d'un monde qui ne peut pas finir. (17)

> (Surrounded by captains and war correspondents. Mad imagination, her face toward the flame in the fireplace. She sloughs off a world incapable of closure.)

> La robe agrafée et le cou couleur de terre cuite. Sur le cours passent les officiers de marine. Cent collines coupées de cent rades. (23)

> (Dress done up, neck a burnt umber. Naval officers cross the promenade. A hundred hills cut by a hundred road steads.)

> Peuple naufragé sur sa vieille terre. De quel nom vivre le centre du monde? En quel débat crier les questions toutes neuves?

Le pêcheur et son filet, le serpent sous le talon. Le soleil du verrier comme un pneu Michelin, et les moutons qui sautent les clôtures du plomb. Mort de la reine, renversée. (40)

(Castaway tribe on the worn earth. In what name to live the world's center? To cry in what congress the new questions?

The fisherman and his net, serpent under heel. Sun of the glass-blower, like a Michelin tire, and sheep leaping lead fences. Death of the queen, toppled.)

It is generally considered appropriate in epic poetry to valorize the actions of the valiant soldiers whose victory will legitimate the subsequent writing of history by the vanquishing side. It is worth noting, however, that in the *Chanson de Roland,* which is considered the first example of epic poetry in French literature (at least in traditional literary history textbooks), the main character, Roland, is eventually defeated and throughout the text his military single-mindedness is often contrasted with that of Olivier (who is not a "jusqu'auboutiste"—willing to resist and fight alone to the bitter end). Likewise, in *Boudica,* the title character is a defeated ("toppled") heroine. In 61 A.D. her armies are defeated in such a drastic manner by the legions of the Roman general Paulinus Suetonius that she chooses suicide rather than be captured by her enemies. Thus *Boudica* cannot be an epic poem dedicated to the glorious victory of the valiant warlords now unquestionably legitimized. It can only be a subdued remembrance of something that once was and no longer is.

It is an ambiguous discourse vis-à-vis military operations. Certainly, there is some honor in standing firm to fight for one's beliefs and to prevent genocide; on the other hand, not all military fights are "noble" fights and it may happen that, in the name of the "defense of principles," unscrupulous leaders condemn gullible, idealistic warriors to their certain demise. *Boudica* is thus a balancing act between the two positions. On the positive side there is:

An 61, saison des humiliés. Le peuple est debout qui était couché. Coeur battant, le courage par à-coups. (5)

(A.D. 61, time of humiliation. The people who lay dormant are now on their feet. Heart racing, courage in spurts.)

On the negative side there is:

> An 61 après Jésus-Crist. Les Mau-Mau contre Tacite. L'outrecui-
> dance et le sac. Le combat des arbrisseaux. (18)

> (The year 61. Mau-Maus versus Tacitus. Cocksureness and pillage.
> Battle of the bushes.)

The motives of the "freedom-fighters" are often open to questions, van-
ity, or stupidity:

> Les petits gars que son odeur excite montent à l'abattoir en chan-
> tant. Francs-tireurs et coureurs à pied, doigts gourds, yeux blancs
> pour cette morue. Guérilleros de mes deux, godelureaux et blancs-
> becs, O condottieri de pissenlits par la racine. (16)

> (Kids excited by her odor clamber to the slaughterhouse singing.
> Free-lancers and foot-runners, fingers numb, in a fit form this trol-
> lop. Guerrillas my ass, lumpkins and greenhorns, O condottieri of
> pushed up daisies.)

Boudica herself is far from being presented as an untouchable heroine:
"Voleuse d'hommes, pétroleuse, papesse de bric et de broc, qu'on
l'étrangle et qu'elle claque" (Man-stealer, arsonist, Pope Joan of this and
of that, if only someone strangles her and she kicks off!; 16).

Because of who he is, Keineg is a remnant of something that should
not have survived the defeat, one of those few who, nevertheless, can still
write the chronicle from an unauthorized point of view. Here also is an
impossible status quo. Keineg should not be the witness of the present,
since what matters in this present has no relevance for him. He is torn
between a past whose future has been snatched away and a future that, in
the long term, will be the grave digger of any past memory. The un-
authorized chronicler, as an outsider, can thus only inscribe the past as
folded into the description of the present: tarnished mirrors carved out of
cultural determinism. Each song ignores chronology, and the tense of the
epic poem is conditional; the past and the future of that past are known,
but the present, the very locus of utterance, is erased: "He told me that
we would be vanquished." When? What takes place in 61 A.D. may as
well be what happens in 1870 or 1968. Thus:

L'extinction de quelques tribus calamiteuses ne saurait émouvoir
Rome. Suetonius peut ravager l'île verte, la plaine des genêts en
fleurs. La Commune peut crever. Ici, dans les milk-bars et les théâtres
d'arrière-garde, on cause. On sort les fourrures. L'aube fibreuse sur le
pays vacant. C'est l'été : aphrodites et décapotables dans le bocage
sans issue. On attend missionnaires et pick-pockets. (21)

(The extinction of a few broken-down tribes would cause no ripple
in Rome. Suetonius may ravage the green isle, the plain of flower-
ing broom. The Commune can go down the drain. Here in milk-
bars and rearguard theaters they discuss. They bring out fur coats.
Stringy dawn over empty landscape. Summer: Venuses and convert-
ibles in the wood with no way out. Missionaries and pickpockets
imminent.)

Géographie du colonisateur, du Finistère clôturé à l'araignée des
routes pour le blé et l'étain. Soudards et supplétifs. Le sous-préfet
énarque, la sous-préfète en victoire de Samothrac Histoire du colo-
nisateur, toujours fougueuse et blonde. O siècles de lumière, les
sauvages dos à dos, le bon plaisir, le droit divin. Tout se passe
comme si. Comme ça. (4)

(Geography of the colonizer, from the fenced-off land's-end to the
web of roads for wheat and tin. Desperadoes and reservists. The
power-elite sub-prefect, the sub-prefect's wife as Winged Victory.
Colonizer's history, always passionate and blonde. O Centuries of
light, savages back to back, our own sweet will, divine right. Every-
thing happens if so. So so.)

There is no such ambiguity ("So so") about the goal pursued by Césaire
in *Cahier*. As René Depestre later writes, "Césaire's text is a call to arms,
an incitation to revolt against the state of submission imposed on black
people by white people. The text is explicit: 'Life is not a spectacle, thus
do not cross your arms as does the passive spectator'" (22).[13]
    We are thus in the realm of word-as-act, of performative discourse.
Language becomes the instrument of the revolution, first a social one,
and then, unavoidably, a political one. If in Keineg's text the imperial

---

13. René Depestre, "Un Orphée des Caraïbes," in *Pour la Révolution/Pour la poésie*
(Ottawa: Leméac, 1974), 146–69.

victory (be it that of the Roman generals or of the French republican subprefects) leads to a critical distance marked by irony, for Césaire the liberation imposes a pure belief in language's power. Manipulating language necessarily leads to changing reality. Language still has a magical effect: to speak is to act, and words have not yet lost their original link to things. Thus, to reverse the current social order in which white authority is imposed on a black majority, white words on black reality, it is necessary to write black on white and thereby rehabilitate the fallen.

First it is necessary to eliminate the whiteness that has befallen the prestigious progenitor of black liberation in the Antilles: Toussaint Louverture.

Ce qui est à moi aussi: une petite cellule dans le Jura
une petite cellule, la neige la double de barreaux blancs
la neige est un geôlier blanc qui monte la garde
devant une prison

Ce qui est à moi
c'est un homme emprisonné de blanc
c'est un homme seul qui défie les cris blancs de la mort blanche
(TOUSSAINT, TOUSSAINT LOUVERTURE)
c'est un homme seul qui fascine l'épervier blanc de la mort blanche
c'est un homme seul dans la mer inféconde de sable blanc
c'est un moricaud vieux dressé contre les eaux du ciel. (25–26)[14]

(What is mine too: a small cell in the French Jura,
a small cell reinforced by the double security of white bars
snow is a white watchman that stands guard in
front of a prison

What is mine
is a lonely man entrapped by whiteness
a man alone defying the white cries of a white death
[TOUSSAINT, TOUSSAINT LOUVERTURE]
alone he mesmerizes the deadly gaze of white death
he is alone in the sterile sea of white sand
an old dark-skinned man standing upright against the waters of the sky.)

14. All references to the text are to Aimé Césaire, *Cahier d'un retour au pays natal* (Paris: Présence Africaine, 1983). All translations are our own.

The last verse, "an old dark-skinned man standing upright against the waters of the sky," accentuates the rebellious nature of the old black leader who, rather than be overwhelmed by a "white death," still finds the strength to stand up against what is crushing him. It is this lost gesture of defiance that has to be revisited as the initial stage in recovering black pride if any hope of equality is to be pursued, if any hope exists that, now, history is finally going to be written with the authority of a printed page, namely black on white.

Et voici soudain que force et vie m'assaillent comme un taureau et l'onde de vie circonvient la papille du morne, et voilà toutes les veines et veinules qui s'affairent au sang neuf et l'énorme poumon des cyclones qui respire et le feu thésaurisé des volcans et le gigantesque pouls sismique qui bat maintenant le mesure d'un corps vivant en mon ferme embrasement.

Et nous sommes debout maintenant, mon pays et moi, les cheveux dans le vent, ma main petite maintenant dans son poing énorme et la force n'est pas en nous, mais au-dessus de nous, dans une voix qui vrille la nuit et l'audience comme la pénétrance d'une guêpe apocalyptique. Et la voix prononce que l'Europe nous a pendant des siècles gavés de mensonges et gonflés de pestilences. (56–57)

(And now suddenly strength and life are soaring in me like a raging bull and favorable rain clouds ascend to the top of our hills. Here they are, all the veins and veinlets busy carrying the new blood and the huge lung of cyclones breathing, the fire long stored in the deepest shaft of volcanoes and the gigantic seismic pulse that beats the measure of a body living my own emblazoning.

Upright, now, my nation and I, hair in the wind, my hand small in its enormous fist; the strength is not inside us but above us in a voice that pierces the night and the listeners like the sting of an apocalyptic wasp. And the voice announces that, for centuries now, Europe has abused us with lies and contaminated us with pestilence.)

In order to regain confidence in the destiny of the black population, it is necessary to foreground the figure of Toussaint Louverture since he is the first one to have the courage to oppose the social system of the plantation that shaped their social and economic profile in the New World. This dimension, however, is not the totality of the black nation since it is only one avatar of negritude, and one that is highly determined by the land and special historical circumstances. It is thus necessary, in order to establish negritude, to delve deeper into the ancestral combat. Thus Césaire goes back to Africa, to the land of the Bambara ancestor, so as to give his fight its real ethnic dimension. Out of the plantation system of exploitation come revolutionary, political, and social ideas (and later: unions, socialism, Marxism, communism) but, as Césaire will clearly say after 1954, these ideas are not specific to the black nation. It is only out of Africa that comes negritude.

> Je tiens maintenant le sens de l'ordalie: mon pays est la "lance de nuit" de mes ancêtres Bambaras. Elle se ratatine et sa pointe fuit désespérément vers le manche si c'est de sang de poulet qu'on l'arrose et elle dit que c'est du sang d'homme qu'il faut à son tempérament, de la graisse, du foie, du coeur d'homme, non sang de poulet. (58)

> (Now I understand the meaning of my ordeal: my nation is the "night lance" of my Bambara forebears. If it enters in contact with chicken blood, the shaft becomes short and the head retrogresses with it and it says that it is human blood that fits its temperament, that it needs man's flesh, liver, heart, and not chicken blood.)

With these claims toward Africa, Césaire goes beyond the simple notion of a country, or a land, that would be circumscribed to the French Antilles. This explains why his negritude is considered much more important for Africa than that of Léopold Sédar Senghor. Thus Guy Ossito Midiohouan writes in the preface to the new edition of the *Cahier* published in Africa that there is a "Césairian négritude" and a "Senghorian négritude." Whereas Senghorian négritude is marked by "reformist ideas," Césairian negritude is "genuinely revolutionary," which accounts for Césaire's place in African literary history.[15]

As a counterpoint to this Caribbean epic that needs resourcing in Africa and presents itself more like the epic of the black nation, Glissant,

---

15. Guy O. Midiohouan, ed., *Aimé Césaire pour aujourd'hui et pour demain* (Saint-Maur: Sépia, 1995).

in *Les Indes,* attempts to propose a text that is the true epic of a specific geographic land, the Caribbean islands. A former student of Césaire at the Victor Shoelcher High School in Fort de France, Glissant attempts to impose the notion of *Antillanité* against the concept of negritude, which is not, as defined by Césaire, geographically specific. This "topological" recentering is signaled by the title of his work since, as explained earlier, the Antilles were first known as the *Indes Occidentales,* a term that disappeared quickly in French but is still present in their English name (West Indies). Glissant's text is organized in a very classic manner. It adopts the rhetorical device of prosopopoeia, as it is Christopher Columbus who is supposedly narrating his "discovery." It begins with the dream of having access to the riches of India by navigating westward; we then follow a loose chronology of the journey, intersected by insights about the past and the future of these islands. It ends with the sad return to the "tristes parapets européens" (gloomy European parapets). Here again, a sense of the marvelous and a magical capacity for divination allow dreamlike sequences to interrupt the narrative, letting Columbus foresee what has happened and what will happen to these lands he is about to discover. As in Keineg's text, time is compressed in such a way that events are not chronologically organized so as to exactly follow historical determinism. This corresponds exactly to what Glissant believes is the Caribbean way to look at what Western civilization calls "history." He believes in the notion of "grands temps" (circular time) in which there is no beginning and no end, just an eternal return of events. His image for what he considers the Caribbean dimension of time is a conical ellipse, a sort of multidimensional spiral, in which events that in a linear description of time would seem far away can, in fact, touch each other or even appear to be simultaneous in a three-dimensional format.

This principle of composition that is chosen for a "Caribbean (hi)story" and gives the text a transhistorical dimension that borders on eternal transcendence, corresponds, in fact, to the very spirit of epic poetry. By definition, epic poetry should offer a presentation of events that, even if situated in time, are in fact of no special time, mixing freely the past and the future. In *Les Indes* Glissant inserts special passages that reinforce the sense that his text is composed from a standpoint outside the Western sense of linear time and away from our usual temporal expectations: "Trois siècles ont noué de paille et de cablure ce venant [...] / Echoué, paysan des Indes surannées, fils de la terre du passé qui jadis fut terre à venir" (Three centuries of navigation have molded this newcomer

[...] / Now beached, farmer of the Indies of yore, son of a land of the past that, once, was land of the future; 126). According to the principles of epic poetry established by Goethe and Schiller in their essay, *Über Epische und Dramatische Dichtung* published in 1797, any comment or description of a present situation would be enough to change the nature of the genre of the poem. The introduction of elements specifically alluding to the present would transfer the epic poem into the genre of the dramatic poem because, for them, any direct consideration of present events can only be tainted by a subjective appreciation and thus introduces in the poem a lyric dimension that should be banned from epic poetry.

This last visit to the canon of epic poetry, if taken literally, runs the risk of destroying our whole demonstration. Certainly, as we discussed at the beginning of this essay, as well as in Chapter 10, it is very difficult nowadays to establish indisputable definitions of genres. However, if we accept as an absolute the absence of discourse in the first person as a litmus test for epic poetry, none of our three texts qualify. Until now our three texts have conformed to the proposed criteria, but all, at one point or another and to varying degrees, allow the expression of an explicit "I" that takes over not so much the act of utterance as the first role in the narrative. This I is not there to present events in an explicitly subjective first-person mode, but to manifest the participation of the author in the story, to make him an element of the epic saga, and to show how the presented events are an inextricable part of his own personal, psychological, and vital constitution. No one can deny that this mixing of life, dream, and psyche through poeticized language is an instance of lyricism. Here, however, as in Chapter 10, we can see that the I is far from being Lamartinian. In these three texts, the events are adopted by the poet; they are what gives the I a transpersonal dimension. The process consists precisely in the personalization of a context that originally is far removed from the personal history of the author. Thus the I's difficult crossover into the text and the various modes of discourse generated in order to negotiate its verbal passage into epic legend.

In Keineg's *Boudica,* most of the utterances are of an indefinite nature through the use of the pronoun *on* ("on sourit aux vieilleries des littératures lacrymogènes" [one laughs at the old tear-gas revolutionary literature]), the infinitive construction ("Autant de langues pour avancer masqué" [So many tongues to walk masked]), and an abundance of absolute nominal phrases ("Anatomie d'une vengeance. Les attaques nocturnes, les têtes de mauvais rêve" [Anatomy of revenge. Attacks by night, nightmare heads]), all this to avoid saying "I" or using any other first-person pronouns or determiners.[16] Keineg makes two exceptions to this rule, precisely in order to allow the reader to understand why Boudica matters to him: "C'est mon histoire entassée jusqu'au plafond, mon souci torride, tonique" (It's my history piled to the ceiling, my burning beneficent anxiety; 10), and "C'est pour elle que je m'étonne, pour elle que je m'évanouis. La maîtresse calcinée, si vraie qu'on la dirait calculée" (She startles me, she stuns me. Mistress burned to death, so matter-of-factly it must have been intentional; 46).

In an interview given in Haiti in the middle of the cold war, Césaire explains to Depestre why, in order to define his negritude, he had to think of himself first as Haitian and second as Martiniquais so as to enter into a closer link with Africa:

> J'ai fait la liaison entre les Antilles et l'Afrique, et Haïti est la terre la plus africaine de toutes nos Antilles. C'est en même temps un pays qui a une histoire prodigieuse, la première épopée noire du nou-veau monde a été écrite par les Haïtiens [...]. *La négritude-en-action*. Haïti est le pays où l'homme noir s'est mis debout pour affirmer, pour la première fois, sa volonté de fonder un nouveau monde, un monde libre. (Depestre 166)

> (I made the connection between the Caribbean and Africa. For me Haiti is the most African of all the islands. It is a land that has an extraordinary history and the first black epic was written by the Haitian people [...] *Negritude-as-action*. Haiti is the country where the black man stood upright to assert, for the first time, his will to create a new world, a world of freedom.)

In the second edition of the *Cahier*, the one commonly read today, the text begins immediately with an I in full control of its ideological bearings and who asserts the direction to be taken. Already, it editorial-izes what will follow: "Va-t-en, lui disais-je, gueule de flic, gueule de vache, va-t-en, je déteste les larbins de l'ordre et les hannetons de l'es-pérance" (Beat it, cop, pig, beat it, I hate the lackey of law and order and

---

16. Because of the particular nature of the English language, which prefers "we" to "one" and calls for the present participle where the French language would use the infini-tive or the past participle, these remarks apply only to the original French version of *Bou-dica* and not to the English translation.

the false angels of hope; 7). In the original version, the one that André Breton admired when he visited the island in 1943, the beginning of the poem was the long self-reflexive part titled "Au bout du petit matin" (At the end of early morning). It is first a moment of intense reflection on the French Antilles, Fort de France, this "flat town lying . . . dormant." This part is characterized by the same indefinite pronouns, infinitive, and nominal phrases already mentioned in the presentation of Keineg's text. Then, progressively, an I surges forth into the utterance, as if, through a sequence of grammatical progressions, the reader were witness to someone gaining in expressive skills and more and more in control of his own speech. The whole passage describing the simultaneous awareness of a fallen statute and of the power of speech culminates in the epiphany of the I producing a performative statement: "Partir. Comme il y a des hommes-hyènes et des hommes-panthères, je serais un homme-juif" (To leave. As they are men-hyenas and men-panthers, I would be a man-Jew; 20). After this strong affirmation, the text returns for a while to the previous dilatory and weak statements in which all traces of identity have been wiped out. It is only later, as we have seen, after the episode of the "nègre comique et laid" that the I can finally express itself in the full register of a discourse-as-action:

> Et *au milieu de tout cela* je dis hurrah! Mon grand-père meurt, je dis hurrah! La vieille négritude progressivement se cadavérise.
> Il n'y a pas à dire: c'était un bon nègre.
>
> Les Blancs disent que c'était un bon nègre, un vrai bon nègre, le bon nègre à son bon maître.
>
> Je dis hurrah! (59, our emphasis)
>
> (And *in the middle of all this* I say "hurrah!" My grandfather dies, I say "hurrah!" The old negritude progressively becomes no more than a corpse. One no longer has to say "He was a good Negro."
>
> The Whites say that he was a good Negro, a really good Negro, the good Negro to his good master.
>
> I say "hurrah!")

In Césaire's text one has the impression that the epic nature of the poem works against what the poem culturally represents. The epic has traditionally been a means for a society to establish its legitimacy and to develop a legend that will give credence to its excellence and eventually justify the conquest of people and ethnic groups that are less worthy. In this case, however, everything points to the fact that the epic construction will empower an I that will, in turn, express its revolt against precisely the type of imperialist culture that has built its strength on piles of epic texts to magnify its own legend. By building an epic of his own, Césaire gains access to a discourse and is finally able to declare: "I say."

The impersonal discourse, indefinitely descriptive, that constitutes the history of the black nation in the French Antilles is characterized by its public nonexistence, by the silence that is imposed on it. It merely survives in an oral tradition, in a devalued language that cannot break the "ceiling" that constitutes the official history of the people who own the plantations. "Tout cela" (all that), as Césaire calls it, has to be said so that the I will find its strength and the power of asserting itself and of exploding, without further delays, into "paroles abruptes" (sharp words). If the epic poem should be without an uttering I, then in *Cahier,* the epic poem falls prey to what it generates.

In Glissant's *Les Indes,* the subversion of chronology and linear history that allows the prediscovery of the new world and its postdiscovery songs to be mixed together also results in hindering any clear recognition of the different uttering subjects that may use the I to express themselves. In many passages it is difficult to distinguish between Columbus, a black slave, a nondescript Antillean, and so on. The I is a floating pronoun pursuing its own migration in a polyphonic field of voices expressing their own *Antillanité* (Caribbean identity). To complicate matters even further, there is also a complex nexus of relations attached to the "nous" (we). For instance, how can one identify which enunciative instance is behind the "we" in this passage:

> Comme ce nègre, disions-*nous,* supplicié
> Lui, dans son plein baril de foudres, tenait langage de prophétie.
> (73, our emphasis)

> (Like this Negro, as *we* said, tortured
> He, full of thunder, uttered words of prophecy.)

Should we interpret this simple example as a case of the central dichotomy that Glissant introduces between the I and the we? For him, the distinction between the I and the we is representative of the radical dichotomy that exists between cultural representations in Europe and in the Caribbean world. In a way, Glissant demonstrates the same dislike of the I that seems to have been central to the old theoreticians of the epic genre. The I is individualistic and it is a representation of an abstract subject based on the sense of a self isolated from all others. It is based on a double abstraction: first on a separation from the social body and second on the intellectual operation that separates the isolated categories that are necessary for classification (and thus possible differentiation). In effect, Glissant can write: "La question à poser à un Martiniquais ne sera pas 'Qui suis-je?,' question inopératoire d'abord, mais 'Qui sommes-nous?'"(The question to be asked to a Martiniquais is not "Who am I?" an ineffective question at the first level, but to ask "Who are we?"; 152–53). Accordingly, *Les Indes* offers a system that links the we to the epic dimension of the dream and the quest for the "Western passage," and the I to the oriented historical conscience of a very rational Western world that is going to make the West Indies into what they have become.

It is therefore not surprising that the prosaic song "The Trade" is totally dominated by an overbearing I: "Je sais, moi qui vous parle [...] que ceux-là furent sanglants et nus" (I know, I who is speaking to you [...] that those were bloodied and naked; 105). Why the introduction of an I, here, in an epic poem? It is not because Glissant wishes to talk to us directly through a structure of utterance, but because, in his system of oppositions, the drama of the trade of black slaves is unfolding in the mouth of the Western world, in the mouth of this I who is the instrument of established and legitimate history. It is this history, according to Glissant, that Western thinking considers to be a fundamental dimension in its description of mankind, since Western history "inscribes edicts and laws," and "marks bodies and territories with the seal of reason" using the founding principle of a linear time as the basis for its legitimacy. These are all aspects that "chaos-time" with its vertiginous vortex refuses, opening the way for the transhistorical communal we of the "Tout-Monde."[17] It is this dimension (pronoun and time) that shapes the specific culture of the Caribbean territory as well as the general composition of *Les Indes*.

Here again, with this last book, it is clear that the use of the pronoun *I* in no way corrupts the epic text so as to confuse it with a lyric one

17. Edouard Glissant, *Traité du Tout-Monde* (Paris: Gallimard, 1997).

in which an autobiographical content would ultimately trace the ideal "contours of a poetic persona, or self," or reactivate this type of poetry "as aestheticizing personal activity," which Roche deemed "inadmissible."[18] With the possible exception of Césaire's text, these poems are not performative in a strict sense, even if there is an intentionality, at a very elementary level, to produce an alternative discourse to the official history. All this offers a different modality of establishing the I: closer to "he" than to "me." It cancels out the selfish self and promotes a self that can only exist through communal relationships, as an element of an ensemble and not in opposition to all others. "All that which is inside, never stops being outside" writes Keineg (41).

If, at the end of the twentieth century, the current poetic movements seem to have forgotten about this contemporary epic poetry, it is probably because contemporary French poetry has been sedentary for so long (as implied by Pinson's title, *Habiter en poète*), with too much invested in the poetic quest of "trouver son lieu" (finding its place). One may remember that Mallarmé wrote to an American correspondent that too much was made of Rimbaud, that he was just an exception irrelevant to the poetry of the period, and that "everything" would have happened anyway without him.[19] By demanding to be legitimized on the basis of some recently influential interpretations, contemporary French poetry has forgotten its hybrid origins and its transgressions, as well as the experiments, the composite forms, and the apparently monstrous results that have left their marks on twentieth-century literature written in French. To say today that we only have a choice between logolatric or lyric poetry is to forget the profusion of poetic forms that exist. They are neither archaic formations nor deviant syntheses, but the familiar creatures of our imaginary creative world. On the periphery of Bonnefoy's fictional city, and beside the windowpane that shines in the sunset and shows us the high road returning the I to its lyrical home, there is a wild and luxuriant world of the we, where certain poets have managed to encapsulate anxiety and human struggles in some new epic formulas.

18. For other definitions of lyric poetry, see Chapter 10.
19. Stéphane Mallarmé, "Lettre à Harrison Rhodes (April 1896)," in *Igitur, Divagations, Un coup de dés* (Paris: Gallimard, 1976), 122–23.

CONCLUSION

In his collection of poems from 1962 entitled *Il n'y a pas de paradis* (There is no paradise), André Frénaud characterizes poetry as a *machine inutile* (useless machine).[1] The poem of this title goes on to describe the machine of words in the following way:

> Une machine à faire du bruit
> qui s'ébroue et supplie et proclame,
> (...)
> construite en mots dépaysés
> pour se décolorer l'un par l'autre,
> pour entrer dans l'épais du grain
> (...)
> pour y pomper l'eau imprenable

1. André Frénaud, *Il n'y a pas de paradis* (Paris: Gallimard, Poésie, 1962).

dont le courant gronde sans bruit,
machine à capter ce silence
pour vous en mettre dans l'oreille
à grands coups d'ailes inutiles. (85)

(A machine for making noise
that flaps and blows, begs and proclaims,
[...]
built out of uprooted words
so that all of them can discolor each other,
so that they can penetrate the densest grain
[...]
so that they can pump up unconquerable water
whose current is rumbling without a sound,
a machine for capturing this silence
for putting some of it in your ears
with great flaps of useless wings.)

The avowed uselessness of poetry in these lines is nevertheless tempered by a description of its effects. For even if the poem's final phrase repeats Mallarmé's avian metaphor of poetry's imprisonment and impossible flight, with the result that poetry remains incapable of expressing whatever ideal (or "paradise") is in vogue, a poem nevertheless affects its readers. Its "noises" still fill the latter's ears with what Frénaud calls a few lines earlier the "rumbling current" of silent water. The obvious oxymoron that is formed by these words points to the fact that water is used here in a figurative sense, and when one places the oxymoron alongside the phrase "unconquerable water" (*l'eau imprenable*) in the previous line, this sense grows clearer. Insofar as water is metaphorized as a possession that cannot be taken (*une forteresse imprenable* [impregnable fortress] is the underlying model for the metaphor in French), it is put forward by Frénaud as an inexhaustible resource. Indeed, it is the epitome of re*source*fulness because water is a standard metonymy for survival, and hence life itself. So the moral of Frénaud's text is in fact positive: poems bespeak living.

Despite their uselessness as vehicles for conveying information, and thus participating in a general consumption of meaning that regulates most of the everyday exchanges between humans, it would seem that poems succeed at another level. They are machines that change their readers' position toward widespread systems of consumption. Instead of being passive receivers of news that is independent of them, it is hoped that readers will be turned into active producers of sense, retracing the rules embedded in each machine-poem in order to enact a verbal performance that is uniquely self-sustaining. How the various types of verbal machinery manage to engage their readers' cooperation is what we have tried to demonstrate in this book. In so doing we have deliberately avoided both strictly intratextual and also self-authorizing interpretations, which ignore the formal causes of the effects that a text produces in its readers. Instead, these two approaches merely slot poetic effects into two overarching models for meaning. On the one hand, intratextual analyses seek recurring thematic patterns within an author's work and thus subsume the linguistic mechanisms that give rise to these patterns under the authority of the individual poet's signature. On the other hand, analyses of meaning based on communal reading values (as in Stanley Fish's theory of interpretative communities) remove literary effects from the poem itself and use them instead to propose a broad overview of literary consumption. In both approaches the value of individual poems is erased.

Returning to Frénaud's machine metaphor, it seems that the uselessness of putting the machines of poetry to work is purely relative. For "useless" is a negative attribute only within a limited definition of life as an economically profitable activity. Viewed in this light, almost any act in nature is equally useless, as Frénaud concedes in the poem immediately preceding the one quoted above, "Inutile nature." Here are its opening lines:

> Pourquoi grogne la truie? Elle ne sème pas
> l'esprit la truie, parce qu'elle grogne.
> Pourquoi meugle la vache? Elle n'adoucit pas la
> terre, la débonnaire, parce qu'elle la lèche.
> (...)
> Pourquoi les chevaux courent, longue crinière . . .
> Qu'ont-ils à faire?
>   (84)

> (Why does the sow grunt? It is not spreading its
> mind around, the sow, because it grunts.
> Why does the cow low? It is not softening any of
> the earth, the meek creature, because of its licking.

> [...]
> Why do horses run, their long manes . . . .
> What have they got that has to be done?)

These questions, and the negative answers that follow them, mark out
two positive traits in the useless machines of nature and those one finds
in a collection of poetry. First, they embody life, and second the witness-
ing of such life produces joy for the beholder, or reader. Every action that
is listed in the above lines is done for its own sake and also defines the
animal in question: cows low and horses run just because they are cows
and horses. That is part of what makes their lives uniquely different from
ours. Moreover, to recognize these differing patterns of action around us
is to acknowledge limits to many all-too-human motives for action,
which are usually quite limited in their scope: for instance, impressing
others with one's mind, which the sow does not do. Admitting that ac-
tions can derive meaning not from short-term goals but from the particu-
lar web of doings that make up a form of life is consequently a lesson in
alternative forms of happiness.

Yet the joy experienced by the reader of "Inutile nature" is also a
joy of language. In the poem's final question, which immediately follows
the ones quoted above, we read:

> Le souffle inaltérablement vrillé par les grillons,
> s'échappera-t-il, se lèvera-t-il?   (84)

> (Breath unfailingly drilled by the crickets,
> will it break free, will it rise up?)

Against the backdrop of phonetic patterns in French, Frénaud has created
a network of [R] and [i] phonemes in this last line—"*inalté*r*ablement,*"
"s'échappe*ra*-t-*il*," "se lève*ra*-t-*il*"—that underscores the paronomasia of
vrillé and *grillons*. The reader is quite unprepared for this density of
sounds and the subsequent creation of a new semantic link between
"crickets" and "drilled" (or "to bore, to whirl," which are the standard
meanings of *vriller*), because up until this last line the verbs that are used
to designate animal sounds are the standard ones associated with each
animal (*grogner, meugler,* and so on). As a result, the poem's concluding
line is foregrounded, with the materiality of its phonemes standing out
just as much as a cricket's sudden sounds stand out against all others. Yet

there is more to the poem's final question. Not only does its recitation lead readers to create within the space of language a transposition of a piercing cry, but it also focuses their attention on the recitation itself. For the breath they use in pronouncing the poem out loud is both an agent and subject for the poem's phonetic performance. The question put forward at the end of the poem is thus a rhetorical one: Will our breath (as speakers) rise above subservience to the sounds of everyday communication and become something richer, deeper, and more self-sufficiently alive? Insofar as the reader's voice has enacted this very shift to a denser phonetic patterning, where sounds are created for their own ends, the answer is definitely yes.

Many of the poems examined in this book use similar mechanisms to restore to their readers a performative competence in the use of language. In modern life it is easy to become a dispenser of information to the detriment of our ability to act through words and change the ties to people around us, as well as to the natural world. It is significant that after the poems "Inutile nature" and "Machine inutile," which underscore the value of sounds and actions, Frénaud places a poem that illustrates one type of performative utterance that restores effective speech. It is a series of toasts to others, titled "Pour boire aux amis" (For drinking in honor of friends). By expanding our use of such speech acts we can better recreate who we are and what we do—a potential already discovered in our reading of Tzara, Deguy, or Denis Roche. By reemphasizing language's inherent performativity these poets effectively reverse the atrophy of verbal power that is so characteristic of a world defined by what Mallarmé called *reportage* (or fact transmission).

This pragmatic dimension of utterances as actions is the foundation on which several of the poets discussed earlier have erected their own forms of poeticized language. From the user manuals proposed by OuLiPo back to Apollinaire's calligrams, modern French poems require their readers to work in unison with the text on the raw material of language, and in so doing they turn these readers into centers of performativity. Whether it be the phonetic poems of Dada, the rule-generated works by Queneau or Roubaud, the scrambled chain of intertexts woven by Apollinaire, Jacob, or Noël, or else the reworked performatives in Chedid's and Jabès's writing, all these poems return to their readers the power of doing things through speech.

Going beyond important recent studies by Gérard Genette, Robert W. Greene, and Jean-Claude Pinson that have unearthed detailed theories of language within works by selected modern poets,[2] we hope to have demonstrated some of the mechanisms used by these and other poets whenever they operate on the one resource that they all share: the French language. It is not the case that the poets discussed here all take a common stance *toward* language—whether it be Cratylist or some other theory. With the possible exception of certain Dadaists, they do not set out to construct a new language or to hypothesize an ideal one that would be totally different from everyday speech. Instead, what unifies contemporary French poets is a set of practices *within* language that exploit (to various effects) some of the basic properties of French.

This is one reason why our book has occasionally developed at length certain key concepts within linguistics: they are crucial to an understanding of how modern French poems function. Although some of our chapters have been inspired by structuralist analyses of the 1970s and 1980s, we have tried to avoid portraying language as a static and closed system, which was an unfortunate consequence of structuralism's insights. For instance, by stressing the importance of an intertextual memory that is part of the semantic component of French, we hope to have shown how a language such as French carries within it an ever-shifting body of citations or semantic oppositions that contemporary poems have absorbed and then recast. Poetry thrives on, and in turn helps propel, the subtle changes that language undergoes through time. Another facet of language's inherent dynamism is the pragmatic dimension to speaking that, as we demonstrated from Chapter 7 onward, forms the bedrock for many of the verbal performances that modern poems produce. Rediscovering the performative power of utterances is just one of the ways in which contemporary French poetry returns us to basics, as it were. Reading such texts is often an apprenticeship in speaking effectively, and it leads us to recognize a basic fact about language that Deguy has phrased

---

2. See Gérard Genette, *Mimologiques* (Paris: Seuil, 1976); Robert W. Greene, *Six French Poets of Our Time* (Princeton: Princeton University Press, 1979); and more recently, Jean-Claude Pinson, *Habiter en poète* (Seyssel, France: Champ Vallon, 1994). Genette's book is in many ways an extension of Roland Barthes's claim, examined in Chapter 5, that contemporary poems hypothesize a reversal of Saussure's axiom that a linguistic sign is always composed of an arbitrary link between signifier and signified. Greene detects two opposed attitudes to language among the six poets he examines: the view (espoused by Bonnefoy and others) that language expresses an extralinguistic reality, and the contrary view (attributed to Ponge) that poetic writing draws out linguistic properties inherent in words themselves. For a discussion of Pinson's characterization of these two opposed tendencies, see Chapter 11.

provocatively. "Language speaks before we do, in accordance with certain turns and figures," he writes.[3] As a result, the appropriate method for poetic knowledge, if there is such a thing, can only be to duplicate and deliberately reactivate, or make audible once more, the very figures through which a language speaks.

3. Michel Deguy, *Actes* (Paris: Gallimard, 1966), 282–83.

select bibliography

The inclusion of works by individual poets, or studies devoted to them, would have made this bibliography excessively long. It is therefore limited to recent general studies. References to more narrowly focused critical works can be found in the notes for each chapter.

Adam, Jean-Michel. *Linguistique et discours littéraire*. Paris: Larousse, 1976.

André, Robert. *Poésie et critique de la poésie*. Marseille: SUD, 1987.

Aspley, Keith, and Peter France, eds. *Poetry in France: Metamorphoses of a Muse*. Edinburgh: Edinburgh University Press, 1992.

Bishop, Michael. *Contemporary French Women Poets*. 2 vols. Amsterdam: Rodopi, Chiasma collection, 1995.

———. *The Contemporary Poetry of France: Eight Studies*. Amsterdam: Rodopi, 1985.

Bohn, Willard. *The Aesthetics of Visual Poetry, 1914–1928*. Cambridge: Cambridge University Press, 1986.

———. *Apollinaire, Visual Poetry and Art Criticism*. Lewisburg, Pa.: Bucknell University Press, 1993.

Bonnefoy, Claude. *La Poésie française*. Paris: Seuil, 1975.

Bouraoui, Hédi, ed. *La Poésie contemporaine en France*. Special issue of *LittéRéalité* 6, no. 2 (fall-winter 1994).

Bourassa, Lucie. *Rythme et sens: Des processus rythmiques en poésie contemporaine*. Montreal: Les Editions Balzac, 1993.

Brindeau, Serge. *La Poésie contemporaine de langue française depuis 1945*. Paris: Editions St. Germain des Prés, 1973.

Cardinal, Roger, ed. *Sensibility and Creation: Studies in 20th-Century French Poetry*. London: Croom Helm, 1977.

Chénieux-Gendron, Jacqueline. *Surrealism*. New York: Columbia University Press, 1990. Originally published as *Le Surréalisme* (Paris: Presses Universitaires de France, 1984).

Christin, Anne-Marie. *L'Image écrite ou la déraison graphique*. Paris: Flammarion, 1995.

Collot, Michel. *La Poésie moderne et la structure d'horizon*. Paris: Presses Universitaires de France, 1989.

Combe, Dominique. *Poésie et récit: Une rhétorique des genres.* Paris: José Corti, 1989.

Cornulier, Benoît de. *Théorie du vers: Rimbaud, Verlaine, Mallarmé.* Paris: Seuil, 1982.

Deguy, Michel. *La Poésie n'est pas seule: Court traité de poétique.* Paris: Seuil, 1987.

Delas, Daniel. "On a touché au vers!" *Littérature* 39 (October 1980): 54–60.

———. *Poétique/Pratique.* Paris: CEDIC, 1977.

———. "Pratiques du poème." In *Le Français aujourd'hui* 114 (1996): 84–93.

Delas, Daniel, and Jacques Filliolet. *Linguistique et poétique.* Paris: Larousse, 1973.

Delas, Daniel, and Jean-Jacques Thomas. *Poética generativa.* Buenos Aires: Hachette, l983.

———. "Poétique générative." *Langages* 51 (1978).

Delaveau, Philippe. *La Poésie française au tournant des années 80.* Paris: José Corti, 1988.

Delay, Florence, and Jacques Roubaud. *Partition rouge.* Paris: Seuil, 1988.

Denis, Philippe, ed. *Poésie/Poetry.* Special issue of *Sub-Stance* 23–24 (1979).

Depestre, René. *Pour la révolution; Pour la poésie.* Montreal: Leméac, 1974.

Eco, Umberto. *Interpretation and Overinterpretation.* Cambridge: Cambridge University Press, 1992.

Edson, Laurie, ed. *Conjunctions: Verbal-Visual Relations (Essays in Honor of Renée Riese Hubert).* San Diego: San Diego State University Press, 1996.

Garnier, Pierre. *Spatialisme et poésie concrète.* Paris: Gallimard, 1968.

Genette, Gérard. *Figures I.* Paris: Seuil, 1966.

———. *Mimologiques, Voyage en Cratylie.* Paris: Seuil, 1976.

Gleize, Jean-Marie. *A Noir: Poésie et littéralité.* Paris: Seuil, 1992.

———. *Poésie et figuration.* Paris: Seuil, 1983.

———. *Le Principe de nudité intégrale: Manifestes.* Paris: Seuil, 1995.

Glissant, Edouard. *Le Discours antillais.* Paris: Seuil, 1981.

———. *L'Intention poétique.* Paris: Gallimard, 1997.

———. *Poétique de la relation.* Paris: Gallimard, 1990.

———. *Traité du tout-monde.* Paris: Gallimard, 1997.

Greene, Robert W. *Six French Poets of Our Time.* Princeton: Princeton University Press, 1979.

Groupe Mu. *Rhétorique de la poésie.* Brussels: Complexe, 1977.

Hagège, Claude. *Le Souffle de la langue.* Paris: Editions Odile Jacob, 1992.

Herrnstein-Smith, Barbara. *Contingencies of Value: Alternative Perspectives for Critical Theory.* Cambridge: Harvard University Press, 1988.

Hocquard, Emmanuel. *Tout le monde se ressemble: Une anthologie de poésie contemporaine.* Paris: P.O.L., 1995.

Hošek, Chaviva, and Patricia Parker, eds. *Lyric Poetry: Beyond New Criticism.* Ithaca: Cornell University Press, 1985.

Hubert, Renée Riese. *Surrealism and the Book.* Berkeley and Los Angeles: University of California Press, 1988.

Jacobs, R. A., and P. S. Rosenbaum. *Transformation, Style and Meaning.* Waltham: Xerox, 1971.

Jacobson, Roman. *Essais de linguistique générale.* Paris: Minuit, 1963.

———. *Questions de poétique.* Paris: Seuil, 1973.

———. *Six Leçons sur le son et le sens.* Paris: Minuit, 1976.

Johnson, Barbara. *Défigurations du langage poétique.* Paris: Flammarion, 1979.

Kristeva, Julia. *Revolution in Poetic Language.* New York: Columbia University Press, 1984. Originally published as *La Révolution du langage poétique* (Paris: Seuil, 1974).

La Charité, Virginia A. *Twentieth-Century French Avant-Garde Poetry.* Nicholasville, Ky.: French Forum, 1992.

Leiris, Michel. *Zébrages.* Paris: Gallimard, 1992.

Leuwers, Daniel. *L'Accompagnateur: Essais sur la poésie contemporaine.* Marseille: SUD, 1989.

Levin, Samuel. *Linguistic Structures in Poetry.* The Hague: Mouton, 1962.

———. *The Semantics of Metaphor.* Baltimore: Johns Hopkins University Press, 1977.

Lewis, Roy. *On Reading French Verse: A Study of Poetic Form.* Oxford: Oxford University Press, 1982.

Lotman, Y. M. *La Structure du texte artistique.* Paris: Gallimard, 1973.

———, ed. *Travaux sur les systèmes de signes.* Brussels: Editions Complexe, 1976.

Martin, Serge, ed. *"Il y a poésie & poésie* [Special Issue]." *Le Français aujourd'hui* 114 (June 1996).

Maulpoix, Jean-Michel. *La Poésie malgré tout.* Paris: Mercure de France, 1996.

Meschonnic, Henri. *Critique du rythme.* Lagrasse: Verdier, 1982.

———. *Les États de la poétique.* Paris: Presses Universitaires de France, 1985.

———. *Modernité, modernité.* Lagrasse: Verdier, 1988.

———. *Politique du rythme.* Lagrasse: Verdier, 1995.

———. *Pour la poétique I, II, III, IV, V.* Paris: Gallimard, 1970–78.

———. "Pour une poétique négative." *Le Français aujourd' hui* (June 1996): 39.

———. *La Rime et la vie.* Lagrasse: Verdier, 1989.

Metzidakis, Stamos, ed. *Understanding French Poetry: Essays for a New Millenium.* New York: Garland, 1994.

Milner, Jean-Claude. *L'Amour de la langue.* Paris: Seuil, 1978.

Minahen, Charles D., ed. *Figuring Things: Char, Ponge and Poetry in the XXth-Century.* Lexington: French Forum, 1994.

OuLiPo. *La Bibliothèque oulipienne.* Geneva: Slatkine, 1981.

———. *OuLiPo: Atlas de littérature potentielle.* Paris: Gallimard, 1981.

———. *OuLiPo: La Littérature potentielle.* Paris: Gallimard, 1973.

Paris, Jean, and Jacques Roubaud. "Introduction à la critique générative." *Change de Forme* (1975): 158–77.

Paulhan, Jean. *Les Incertitudes du langage.* Paris: Gallimard, 1970.

Pinson, Jean-Claude. *Habiter en poète.* Seyssel: Champ Vallon, 1994.

Rabaté, Dominique. *Figures du sujet lyrique.* Paris: Presses Universitaires de France, 1996.

Richard, Jean-Pierre. *Microlectures.* Paris: Seuil, 1979.

———. *Onze études sur la poésie moderne.* Paris: Seuil, 1964.

Riffaterre, Michael. *Essais de stylistique structurale*. Paris: Flammarion, 1971.

————. *La Production du texte*. Paris: Seuil, 1979.

————. *Semiotics of Poetry*. Bloomington: Indiana University Press, 1978.

————. "La Trace de l'intertexte." *La Pensée* 215 (October 1983): 4–18.

Roubaud, Jacques. *Poésie, et cetera: Ménage*. Paris: Stock, 1995.

————. *La Vieillesse d'Alexandre*. Paris: Maspéro, 1978.

Rubin, David Lee. *The Ladder of High Designs: Structure and Interpretation of the French Lyric Sequence*. Charlottesville: University Press of Virginia, 1991.

Ruwet, Nicolas. *Langage, musique, poésie*. Paris: Seuil, 1972.

Scott, Clive. *French Verse-Art: A Study*. Cambridge: Cambridge University Press, 1980.

————. *Reading the Rhythm: The Poetics of French Free Verse 1910–1930*. Oxford: Clarendon Press, 1991.

Stamelman, Richard. *Lost Beyond Telling: Representations of Death and Absence in Modern French Poetry*. Ithaca: Cornell University Press, 1990.

————, ed. *French Poetry since the War: The Poetics of Presence and Passage*. Special issue of *L'Esprit Créateur* 32, no. 2 (summer 1992).

Steinmetz, Jean-Luc. *La Poésie et ses raisons*. Paris: José Corti, 1990.

Thomas, Jean-Jacques. *La Langue, la poésie: Essais sur la poésie française contemporaine*. Lille: Presses Universitaires de Lille, 1989.

————. *La Langue volée: Histoire intellectuelle de la formation de la langue française*. Bern: Peter Lang, 1989.

Todorov, Tzvetan. *Théories du symbole*. Paris: Seuil, 1977.

Van Dijk, T. A., ed. *Pragmatics of Language and Literature*. Amsterdam: North Holland, 1976.

Williams, Adelia. *The Double Cipher: Encounter between Word and Image in Bonnefoy, Tardieu and Michaux*. New York: Peter Lang, 1990.

Winspur, Steven, ed. *Mallarmé, Theorist of Our Times*. Special issue of *Dalhousie French Studies* 25 (fall–winter 1993).

Zumthor, Paul. *Introduction à la poésie orale*. Paris: Seuil, 1983.

————. *Langue, texte, énigme*. Paris: Seuil, 1975.

index